The Handbook of
International Marketing Communications

The Handbook of International Marketing Communications

EDITED BY SYLVESTER O. MONYE
South Bank University

Copyright © Blackwell Publishers Ltd 2000
Editorial apparatus and arrangement copyright © Sylvester O. Monye 2000

First published 2000

2 4 6 8 10 9 7 5 3 1

Blackwell Publishers Ltd
108 Cowley Road
Oxford OX4 1JF
UK

Blackwell Publishers Inc.
350 Main Street
Malden, Massachusetts 02148
USA

British Library Cataloguing-in-Publication Data

A CIP catalogue record for this book is available from the
British Library.

Library of Congress Cataloging-in-Publication Data

The handbook of international marketing communications / edited by
Sylvester O. Monye.
p. cm.
Includes bibliographical references and index.
ISBN 0–631–20913–1 (alk. paper). — ISBN 0–631–20091–6 (alk.
paper)
1. Communication in marketing. 2. Export marketing.
3. Marketing. 4. Advertising. 5. Communication, International.
I. Monye, Sylvester O.
HF5415.123.H36 1999
658.8'48—dc21   99–32754
                                       CIP

Typeset in 10 on 12pt Galliard
by Graphicraft Limited, Hong Kong
Printed in Great Britain by MPG Books, Bodmin, Cornwall

This book is printed on acid-free paper.

Contents

4 American Culture and Advertising   45
Dag Bennett

5 Global Advertising   69
Sylvester O. Monye

PART 2   Aspects of International Marketing Communications

List of Contributors

Colin Angwin is a cross-border direct marketing consultant.

Suleiman Attour is a doctoral researcher at City University London. His research interests are in marketing and international advertising.

Michael J. Baker was Professor of Marketing and Head of the Department of Marketing from its inception in 1971 to 1988. After serving as Dean of the School of Business Administration/Strathclyde Business School, 1978–84, he was appointed as Deputy Principal in 1988 and Senior Adviser to the Principal in 1991. He is former Chairman of SCOTBEC (Scottish Education Council), past Chairman of the Chartered Institute of Marketing, and Governor of the CAM Foundation. Professor Baker's main research interests include innovation and technology transfer, competitiveness, and the formulation of marketing strategy. He is the author/editor of over thirty books, many of which have appeared in multiple editions. He holds several directorships and has worked as a consultant/ adviser to many major public companies.

Neil Barnard is a consultant, specializing in market analysis and advertising and its evaluation. As a visiting research associate at South Bank University, he was involved in the industry-funded project 'Justifying our Advertising Budgets' that led to various published papers. Previous appointments include Marketing and Advertising Analyst at Young & Rubicam, Kellogg's Research Fellow at the London Business School, and Analysis Section Manager at Beecham Products.

Dag Bennett is Senior Lecturer in Marketing at South Bank University, London. He received an MBA in International Business and Marketing from Indiana University, USA, a BA from Carleton College, USA, and a Sivil Okonom first degree from Norges Handelshoyskolen, Norway. His on-going research is on Eastern Europe consumer behaviour and marketing in developing markets. His articles have appeared in conference proceedings and business journals such as *Business Horizons*. He has also contributed chapters to textbooks and marketing readers. In addition to academic pursuits, Dr Bennett is Executive Director of Fair Trade Links, a co-operative trading company, and also does consulting with companies such as General Motors, J. Walter Thompson, and Heineken.

Sam Black, MBE, is one of the leading pioneers of public relations practice in Britain. Public relations bodies and academic institutions throughout the world have honoured him. He has played a significant role in the development of both the Institute of Public Relations (IPR) and the International Public Relations Association (IPRA) since their inception in 1948 and 1955 respectively. Since 1975 he has concentrated on the development of public relations education at the graduate and undergraduate levels. Sam Black is an Honorary Professor of Public Relations at the University of Stirling and he has received similar acknowledgement at other universities in the United Kingdom, Spain, and China. Recent books bring his total to fourteen. They include: *The Essential of Public Relations, International Public Relations Case Studies, Introduction to Public Relations,* and *Exhibitions and Conferences from A to Z.*

Lakhdar Boukersi is Principal Lecturer in Marketing at South Bank University, London. He received a Ph.D. in International Marketing from UMIST, Manchester, UK, an MBA in International Business from the University of Bridgeport, CT, USA, and a BA (Hons) in Finance from the University of Algiers, Algeria. His research interests include the application of marketing management in developing economies, the impact of international trade fairs on export development, and Japanese trading companies. His papers have appeared in respectable journals.

Rosemary Burnley is Senior Lecturer in Marketing at the University of Luton. She holds a master's degree from Glasgow University and a Ph.D. from the University of Salford. She is an external examiner for the MA in Export Marketing Management at Buckinghamshire Business School. Her current research interests include international relationship marketing, internal marketing communications, and financial services marketing in developing countries. She has presented and published a number of articles in this field. Her current consulting activity is in the development of international marketing programmes for Bulgarian universities.

James M. Curran is a doctoral researcher at the University of Rhode Island, USA. His current research interests are in marketing management and sales management, and he has published in these fields.

Andrew S. C. Ehrenberg is Professor of Marketing at South Bank University. Previously he spent twenty-three years at the London Business School and fifteen years in industry. He has also held academic appointments at Cambridge, Columbia, Durham, London, NYU, Pittsburgh, and Warwick. A former chairman of the Market Research Society, Professor Ehrenberg was a gold medallist in 1969 and 1996. With his colleagues he has published ten books and over 300 papers in learned journals such as *Nature* (five), and *JMRS, Admap, Journal of the Royal Statistical Society, JAR, JMR/JM* (about twenty in each). He is a frequent speaker and active consultant on both sides of the Atlantic, and now leads a small research team for the SBU's 'R&D Initiative'. The R&D I is supported by some seventy leading companies including Anheuser-Busch, Bristol Myers, CBS, Colgate, DDB, GM, GMI, Kodak, Kraft, IRI, NBC, O&M, and P&G in the United States, and

Abbey National, AGB, Barclays, BBC, BP, BT, Coca Cola, Diageo, Esso, Halifax, Millward Brown, NatWest, News International, O&M, PepsiCo, RI, Shell, Sony, and Unilever in the United Kingdom.

Frances Ekwulugo is Senior Lecturer at the Watford School of Business and holds a master's degree from the University of Kent. Her current Ph.D. research is in the area of new product development in the financial services sector. With many years of practical experience in export management, she consults extensively for SMEs in the UK. She acts as an external examiner for both the Institute of Credit Management and the Institute of Export. She specializes in international marketing and export management.

Greg Harris is Lecturer in Marketing at City University Business School. Prior to entering academia in 1983, Greg worked for ten years in advertising with D'Arcy, Masius, Benton and Bowles, where his clients included such companies as Mars, Weetabix and Brooke Bond and Oxo. After leaving Masius, he went to teach marketing at the London Business School, where he was also awarded his Ph.D. for a thesis on the issue of international advertising standardization. His current research is focused on the role of communications in the marketing of financial services. His articles have been published in the *Journal of International Marketing*, the *International Journal of Advertising*, the *Journal of Marketing Management*, the *Journal of Financial Services Marketing*, and the *Journal of Brand Management*. He has taught on executive programmes for a range of companies including Unilever, Nestle, IDV, Yardleys, and Toshiba.

Eugene M. Johnson is Professor of Marketing at the University of Rhode Island, USA. He received his BS and MBA degrees from the University of Delaware and his doctorate (DBA) from Washington University. Professor Johnson's extensive research and consulting activities include studies of service marketing, sales management, marketing planning, bank marketing, and telemarketing. He is a contributor to the *Handbook of Modern Marketing* and is author of twelve books including *Managing Your Sales Team*, *Profitable Services Marketing* and *Sales Management: Concepts, Practices and Cases*. Eugene Johnson's research on service marketing, sales management, and telemarketing has been published in the *Journal of Services Marketing*, *Bank Marketing*, *Marketing News*, *Sales and Marketing Management*, the *Journal of Personal Selling and Sales Management*, the *International Journal of Bank Marketing*, and other publications.

Petra Mayer is a consultant at a Munich-based strategy and marketing consultancy specializing in information technology and telecommunications. Her specialism is the use and exploitation of new media and the Internet for internal and external communications, electronic commerce and procurement. She is also the Co-ordinator at UK-based Brodeur a Plus, the EMEA lead agency of Brodeur, one of the world's leading technology marcoms consultancy groups. Her experience there includes European service marketing and communications, new business development, operational and organizational efficiency, and culture change. Ms

Mayer received her bilingual MBA in European Management from South Bank University, London, and her MA in Modern Languages and Linguistics from the Ludwig Maximilians University of Munich.

Sylvester O. Monye is Principal Lecturer in Marketing and International Business at South Bank University, London, and Visiting Professor of Marketing and International Business at Assumption University of Thailand, Bangkok. He studied economics at the University of London, obtaining M.Sc. and Ph.D. degrees at the University of Strathclyde, Glasgow, and an MBA at South Bank University, London. Dr Monye's research and consulting activities include studies of sales management, licensing, franchising, globalization of marketing, and technology transfer. He is author of *The International Business Blueprint,* and his studies have been published in the *Journal of Technology Transfer, International Marketing Review, Precision Marketing, les Nouvelles, Franchising Research: An International Journal,* the *African Journal of Finance and Management,* the *Journal of Selling and Major Accounts Management,* and other publications.

Nana Owusu-Frimpong studied Business Administration at the Universities of Brighton and Durham. In 1994, he received his Ph.D. in Business Administration for a thesis on marketing of financial services from the University of Durham. He is Senior Lecturer in Marketing at South Bank University, London, and teaches marketing strategy and marketing of financial services. In recent years, his consultancy and research interests have focused on customer satisfaction measurement and the development of marketing in former Communist countries of Eastern Europe. He has published a number of articles in this field.

John A. Scriven has been a senior research fellow at South Bank Business School since January 1993, specializing in the study of brand performance measures and the effects of marketing inputs, particularly price and advertising. He has over twenty years of commercial experience in a series of domestic and international marketing, market research and marketing planning positions with three major corporations: United Biscuits, RJR/Nabisco, and PepsiCo. Recent published papers include 'How consumers respond to price' (MRS Conference, March 1995), 'Brand loyalty under the microscope' (EBEA, 1996), and four papers in the Justifying our Advertising Budgets series. He has also produced a series of reports for participants based on extensive experimental work on the South Bank Pricing Project.

Chris C. Simango is Senior Lecturer in Corporate Strategy and International Business at De Montfort University, Milton Keynes, Buckinghamshire. He is a graduate in Aeronautical Engineering (Civil Aviation), BBS (Hons), Dip. Development Studies, Dip. Foreign Trade, Dip. Chartered Institute of Transport, Dip. Materials Management and Purchasing, Dip. General Management and M.Sc. His Ph.D. research area focuses on American, European, and Japanese multinational enterprise corporate strategies in the pharmaceutical industry (ethical and

OTC drugs). He has broad consulting experience in the pharmaceutical industry and foreign direct investment and multinational corporate strategies in southern Africa. Some of his publications have appeared in such journals as the *European Business Review, Industrial Development Authority, Health Care, Drugs and Perspectives*, and the *Journal of Pharmaceutical Marketing*.

PART 1

General Overview: Issues and Concepts

1 International Marketing Communications: An Introduction and Overview

SYLVESTER O. MONYE

Introduction

After nearly forty years of intense academic research and debate on the pattern and strategic direction of international business, there is still no consensus on how best to approach the subject of globalization. While most agree on the direction of the forces shaping the world markets, strategic responses to these forces still cause considerable disagreement (Czinkota and Ronkainen, 1995). This disagreement centres on whether it is better to standardize products and services, and pursue a consistent marketing programme and strategy everywhere for maximum economic benefit for the firm, or to adopt a customer-focus strategy by making market-specific adaptations where necessary.

Proponents of globalization believe there are merits in applying a standardized strategic approach in international markets because of the emerging 'global consumer' – a consequence of increasing commonality in educational background and lifestyles of consumers occasioned by advances in transport and telecommunications technology (Dichter, 1962; Elinder, 1965; Levitt, 1983; Ohmae, 1985). It is passionately argued that the emerging similarities among nations far outweigh the remaining differences. As a result, the success and long-term development of a multinational operation depend on the know-how and capability in pursuing a standardized strategy in this global village. Indeed, some studies have shown that a consistent and respectable brand image is vital to a successful globalization strategy (Levitt, 1983; Aaker and Keller, 1990; Park et al., 1991). For example, the sportswear company Nike maintains a strong and standardized fitness-cum-performance image in all the markets it serves. It is believed that this functional image of fitness and performance is the basic concept underlying Nike's product development, styling, advertising, promotions, merchandising, pricing and so forth (Roth, 1995). It is, therefore, of strategic importance that international firms maximize the use of the various elements of the communications mix in their international communications strategy. It is noteworthy that discounted sales offers, a Western-style short-term sales promotion technique hitherto shunned for cultural reasons, are now gaining favour with both consumers and marketers alike in Japan. In the past, the Japanese believed companies offered discounted products only when these were damaged or less valuable. Such marketing techniques were, therefore, stigmatized. It is plausible to argue that changes in attitudes and responses to marketing campaigns in a traditional society such as Japan lend support to the notion of the emerging global village.

There are also those who question the wisdom and validity of the so-called economic merits in the standardization of international marketing programmes and strategy. Furthermore, academics and practitioners often wonder whether promotional tools, which include advertising, personal selling, direct marketing, sales promotion, public relations, trade exhibitions and publicity, can be standardized in all world markets without disastrous consequences for the firm. It has to be said that a consistent and respectable global brand image does not imply or require a standardized promotional strategy in all markets. One of the most fundamental tasks of international marketers is to communicate a range of messages about value, quality, reliability and brand image to a whole variety of global audiences. With the exacerbation of nationalistic tendencies and tribalism within countries, and the differences in sociocultural, political and economic systems between the nations of the world (Buzzell, 1968; Anholt, 1995; Rodwell, 1996), the case for globalization has become more complicated and sometimes confused. While there are potential benefits in the strategy of standardization of international marketing programmes, developing and implementing such a strategy is a complex undertaking exacerbated by the multi-environmental factors that businesses face. Each stage of the communications process is vulnerable to the effect of noise which may cause distortion in the encoding, delivery and reception of a message.

The Book

In this book, we take a holistic approach to the subject of international marketing communications by drawing together all facets of this important subject, thus producing a comprehensive volume that offers scope, depth and quality. This is based on the belief that no element of the communications mix can be easily isolated or utilized optimally and successfully on their own. The elements of the communications mix must be taken as part of a total concept. *The Handbook of International Marketing Communications* consists of sixteen chapters set in two parts and representing a broad and detailed overview of international dimensions of marketing communication. Part 1 deals with general issues affecting the environment for international marketing communications in general and advertising in particular. The tendency in general marketing literature is to oversimplify the consequences of cultural imperatives in the analysis of factors affecting the globalization of marketing communication. The international orientation of this book means that the role and impact of culture on the subject is well covered. Thus, it is neither possible nor desirable to assume that discussions relating to cultural issues in one chapter will suffice in another. This makes for a certain degree of overlap between chapters, which is mutually reinforcing. In part 2, aspects of the communications mix are dealt with, within an international context. Topics for this book have been specifically selected to provide a detailed treatment of the various issues in international marketing communications, both in scope and depth, to ensure that the international dimension of their coverage goes beyond the treatment one would normally find in general marketing communications books. Issues related to culture, language, standardization and adaptation have been examined in these chapters but from different perspectives and with varying degrees of emphasis. Thus, one of the strengths of this volume, which is intended for academics, practitioners and students of marketing and international business, is that readers may find each chapter a valuable stand-alone resource. Contributors to this volume are distinguished academics and practitioners who have an excellent track record in research and publications.

In chapter 2, Michael Baker looks at the nature of marketing communication and how it works both in domestic and international settings. He suggests that in developing an effective marketing communications strategy, the marketer has to deal with issues arising from at least two basic problems: first, potential buyers are likely to differ from one another in many important respects, both demographic and psychosocial; second, there is likely to be considerable variation in the levels of knowledge and awareness of the intended audience at any given point in time. As a consequence individuals will vary in their response to marketing communications. It is, therefore, imperative that a marketer contemplating entering foreign markets should pay as much care and attention to developing a clear understanding of their audience's needs as they would in their domestic market.

Chris Simango provides a detailed discussion on the important subject of cross-cultural advertising in chapter 3. He develops a historical perspective on the origins of cross-cultural studies, sub-cultural issues and cross-cultural advertising with emphasis on the symbiotic relationship between them. The chapter provides a useful platform for the understanding of the key issues in the debate on whether to standardize or localize international advertising campaigns by focusing on the salient and specific factors that are relevant to the success of cross-cultural advertising in particular and international marketing in general.

With over 40 per cent of total global advertising expenditure being spent in the United States alone, the influence of American culture on the industry extends beyond the Americas. Dag Bennett examines the source of this influence in chapter 4. He traces the origin of American culture to a number of complex and interrelated factors ranging from the civil war, which erupted over the difficulties of maintaining a federal system that subordinated the rights of states to those of the nation, to individualism, which has its roots in Protestantism which esteems individual achievement, a value so visible in American advertisements. Bennett argues that as the United States leads the way in the global economic transformation through the information revolution, it remains the nexus of ownership and influence in the communications networks and media companies – the vehicles of cultural expression.

In chapter 5, Sylvester Monye examines the more specific topic of global advertising. He argues that the simple task of transmitting information designed to make a positive impact on the consumer becomes a multidimensional and complex exercise when it is internationalised because it means communicating with consumers across the world. The chapter examines the economic and sociocultural imperatives underlying regulations of advertising world-wide, and concludes that the debate on global advertising should not and must not be reduced to an either/or argument. As a consequence, an open strategy approach to global advertising is recommended because it enables a firm to customize or standardize marketing communications programmes when and where it is necessary to do so, using a six-alternative strategy framework.

Chapter 6 focuses on the role of branding and packaging in international marketing communication. Frances Ekwulugo submits that branding is an integral part of marketing management which must revolve around the basic nature of the consumer and the sort of appeal which the firm wishes to communicate to its consumers. Brands tell you about a product's quality, reliability and value, thus facilitating the communications process. Over the last ten years or so, companies have been taking advantage of successful brands by using them in a generic manner through brand extension strategy. The acceptance of new products by consumers is enhanced if they are associated with successful brands because users assume new products offer the same level of quality and reliability as existing ones, making the communications task much simpler and less expensive. Ekwulugo also considers the strategic role of packaging in international marketing communications.

International public relations is a subject which is grossly neglected and not often discussed in international marketing literature. This deficiency is partly caused by the belief that there are no differences between international public relations and the professional work carried out in one's own country. Despite the rather long history of this profession and the formation of an international validating body – the International Public Relations Association which was formed in 1955 – the international dimension of this profession has not generated sufficient interest and publications from academics. In chapter 7, Sam Black provides a state-of-the-art analysis of the unique characteristics of this important piece of the promotion jigsaw. He describes the peculiar nature and practice of international public relations, and the processes of organizing an effective campaign. A number of case examples are introduced to demonstrate the global practice of public relations. Black concludes that the theory and philosophy of public relations practice are similar whether the field of activity is at home or abroad, but that it does require the use of imagination and creativity to prepare programmes that can achieve stated objectives.

Trade exhibitions are generally recognized by both academics and practitioners in marketing as one of the most effective media for the promotion of consumer durable goods and industrial products. Despite this awareness, academic research in this important area of marketing is at best scanty and at worst non-existent. Lakhdar Boukersi attempts to compensate for this lack of attention to the subject in the literature in chapter 8. He writes on the nature and strategic importance of trade exhibitions as a vehicle for international marketing communications. He argues that the trade exhibition is not only an integral part of the marketing mix but also a key element of the communications mix. Recognizing the limitations associated with measurement issues in trade exhibitions, Boukersi observes that advances in computer application, digital technology and multimedia techniques are expected to reduce the significance of this problem.

In chapter 9, Eugene Johnson and James Curran explore the place of personal selling in international marketing communications programmes. It is suggested that, unlike the other promotion techniques that involve a mass appeal to a general customer base, personal selling is geared toward providing more individualized attention to each customer and the customer's needs. Thus, as a promotional technique, personal selling is dependent on the successful interpersonal interaction between the representative of the company and the customer. Although more expensive than other promotional methods on a per capita basis, it is the most effective method available for expensive and complex products. Johnson and Curran suggest that while the selling process in most countries throughout the world is the same and that the skills required may remain constant, levels of commitment to international markets and the strategies under which they are practised can vary widely.

Sponsorship is an essential element of the promotion mix that is particularly critical for the success of publicity and public relations activities. The specific role of sponsorship in international marketing communications is analysed by Nana Owusu-Frimpong in chapter 10. He compares the theory and practice of sponsorship and its impact on the public. Sponsorship is used by many organizations to enhance both their image and other marketing communications activities because it benefits from the public relations spin-offs of these activities. It is not a substitute for advertising. Rather it is a complementary activity that can help in sustaining goodwill, reputation and understanding generated through advertising. Frimpong maintains that the results of a sponsorship campaign – as indeed any form of marketing communications – can be measured if the objectives and benchmarks are well stated.

One important element of the communications mix that is often ignored in international marketing literature is publicity. Rosemary Burnley attempts to deal with this obvious deficiency in chapter 11 by presenting a detailed analysis of the nature, role and importance of publicity in international marketing communications. She argues that publicity is neither advertising nor public relations but involves corporate image advertising, public affairs and opinion making. Although publicity is a key tool in the conduct of public relations campaigns, it is more about generating a favourable media coverage by supplying information that is factual, interesting and newsworthy to radio, television, newspapers and other media. Burnley notes that conducting an international publicity campaign is a different proposition as cultural differences, language barriers, different laws and media availability present a set of unique problems. These issues must be understood and accommodated if publicity is to generate the desired media impact and coverage.

In a fiercely competitive world, there is a growing recognition of the role and importance of personalizing communication with customers. This is achieved through direct marketing. Uniquely, this approach uses marketing and selling methods in combination to build a direct relationship between marketers and customers. Until relatively recently, however, not much had been written about this important communications tool. In chapter 12, Colin Angwin examines the international dimension of direct marketing as a communications tool. He identifies and describes the characteristics of international direct marketing and offers suggestions on how to develop and implement a successful international direct marketing campaign.

In chapter 13, Andrew Ehrenberg, John Scriven and Neil Barnard examine two contrasting theories of how advertising works with a particular emphasis on advertising established brands. They suggest that the view of advertising as a strong force – that it is persuasive, aimed at brand-building and increased sales – is commonly held but unachievable. Instead, Ehrenberg et al. submit a contrasting picture of advertising as mainly for brand maintenance and to defend market share – presenting advertising as a weak force (but effective), reinforcing and at times 'nudging' the number of consumers to whom the brand is salient in the longer term. In their words, the idea that for the advertising of an established product to 'work' always means producing something extra – more sales, added values, differentiation, brand-building, repositioning and so on – is sheer make-believe. This point of view is based on detailed evidence that the authors have accumulated over the years in their study 'Justify Our Advertising Budgets'. The evidence from this study on the behaviour of consumers, and hence their response to advertising, is highly significant because of the principles which have been established. The results of this study, published in the JOAB Reports 1–8, have universal application, and can, therefore, be used in markets across the world. The data from this study cast a huge cloud over validity of the best-known model in persuasion studies – the AIDA model. The case made in this chapter represents a refreshing, albeit somewhat controversial, departure from the traditional understanding of how advertising works.

In recent years, content analysis has gained wide acceptance in both advertising and marketing journals as an important technique for detecting cross-country/cross-cultural differences between markets because of the on-going debate on standardization versus adaptation of the execution elements of advertising. In chapter 14, Greg Harris and Suleiman Attour present a systematic review of the literature on content analysis. They note that although the recommendations for cross-cultural methodologies have been repeatedly emphasized in previous articles on cross-cultural research, their application in empirical studies has been widely ignored. Harris and Attour suggest that methodological issues should be adhered to, in order for future research to make valid contributions to the advertising standardization debate and advance the body of knowledge in international advertising.

The nature, scope and the use of the Internet in marketing communications in the twenty-first century are examined in chapter 15 by Sylvester Monye and Petra

Mayer. They suggest that the increased application of cutting-edge technology, both in the creation of advertising and the use of the information superhighway as a medium of communication, is one of the most exciting and yet challenging developments in recent years in the field of marketing communications. It is also noted that the Internet has emerged as one of the fastest growing media ever in the history of mass communication possibly because of its unique characteristics such as interactivity and individuality, which make it a very powerful medium indeed. As a consequence, media planners are now adapting their plans to take into account the growing number of Internet users. In its relatively short history, the medium has been used for various forms of marketing communications ranging from infomercials, display advertising and advertainment, electronic mail to on-line publications. From the analysis in the chapter, it is clear that the Internet will have a profound effect on international marketing communications over the next twenty to thirty years. However, Monye and Mayer suggest that despite the popularity of the medium, it is not expected to replace the traditional communications media.

In chapter 16, Greg Harris and Suleiman Attour examine the practices of multi-national corporations *vis-à-vis* advertising standardization over the last 30 years. They identified the following: (i) limited available empirical data regarding the practices of multinational companies; (ii) questions about the operationaliza-tion of standardization, with various definitions of standardization being used; (iii) polarization of the issue; and (iv) confusion between companies' policies and practices. Whereas most studies of advertising standardization are based either on the technique of surveying the views of company executives or content analysis, Harris and Attour analyse both methods using data from France, the United Kingdom, Germany, Spain, Italy, Greece, Saudi Arabia, United Arab Emirates, Kuwait and Lebanon. The results of this study suggest a generally higher level of advertising standardization than expected.

Summary

The role of marketing communications in international marketing strategy has never been greater than in the emerging global and fiercely competitive environ-ment. A connecting fact in the literature is the understanding that the various elements of the communications mix cannot and should not be isolated if they are to be utilized optimally and successfully. These must be taken as part of a total concept for optimal results. *The Handbook of International Marketing Communications* provides a unique and comprehensive volume of essays that cover the various facets of international marketing communications and their interconnectedness. The on-going debate on standardization versus adaptation and the relevance of these issues to the various elements of the communications mix represent the dominant theme in this book. It is clear from the analyses therein that neither standardization nor adaptation should be embraced without due consideration to the unique conditions in and characteristics of each market.

REFERENCES

Aaker, D. A. and Keller, K. L. (1990) Consumer evaluation of brand extensions. *Journal of Marketing*, 54(January), 27–41.

Anholt, S. (1995) Global message – pan-European advertising. *Grocer*, 217(7199), 38–40.

Buzzell, R. D. (1968) Can you standardize multinational marketing? *Harvard Business Review*, 46(November/December), 102–15.

Czinkota, M. R. and Ronkainen, I. A. (1995) Introduction and overview. In M. R. Czinkota and I. A. Ronkainen (eds), *Readings in Global Marketing*. London: The Dryden Press, pp. ix–xv.

Dichter, E. (1962) The world consumer. *Harvard Business Review*, 40(July/August), 113–22.

Elinder, E. (1965) How international can advertising be? In S. Watson Dunn (ed.), *International Handbook of Advertising*. New York: McGraw-Hill.

Levitt, T. (1983) The globalization of markets. *Harvard Business Review*, April/May, 92–102.

Ohmae, K. (1985) *Triad Power – The Coming Shape of Global Competition*. New York: Free Press.

Park, C., Milberg, S. and Lawson, R. (1991) Evaluation of brand extensions: the tool of product feature similarity and brand concept consistency. *Journal of Consumer Research*, 18(September), 185–93.

Rodwell, T. (1996) Local flavour for a global advertising is common sense. *Marketing*, December 19, 16.

Roth, M. S. (1995) Effects of global market conditions on brand image customization and brand performance. *Journal of Advertising*, 24, 55–76.

2 International Marketing Communications Explained

MICHAEL J. BAKER

Introduction

In this chapter we address three basic issues:

- What is marketing communication?
- What techniques and methods are available?
- What influence/impact does an international environment have?

While some authors, such as DeLozier (1976), consider that all the marketing mix variables, and indeed all company activities, may be regarded as marketing communications, we follow the more usual and widely held view that marketing communication consists of the promotional activities pursued by the firm. As such, marketing communication includes personal selling, mass selling (comprising advertising and publicity), public relations and sales promotion. In a chapter of this kind it is not possible to discuss these different kinds of marketing communication in any detail but their salient features will be described with commentary on their advantages and disadvantages. Once this has been done we will then examine how operating in an international environment may influence the use of the different methods and techniques. Essentially this question centres on the issues of standardization versus adaptation. However, before we can address these issues it is necessary first to define what we mean by communication.

Communication Defined

Perhaps the best-known and widely used model of communication is that proposed by Wilbur Schramm in *The Process and Effects of Mass Communication* (1955). Schramm defined communication as 'the process of establishing a

Figure 2.1 Simplified communication model.

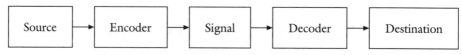

Figure 2.2 Communication channel model.

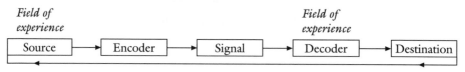

Figure 2.3

commonness or oneness of thought between a sender and receiver'. Pictorially the simplest model of the communication process is shown in figure 2.1. However, this simple model ignores the fact that it is necessary to convert ideas into a symbolic medium to enable them to be transmitted via a communication channel. To allow for this we must introduce two more elements into the model – encoding and decoding – as shown in figure 2.2.

As Schramm points out, this model can accommodate all types of communication so that in the case of electronic communication the encoder becomes a transmitting device – microphone, fax, etc. – and the decoder a receiver – radio, television, telephone, etc. In the case of direct personal (face-to-face) communication, then one person is both source and encoder while the other is decoder and destination and the signal is language. It follows that if an exchange of meaning is to occur, then both source and destination must be tuned into each other and share the same language. Put another way, there must be an overlap in the field of experience of source and destination – a fact which is of particular significance when considering communication in an international context. Schramm illustrates this concept of the field of experience as shown in figure 2.3.

All three models presented so far represent communication as if it were unidirectional. Of course communication is designed to have an effect and we must introduce the notion of *feedback* into the model for it is through this that the sender determines how its signals are being interpreted. In personal communication, as in direct selling, feedback is usually instantaneous through gesture or verbal acknowledgement. But in impersonal communication through the mass media the impact or effect of a communication may have to be inferred from other indicators such as the audience size for a broadcast, the opportunities of seeing a poster, or the readership of a print medium.

An implicit but not immediately obvious element in Schramm's model is the concept of the *channel* or, more correctly, *channels* of communication, for messages are rarely transmitted through a single channel. Channels include all media through which messages are communicated so that in a personal communication we have to take into account not just the words used but also the intonation of the sender's voice and any accompanying gestures. In impersonal communications (advertising) the channel tends to have the specific connotation of the *media classes* which may be used. We return to these later.

The marketer's version of Schramm's model employs rather different terminology and is usually stated as:

Who . . .   says what . . .   how . . .   to whom . . .   with what effect
Communicator   Message   Channels   Audience   Feedback

Kotler (1988) defines these basic elements as follows:

- *Communicator:* the sender or source of the message.
- *Message:* the set of meanings being sent and/or received by the audience.
- *Channels:* the ways in which the message can be carried or delivered to the audience.
- *Audience:* the receiver or destination of the message.

From his model Schramm derives four basic 'conditions of success in communication . . . which must be fulfilled if the message is to arouse its intended response'. These are:

1 The message must be so designed and delivered as to gain the attention of the intended destination.
2 The message must employ signs which refer to experience common to source and destination, so as 'to get the meaning across'.
3 The message must arouse personality needs in the destination and suggest some ways to meet those needs.
4 The message must suggest a way to meet those needs which is appropriate to the group situation in which the destination finds itself at the time when he/she is moved to make the desired response.

These four requirements correspond closely to the basic elements of the so-called *hierarchy of effects* models which see attitude formation and/or behaviour as the outcome of a process in which the receiver of a communication is moved from a state of *unawareness* to *awareness* to *interest* to *desire* to *action*. While models of this kind do not enjoy universal support (see, for example, Keith Crosier's critique in *Marketing: Theory and Practice*, 1995) they are widely used in practice, particularly by marketers who find the model intuitively appealing as a representation of the issues involved in securing a sale. Certainly, hierarchy of effects models appear both to inform and influence most practitioners' views as to how marketing communications work – the issue we deal with in the next section.

How Marketing Communications Work

One of the earliest explanations of how marketing communications in general, and advertising in particular, work is based upon stimulus–response theory. According to this theory the marketing communication is a stimulus which prompts a response in the receiver. Depending on the experience derived from that response, the receiver will learn and that learning will condition their response on the next occasion they receive the same stimulus. Thus if the cue is a message encouraging the receiver to buy/consume a new product and they do this, then, if the satisfaction is equivalent to or greater than the buyer's expectations, they will be likely to respond positively if they encounter the cue again. Indeed, if the learned experience is especially satisfying, then the buyer may well seek out the product again without any external cue prompting them to do so. In other words they have 'learned' both positive attitudes and behaviour towards the new product.

As noted earlier, hierarchy of effects models sees communication as a cue, which initiates a process that, ultimately, may lead to behaviour. The qualifier 'ultimately' is very important because the receiver may break off the communication at any stage of the process. Critics of the theory appear to think that its supporters see action as only occurring after the receiver has developed interest and an attitude (desire) towards the object under consideration. Clearly, this is not the case nor, if one reaches the stage in the process of forming an attitude, need one's response be positive as interest may lead to dislike and a negative response. In addition to this apparent misconception the critics also dismiss hierarchy of effects models on the grounds that they assume attitude formation always precedes behaviour. In many cases of what are called *low involvement* situations the receiver of a stimulus may well act first and defer making a judgement as to whether the experience is good or bad, i.e. form an attitude, until they have direct experience. If, for example, one is presented with a new food product, the only way in which one can really judge whether or not one might like it is to try it – a friend's opinions may be considered but they are no substitute for direct experience. Given that the perceived risk of trying something for oneself is low (low involvement), then one will defer judgement (the formation of an attitude) until after one has gained direct experience.

While the debate between the theoreticians is likely to rumble on, from the practitioners' point of view the learning model is intuitively appealing with the result that marketers frequently set objectives in terms of moving potential customers from a state of unawareness to awareness, then up the hierarchy to a buying decision.

In developing effective marketing communications the marketer faces at least two basic problems. First, potential buyers are likely to differ from one another in many important respects, both demographic and psychosocial. Second, there is likely to be considerable variation in the levels of knowledge and awareness of the intended audience at any given point in time. As a consequence individuals will vary in their response to marketing communications and this will have a major bearing on both the content of the messages to be communicated and the channels to be used.

Many communication experts subscribe to McLuhan's (1965) thesis that 'the medium is the message' and so would argue that once a target audience has been identified, the primary decision is the selection of the medium or channel to be used. Conversely others point out that media planning is a complex activity only because there are so many similar media, making choice between them difficult. This being so, then it is the message that must be selected first and this will help identify the most appropriate medium to reach the target audience. In practice both approaches are followed but, on balance, the channel seems to exercise the greater influence.

In general, channels may be divided into two major categories: *personal* and *non-personal/impersonal*. As the term implies, personal channels embrace all those situations in which direct face-to-face communication takes place, while non-personal communication comprises all those situations where the message is transmitted *without* face-to-face contact. Advertising, packaging, sales promotion, publicity, etc., all fall into the latter category. The evidence suggests that both types have a role to play, with non-personal communication being most effective in stimulating awareness and interest and personal communication in creating desire and action. Personal communication is also seen to be most effective where there is high perceived risk, i.e. the consequences of making an incorrect decision are regarded as particularly negative. In a selling situation the perceived risk is likely to be seen as high when the intending buyer has no prior experience of a product, its performance is complex and hard to assess without direct experience, and/or the price is high. Perceived risk is also likely to be high where the product/service has social connotations, which link it with social groups. As a generalization, then, personal communication tends to be preferred when selling shopping and speciality goods, while impersonal communication dominates the promotion of convenience goods.

However, it is also clear that most sales/marketing campaigns use a combination of both personal and impersonal communications. Research by Lazarsfeld (*The People's Choice*, 1944) showed that impersonal channels are often mediated in their effect by personal channels, a phenomenon known as the *two-step flow of communication*. According to this model certain members of the audience act as filters and amplifiers for messages. These people are termed *opinion leaders* and perform a particularly important role in marketing communications. Opinion leaders generally acquire information on their area of interest from impersonal sources and then become personal sources in communicating their views to others that seek their opinion. Obviously the preferred tactic would be to direct one's communication to the opinion leader but, in practice, it is often difficult to identify who may fill this role as nearly everyone is seen as an opinion leader in some field or other. That said, impersonal communication is less expensive than personal communication, so sellers see advertising as a cost-effective method for broadcasting information, which will be picked up and used by opinion leaders.

The main problem with mass media, however, is that the intended audience is subjected to an information overload, with the result that most of this information is screened out by the psychological defence mechanisms of *selective perception*, *retention* and *distortion*. As a result the power of mass communication as a persuasive influence is largely discounted nowadays, and the mass media are seen primarily as leading to learning and reinforcement over time. It is recognition of this fact that has resulted in the enormous explosion in direct marketing in recent years using the potential of modern information technology to enable the seller to make direct contact with the potential buyer.

As noted earlier, while the channel decision is critically important it cannot be separated from the message to be communicated. Clearly if the message is to attract the audience's attention, then it must be meaningful to them after allowing for possible distortion in transmission and selective interpretation by the receiver. It follows that the message is an infinitely variable element in the communication process that must be tailored to the differing needs and level of knowledge/experience of a constantly changing audience. One school of thought argues that message structure and content should be *consonant* and conform with held beliefs, aspirations, etc. – i.e. 'pleasant messages'. The other school of thought argues the opposite and believes messages should be *dissonant*, as such messages are more likely to attract attention as they create discomfort in the receiver. In practice both approaches are readily to be seen and are often used simultaneously by the same sender, e.g. the use of fear appeals to discourage smoking as well as messages stressing the benefits and offering encouragement to smokers to stop.

The final element in our model of communication is the communicator or sender themselves. Their influence is both direct – identification of the audience, selection of channel, choice of message – and indirect – the way they are perceived by the audience as the source of the message (the *source effect*). The source may not be the communicator but the origin of the message as perceived by the audience, cf. a 'testimonial' advertisement. Perception of the source is important as it influences the audiences' view of *source credibility* – a concept developed by Kelman and Hovland (1953) comprising the two elements of expertness and trustworthiness, both of which affect the receivers' interpretation of the message. The higher the source credibility, the greater the likelihood the message will be received and accepted.

The above discussion of how marketing communication works is a greatly simplified version of a complex topic which is the subject of many major textbooks. If, however, one is concerned to examine the use of marketing communications in an international context, then it is necessary first to establish some of the basic principles before looking at the particular case which is the focus of this book: international marketing. By the same token it will be helpful to review the alternatives open to a seller wishing to make contact with potential buyers; this we do in the next section.

The Marketing Communication Mix

Earlier we noted that some authorities consider that all marketing activities may be considered as marketing communications but preferred to take a more restricted view. In this section we propose to restrict our view of the elements of the marketing communication mix still further. For the purposes of this section we will confine the discussion to those activities conventionally regarded as part of the 'promotional' mix, namely *advertising, personal selling, public relations/publicity* and *sales promotion.*

In developing a promotional mix the main objectives to be considered include the following:

1 To increase sales.
2 To maintain or increase market share.
3 To inform and educate.
4 To stimulate awareness, recognition, acceptance or insistence.
5 To create and reinforce favourable attitudes.
6 To remind and reassure.

Clearly there is considerable overlap between these objectives but the distinction between them is important because an emphasis upon any given objective will call for a different promotional mix. While information and education may be best disseminated by means of mass media advertising, increasing sales may call for personal selling, direct mail and sales promotion. To assess the contribution that each of the various methods may make it will be useful first to define them and then summarize some of their salient characteristics.

Advertising

Any paid form of non-personal presentation and promotion of ideas, goods or services by an identified sponsor.   (American Marketing Association)

This very succinct definition merits some elaboration. First, advertising is paid for, it is a commercial transaction, and it is this which distinguishes it from publicity that is not paid for, at least not directly. It is non-personal in the sense that advertising messages visual, spoken or written, are directed at a mass audience, and not directly at the individual as is the case with personal selling. Direct mail is, of course, targeted at the individual but is still regarded as an impersonal source in the terms of this definition. Finally, advertisements are identifiable with their sponsor or originator, which is not always the case with publicity or propaganda.

Notable characteristics of advertising include the fact that it has the capability of reaching very large audiences and can communicate both simple and complex messages using a wide range of media. It is also a tool over which management can exercise high levels of control via the design of the message, the choice of channel and the precise timing and nature of the message delivery. Costs vary considerably from the classified advertisement in the local newspaper to the one-minute commercial broadcast nationwide at prime time. However, when costs are expressed in terms of the audience size (*cost per thousand*) they can be relatively modest. Nonetheless, given the cost of reaching mass audiences, there can be no doubt that advertising costs can act as a distinct barrier to entry – consider the cost of a global campaign to compete with Coca-Cola!

As noted, advertisers have access to a wide range of channels. Their main characteristics are summarized in table 2.1.

Table 2.1 A summary of media characteristics

Type of Media	Strengths	Weaknesses
Print		

Newspapers	Wide reach
	High coverage
	Low costs
	Very flexible
	Short lead times
	Speed of consumption
		Short lifespan
		Advertisements get little
		  exposure
		Relatively poor reproduction,
		  gives poor impact
		Low attention-getting properties

Magazines	High-quality reproduction
	  which allow high impact
	Specific and specialized
	  target audiences
	High readership levels
	Longevity
	High levels of information can
	  be delivered
		Long lead times
		Visual dimension only
		Slow build-up of impact
		Moderate costs

Television	Flexible format, uses sight,
	  movement, and sound
	High prestige
	High reach
	Mass coverage
	Low relative cost so very
	  efficient (potentially)
		High level of repetition necessary
		Short message life
		High absolute costs
		Clutter
		Increasing level of fragmentation

Radio	Selective audience, e.g. local Low costs (absolute, relative and production) Flexible Can involve listeners	Lacks impact Audio dimension only Difficult to get audience attention Low prestige
Outdoor	High reach High frequency Low relative costs Good coverage as a support medium Location orientation	Poor image (but improving) Long production time Difficult to measure
Transport	High length of exposure Low costs Local orientation	Poor coverage Segment-specific (travellers) Clutter
Instore POP	High attention-getting properties Persuasive Low costs Flexible	Segment-specific (shoppers) Prone to damage and confusion Clutter

Personal selling

Oral presentation in a conversation with one or more prospective buyers for the purpose of making a sale. Its function is to provide specific inputs that non-personal selling cannot offer at the individual level. It takes several forms: sales calls by a representative, assistance from a sales clerk, etc. It can be used for many purposes, such as creating product awareness, arousing interest, developing product preferences, negotiating prices and other terms, closing a sale, and providing post-transactional reinforcement. Above all else it promotes a dialogue between buyer and seller and the opportunity to clarify and elaborate when required.

This potential for interaction represents one of the greatest strengths of personal selling as the seller can tailor the information given precisely to the needs of the intending buyer. At the same time the involvement of a salesperson is also the source of the method's greatest weakness – its cost. In addition, delegating the responsibility to a salesperson reduces the seller's control over the exchange process. While training can help reduce the potential for salespersons to misrepresent their principals, the formers' desire to 'close the sale' can easily become a source of misunderstanding between buyer and seller.

Public relations

> The planned and sustained effort to establish and maintain goodwill and mutual understanding between an organization and its publics.   (Institute of Public Relations)

In everyday usage the term is often used interchangeably with publicity. But the IPR definition sees public relations as having a broad and strategic focus, whereas publicity is usually regarded as having a narrow and tactical application.

Unlike advertising, organizations do not pay directly for information about themselves, which is disseminated by means of a public relations effort. The use of such information is at the discretion of the editor, producer, etc., responsible for a medium's editorial content; this means that the information communicated frequently is seen as having greater credibility than if it had emanated direct from the source (the *halo* effect). On the other hand, the publicist has no control over the timing or content of the material published by a medium based on their public relations release. However, because one does not have to pay for media time or space, the actual cost of public relations is comparatively low and confined to time involved in preparing and distributing releases together with the costs of any professional advice.

Sales promotion

> Sales promotion is a facet of marketing, which is adding value, usually of a temporary nature, to a product or service in order to persuade the end user to purchase a particular brand.   (Institute of Sales Promotion)

This is a highly elastic definition, which embraces a wide range of activities. Free samples, price deals, banded offers and the like give the consumer an economic incentive to buy the product, whereas brochures and exhibitions provide information but no direct material gain.

Sales promotion expenditure is often referred to as *below the line* to distinguish it from advertising expenditures, which are *above the line*. Traditionally, advertising expenditures accounted for the lion's share of the promotional spend, but, in recent years, there has been a marked swing towards sales promotion, which is now estimated to account for two-thirds of promotional expenditure in the UK. Fill (1995) suggests a number of reasons for this change including *short-termism*: sales promotion has an immediate and measurable effect. Other forms of promotion take longer to work and their effect is less direct and more difficult to measure. Thus, increased *managerial accountability* tends to favour the method, which can be monitored most effectively. This trend is reinforced by the retailers' desire to track brand *performance* using modern information technology such as barcode scanners, electronic shelf-checking equipment and computerized stock systems because of the *competition for shelf space* and *brand expansion*.

Sales promotion can be very effective when used as a short-term tactical weapon. It is also a method over which the promoter can usually exercise a high degree of control, albeit that there will always be spectacular failures like Hoover's Free Flights campaign to prove the contrary.

From these definitions and short descriptions it is clear that the marketer has a rich array of promotional tools from which to choose when developing a promotional campaign. The issue we must now address is how might operating in an international environment influence decisions concerning the promotional mix.

Marketing Communications in an International Environment

In marketing it is widely accepted that there are only two core strategies – *standardization* and *differentiation*. With the division of labour, so clearly exemplified in Adam Smith's description of the transformation of pin making from a craft to an industrial process, standardization was pursued single mindedly as offering the best solution to the fundamental economic problem of maximizing satisfaction from the use of scarce resources. As we have described elsewhere (Baker, 1995), this pursuit of standardization is frequently regarded as reflecting a production orientation in that the final decision as to the precise nature of goods and services is made by the producer in pursuit of the economies of scale in order to maximize output and, thereby, profitability. In turn, marketing was 're-discovered' when supply began to catch up with and even overtake demand due to a slowing down of population growth in the advanced industrialized countries and a continuing acceleration in productivity as a consequence of technological innovation.

Faced with the prospect of oversupply, producers recognized the need to differentiate their output so that intending buyers could distinguish it from that of their competitors, and differentiation became a key element in the firm's competitive strategy. It should be stressed that standardization was pursued originally as a means to reducing costs with the objective of making products more widely available to the mass market. If goods are standardized, then, as economic theory predicts, buying decisions will be based on price which means that the most efficient firms with the lowest cost base will drive their less efficient rivals from the market place. For this reason, standardization is usually described as if it is synonymous with a strategy of *cost leadership* – it is not. Standardization was seen as a source of cost leadership – it also meant that if one could not differentiate between different suppliers in terms of product characteristics and performance, then one would choose the product with the lowest price. But, if suppliers do differentiate their products, this does not mean that price becomes irrelevant to the intending buyer. Far from it! In making buying decisions, firms and individuals are concerned with a much more complex concept of value which is the product of the relationship between costs and benefits. Thus, in today's highly competitive marketplace, it is not a choice between cost leadership and differentiation, as authors like Porter (1980) would have us believe, but the pursuit of both cost leadership *and* differentiation. We reiterate, there are only two generic strategies – standardization and differentiation – and these are at the heart of any debate about competitive strategy both at home and abroad.

Since Levitt (1983) published his 'The globalisation of markets', the concept has been enthusiastically taken up and developed by theoreticians and practitioners alike. As Usunier (1996) observes, 'Globalisation is a simple word which has achieved great success' in at least three distinct ways. In terms of demand, it predicates a convergence of tastes and preferences; in terms of supply, products and services are seen as becoming more standardized and, third, competition increasingly takes place on a global scale as multinational corporations (MNCs) seek to protect and grow their businesses. Each of these issues will be examined separately to establish what impact, if any, they are likely to have on the choice and implementation of promotional strategy in an international environment.

Globalization and Demand

In his seminal book *International Marketing: A Cultural Approach*, Usunier (1996) explores four aspects of globalization, all of which have relevance to the promotional mix decision, namely:

1 The impact of globalization on consumer behaviour. Is there, as Levitt claimed, a convergence in tastes and a concomitant diminution in cultural differences?
2 Is globalization resulting in a move away from competition at the local and regional level to competition on a global scale?
3 Is globalization resulting in policies of standardization in developing and delivering marketing strategies?
4 Is globalization leading to centralization of control?

In seeking to answer these questions, Usunier reviews both the conceptual literature and the empirical evidence, and draws a number of broad conclusions along
the following lines. (It should be emphasized that the following summary is the
author's interpretation of Usunier. The reader is strongly recommended to refer
to the original source for a much more detailed and fully documented review.)

In addressing the issue of the possible convergence in consumer tastes and
behaviour, three sub-issues emerge. First, how do products differ in terms of
cultural perceptions? Second, what evidence is there for convergence? Third, do
consumers have completely free access to 'global' products or do intermediaries
control their availability?

With regard to the question of cultural perceptions, it is apparent that some
products are culture bound while others are culture free. While quality (performance) and price have universal appeal, culture bonds may be particularly strong
under certain circumstances, especially where 'A rich cultural context surrounds
the product . . .' and 'There is an investment of consumers' cultural and often
national background and identity in the consumption act'. Food and eating habits
are clear examples of this tendency, and are reinforced internationally by the
emphasis on their geographical and ethnic associations, i.e. it is this which differentiates between them. Evidence suggests that standardization (global) strategies
work better for industrial and high-technology products like computer hardware,
machine tools and heavy equipment, but that differentiation is better suited to
consumer products like clothing, confectionery, food and household cleaners.
Language, a major constituent of culture, also plays an important part, especially
when it admits or denies one access to a 'product' such as the print medium, a
broadcast, instructions for use, etc. Clearly, there is no single answer to the question and each situation needs to be examined separately, although, inevitably, all
will fall into one or other of our two categories 'standardized' or 'differentiated'.

As to the issue of converging tastes, an equally mixed picture emerges. While
numerous studies, both academic and practitioner-based, have been undertaken,
the results indicate that while some products have a universal appeal, many do
not. Similarly, persons with a cosmopolitan lifestyle, affluent and with opportunities for foreign travel may enjoy similar tastes, but they represent a minority in
most countries. Usunier concludes that the globalization process is *pushed* on
consumers rather than *pulled* by them, from which one can infer that sellers will
target those market segments in other markets which conform most closely to
those where they are successful in their domestic market. For the rest, cultural
differences such as language, eating habits, political institutions, ethnic differences, etc., will represent obstacles that the seller may well consider too great to
overcome. In other words, the examples cited to justify the claim that tastes are
converging may only confirm that, within different countries, you will find subgroups of consumers with similar tastes to those in other countries – hardly
evidence for a worldwide convergence in tastes and consumption behaviour!
Usunier concludes that there are severe methodological problems in designing
and implementing research which would provide any kind of conclusive evidence
on the issue. In light of these, it seems likely that practitioners will continue to
take a pragmatic and ad hoc approach to market entry decisions.

While there is support for the view that some products have universal appeal and that lifestyles, especially 'the American way of life' as communicated through films, television, etc., are being emulated and copied in other countries, there is also evidence of a countervailing trend of ethnic groups and nationalities resisting what they see as a take-over of their cultural heritage. The French opposition to 'Franglais' is a harmless example of a concern for national identity. The break-up of the former Yugoslavia and tribal wars in Central Africa and elsewhere is a sad, but clear indication that the world consumer is more a figment of the imagination than reality.

The second question posed earlier was: 'Is there evidence that competition is becoming global rather than local or regional?'. Here the answer is clear-cut. 'Clear evidence from macroeconomic figures shows that competition is globalising, both at a world-wide level and at a regional level' (Usunier, 1996). While this trend is dependent on freedom of international trade, all the signs are that efforts will be maintained to achieve this provided that a reasonable equilibrium in the balance of trade between nation states can be established.

Given that competition is becoming global, the third question remains: 'What impact is this having on international marketing strategy?'. As noted earlier, this question comprises two dimensions: the degree of standardization to be used and the organizational issues involved in implementing the chosen strategy.

The question of standardization versus adaptation is, of course, central to the whole debate. We have argued that in rapidly growing markets with high levels of unsatisfied demand, standardization offers the better solution to solving the central economic problem of maximizing satisfaction from the consumption of scarce resources. At an earlier stage of technological development, this belief was reinforced by the fact that significant economies of scale and experience could be achieved in the production process as a result of standardization. Today, such economies are more elusive. As a result of technological innovation in areas such as computer-aided design and manufacturing (CAD/CAM), and the development of flexible manufacturing systems (FMS), it has become possible to create variety without incurring additional cost, reducing the case for standardization in manufacturing. However, while economies of scale in manufacturing have largely disappeared, they still exist in procurement, distribution and marketing, and it is this that largely underpins multinational standardization strategies and the case for centralized versus decentralized control of the organization.

Research into this issue reveals a similar pattern to that discussed earlier concerning the product – in some cases a standardization strategy is more successful, in others it pays to adapt! In other words, there is no single answer and every case needs to be analysed on its particular merits.

Adaptation or Standardization?

The *International Advertising Strategies of Multinational Corporations* was the subject of a major study by Hite and Fraser in 1988 and its findings are still regarded as an authoritative statement of practice. Based on a sample of the

Table 2.2 Summary of international advertising strategies

	Per cent	Number
Firms which advertise internationally	66	(99)
(1) Using all standardized advertising	8	(8)
(2) Using all localized advertising	36	(36)
(3) Using a combination strategy	56	(55)
Preparation of advertising campaigns		
(1) Foreign advertising agency	50	
(2) US advertising agency	27	
(3) International agency/network	21	
(4) Corporate in-house agency	20	
(5) Foreign affiliates in-house agency	18	

Importance of changing items to blend with culture	Strongly agree (%)	Agree (%)	No (%)	Disagree (%)	Strongly disagree (%)
(1) Language	77	18	1	4	0
(2) Product attributes	23	36	13	19	10
(3) Models	15	54	12	12	7
(4) Scenic background	10	48	22	13	7
(5) Colour of ad	8	25	42	17	9

Importance of environmental factors regarding transfer	Very	Fairly	Somewhat	Not	Average[a]
(1) Acceptance of trademark or brand name	66%	24%	7%	3%	2.5
(2) Transferability of slogan	52%	24%	16%	8%	2.2
(3) Level of consumer education	28%	54%	11%	7%	2.0
(4) Attitudes toward US	39%	26%	23%	11%	1.9
(5) Degree of nationalism in country	28%	44%	20%	7%	1.9
(6) Competence of personnel in foreign office	27%	38%	18%	16%	1.8
(7) Rate of economic growth	21%	38%	26%	14%	1.7
(8) Independence of media from government control	22%	18%	38%	21%	1.4
(9) Attitude toward work and monetary gain	14%	19%	49%	18%	1.3
(10) Eating patterns of market	13%	28%	8%	50%	1.0
(11) Attitudes toward authority	7%	12%	27%	54%	0.7

[a] Very = 3, fairly = 2, somewhat = 1, not = 0.

418 *Fortune* 500 business firms involved in international trade, 150 useable responses were received, fairly evenly distributed across business types. The main findings from the survey are summarized in table 2.2.

Of the 66 per cent of the respondents who advertise internationally, only 8 per cent use completely standardized advertising, with the remainder using some form of adaptation. Ninety-five per cent of the international advertisers agree that it is important to change the language to suit the context, and more than half consider it important to change models, scenic backgrounds and product attributes. The third part of the table summarizes the importance of factors influencing transferability in rank order of importance. The acceptability of trademarks/brand names, slogans, levels of education of consumers, attitudes towards the United States as the country of origin, the degree of nationalism in foreign markets, and competence of personnel in foreign offices are all rated important. The remaining factors have declining degrees of importance with perhaps the surprising finding, in light of earlier comments, being the unimportance attached to eating patterns. Hite and Fraser explain this by the fact that the majority of the firms in the survey do not compete in food-related industries. That said, this factor emerged as the most important determinant of whether or not advertising strategies will transfer from one foreign market to another. (This was the outcome of a discriminant analysis, the full results of which are contained in the paper.)

In the discussion of their findings, the authors also compare their results with those of earlier surveys and point to some important changes in emphasis between the different studies. Undoubtedly, such changes have continued to occur, but, one of the more recent studies of the effects of culture on cross-cultural advertising confirms that adaptation is necessary to accommodate differences between different countries (Albers-Miller, 1996).

Summary

In the final analysis, the best advice we can offer to the marketer contemplating entering foreign markets is that they should pay as much care and attention to developing a clear understanding of their audience's needs as they would in their home market. Without such understanding, there is little likelihood of developing an effective international marketing strategy and still less of devising an effective promotional mix.

REFERENCES

Albers-Miller, N. D. (1996) Designing cross-cultural advertising research: a closer look at paired comparisons. *International Marketing Review*, 13(5), 59–75.

Baker, J. (ed.) (1995) *Companion Encyclopaedia of Marketing*. Routledge.

Crosier, K. Marketing communications. In M. J. Baker (ed.), *Marketing: Theory & Practice*, 3rd edn. London: Macmillan, pp. 216–49.

DeLozier, M. W. (1976) *The Marketing Communications Process*. New York: McGraw-Hill.

Fill, C. (1995) *Marketing Communications*. Hemel Hempstead: Prentice Hall.

Griffin, T. (1993) *International Marketing Communications*. Oxford: Butterworth-Heinemann.

Hite, R. E. and Fraser, C. (1998) International advertising strategies of multinational corporations. *Journal of Advertising Research*, August–September, 9–17.

Kelman, H. C. and Hovland, C. I. (1953) Reinstatement of the communicator in delayed measurement of opinion change. *Journal of Abnormal & Social Psychology*, 48(July), 327–35.

Kotler, P. (1998) *Marketing Management*, 6th edn. Englewood Cliffs, NJ: Prentice-Hall.

Lazarsfeld, P. F. et al. (1944) *The People's Choice*. Sloan and Pearce.

Levitt, T. (1983) The globalisation of markets. *Harvard Business Review*, May–June.

McLuhan. M. (1965) *Understanding Media: the Extension of Man*. New York: McGraw-Hill.

Porter, M. (1980) *Competitive Strategy: Techniques for Analyzing Industries and Competitors*. New York: Fress Press.

Schramm, W. (1955) *The Process of Effects of Mass Communication*. Ill.: University of Illinois Press.

Usunier, J.-C. (1996) *International Marketing: A Cultural Approach*, 2nd edn. Hemel Hempstead: Prentice Hall.

3 Cross-Cultural Advertising

CHRIS C. SIMANGO

Introduction

The main objective of this chapter is to discuss cross-cultural advertising focusing on regional market structures (economic alliances), and international and global markets. The chapter also discusses some historical perspectives and origins of cross-cultural studies, cross-cultural analysis, subcultural issues, languages (back-translation problems) and cross-cultural advertising. More emphasis is given on the symbiotic relationship that exists among these disciplines. Thus, the chapter is not intended to be a stand-alone but forms an integral part of the entire book, focusing on some salient and specific factors that contribute to cross-cultural advertising, cross-cultural studies, cross-cultural analysis and international marketing advertising in general. Thus, it could be said that cross-cultural studies and analysis are intertwined with cross-cultural advertising since one might argue that the latter was developed as a result of the former (see the next section). Chapter 5 in this book, by Monye, on global advertising, should be used as an immediate link with cross-cultural advertising, and as an eclectic framework within which to appreciate and understand the extent to which advertising can be applied in a standardized or localized form, at the global or international level.

For example, market segments of British national consumers differ as a result of significance in the number of subcultures (multicultural nation) that are in existence in Great Britain. If such diversity exists between segments of a single nation, then even more diversity should exist among the members of two or more countries, such as those in the European Union (EU), North American Free Trade Agreement (NAFTA), Asia Pacific Economic Cooperation (APEC) and the emerging Southern African Development Community (SADC) member states. The international or global marketing manager or analyst must understand and appreciate the differences inherent in different nations (that is to say, cross-culturally) in order to choose, develop and implement suitable marketing strategies and advertising campaigns that are culturally congruent and effective enough to penetrate overseas markets.

Cross-Cultural Studies: A Historic Perspective, Development and Origins

It could be suggested that cross-cultural advertising has evolved and developed as a result of a cross-cultural survey project that was initiated and carried out in America in 1937, by Murdock, an American anthropologist who specialized in comparative ethnology, the ethnography of African and Oceanic peoples, and social theory. According to the report in *Encyclopedia Britannica* (1991), Murdock is perhaps most notable as the originator (in 1937) of the Cross-Cultural Survey, a project of the Institute of Human Relations of Yale University, in which a vast amount of anthropological data were catalogued so that any known aspect of a society's social structure could be quickly summoned from the data bank. The work by Murdock was broad in the sense that it was heavily dependent on other disciplines in the social sciences, especially the study of languages, sociology, social psychology and psychoanalysis. It could be argued that although the variables in the studies carried out by Murdock did not explicitly include the mordent business environmental imperatives such as technology, political systems, nature of competition and diverse global regulatory frameworks, it could be concluded that culture is generally and broadly moulded by characteristics of market structures that prevail in a given economy at a given time. Structural adjustments thus directly influence how consumers perceive well-established and newly introduced products. As needs and expectations in some countries change, cross-cultural advertising might also change according to macro and micro demands imposed on society, but the rate of change varies from country to country. However, it could be noted that regulatory frameworks might restrict consumer choice; for instance, erosion of effective disposal income normally retards or reduces effective demand. Price controls by governments might force consumers to search for substitutes. As a result of such measures, a company that uses, for example, standardized advertising in Spain and Italy might have to adjust the appeal in order to suit some changes in attitude and perception within these specific market segments. The same applies to countries that have a welfare system whereby unemployed people are given a fixed income per week or per month, such is in Great Britain and other EU member states.

In terms of cross-advertising, the study cited above has been used by academics and practitioners as a framework within which to understand and appreciate cross-cultural analysis and cross-cultural advertising. Through refining, understanding and appreciating the degree to which cultural universals and self-reference criterion impinge on how messages appeal to prospective target audiences, more companies are paying more attention to the extent to which advertising could be standardized or multicountry focused (Cateora, 1990). This has incrementally enabled academics and practitioners to understand and fine tune how they could position their ads in domestic (multiculture economies such as the United States and Great Britain) and international market segments in order to inform and trigger trial purchases. However, it could be noted that cross-cultural advertising has its inherent problems and can be complex in practice. As firms become international or global (very few) marketing managers or analysts seek to stand-ardize various elements of the marketing mix across many nations. This makes cross-advertising become more complex and cross-cultural studies become more important. An international company needs to determine whether advertising should be standardized or adapted in order to manage the marketing mix more effectively and efficiently. Thus, market structures and external environmental characteristics that prevail across diverse cultures should (must) be compared for differences and similarities prior to contemplating or developing an international or global advertising appeal or strategy.

Familiarities with similarities and differences in cultures and subcultures will reduce trial purchase resistances that are associated with perceived risk (the degree of uncertainty perceived by the consumer on the basis of various informational cues associated with the product), and could also help the international market-ing manager to identify perceptual blocking (the subconscious screening out or blocking of stimuli that are threatening or inconsistent with the consumer's values, beliefs or attitudes). Broader understanding of the issues raised above would enable a company to position its product lines in a more appropriate way, and according to the way in which culture and subcultures impinge on cross-cultural advertising appeals. This could result in more efficient and effective alloca-tion of resources in the sense that managers will be proactively aware of cultural universals and cultural exclusives related to particular markets and products. Brand names could be set and developed according to the manager's familiarity with the language and awareness of problems that are associated with backtranslation. For example, Tula is a popular brand name for women's leather bags in Great Britain, and this brand name does not have any specific meaning in the United Kingdom. The same name, or word (Tula), is spelt in the same way in South Africa and Zimbabwe, but has a definitive meaning in these countries, i.e. shut up or keep quiet. Owing to cross-cultural differences, such a brand name will not be accept-able in the two markets, Zimbabwe and South Africa.

Cross-Cultural Research and Cross-Cultural Advertising: An Overview

Practitioners must be familiar with the difficulties that are associated with con-ducting research within a culture (such as multiculture nations like the United Kingdom and United States), cultures and subcultures. For example, to carry out research on cross-cultural analysis in the United Kingdom, South Africa, Nigeria, Zimbabwe, the United States and Japan, on for instance high or low perceived risk, different survey methods will be required. The process tends to be more complicated because of diverse differences in business practices, cultures, respondent selection, translation (backtranslation) and sources of comparability. This also raises a serious question about the reliability of data collected in cross-cultural studies meant for the purpose of cross-cultural advertising. Davis et al. (1981) argue that there is evidence to suggest that insufficient attention is given not only

to non-sampling errors and other problems that can exist in improperly conducted cross-cultural studies, but also to the appropriateness of consumer research
measures that have not been tested in cross-cultural contexts. Such inherent problems will have an impact on choosing and developing cross-cultural advertising
strategies and programmes because culture and other related external environmental imperatives influence the two components of advertising strategy, namely,
strategic decisions (positioning, main theme) and tactical decisions (creative execution and media buying). This is reinforced by Parameswaran and Yaprak (1987) who
concluded in their survey of cross-cultural comparison that 'the same scales may
have different reliabilities in different cultures, and that the same scales may exhibit
different reliabilities when used by the same individual in evaluating products
from different cultures'. These pose problems in terms of validating standardized
benchmarks for standardized research instruments used in different countries.

Such complex issues as discussed above could pose so many problems in
terms of designing and choosing a standardized or localized advertising appeal.
Parameswaran and Yaprak went on further to warn us against using simple comparisons of research in cross-national marketing and that cross-cultural research data
comparisons should be attempted only after accounting for necessary adjustments
for possible variability. However, it is not very clear what sort of specific adjustments could be made in order to reduce these inherent difficulties mentioned
above. Cheron et al. (1987) are aware of and confirmed that researchers are
focusing on the difficulties raised above and other problems, including research
methodologies which are being evaluated as the degree of their applicability for
cross-cultural studies. One of the main problems facing researchers in cross-
cultural advertising is the limitation in which research findings could be quanti-
fied given the difficulties cited in this section. In order to illustrate and reinforce
some of the problems mentioned earlier, exhibit 3.1 gives some classic examples
of problems that are associated with cross-cultural advertising, developing and
implementing international marketing strategy, and the extent to which product
positioning is directly influenced by product usage, beliefs, values and norms in
the Japanese market segments. Such problems could be reduced if marketing
researchers carry out effective (information is the raw material for decision making) cross-cultural market research in order to identify both cultural universals
and exclusions that prevail in overseas markets prior to implementing international advertising strategies in specific host nations. As a result of not fully understanding cross-cultural implications, many companies fail to penetrate international
market segments even if their products have the potential to be modified and,
hence, adjust advertising appeals according to local conditions so as to stimulate
trial purchases.

Exhibit 3.2 shows an outline of some sources of broad information that may be
derived from answering some of the specific marketing-oriented questions raised.
It should be noted that the context for answering these questions tends to vary
from nation to nation as a result of different environmental imperatives that prevail
at any given time.

Exhibit 3.3 shows seven basic factors that an international or global marketing
practitioner must consider when planning cross-cultural consumer research.

EXHIBIT 3.1 LEARNING HOW TO PLEASE THE BAFFLING JAPANESE

If you are going to do business in another culture, you must know your market. Marketing research would have helped avoid most of the problems these companies had.

A baby powder company fretted about the relatively low demand for baby powder until it did some research on how the Japanese live. In their small homes, mothers fear powder will fly around and get into their spotlessly clean kitchens. The company had to settle for selling its products in flat boxes with powder puffs so that mothers could apply it sparingly. Adults won't use it all. They wash and rinse themselves before soaking in hot baths – after which powder makes them feel dirty again.

A cake mix company designed a mix to be prepared in electric rice cookers which all Japanese have rather than ovens which few have. The product flopped. Why? The Japanese take pride in the purity of their rice, which they thought would be contaminated by cake flavours. It was like asking an English housewife to make coffee in her teapot.

One company that was ready to launch a new peanut-packed chocolate bar aimed at giving teenagers quick energy while cramming for exams found out in time that a Japanese old wives' tale held that eating chocolate with peanuts can give one a nosebleed. The product was never marketed.

Source: *Fortune* (5 October 1981), p. 122.

Although the factors listed in exhibit 3.3 seem very straightforward, the composition of external environmental forces and interpretation will vary from nation to nation and, thus, complicates cross-cultural research and data analysis. Languages vary in the degree of specificities and backtranslation problems could be a major concern when targeting certain markets in terms of product positioning. Words might not have a common literary meaning when they are used in other international markets. For example, in Zimbabwe, traffic lights are commonly referred to as robots, which is contrary to what they are called in the United Kingdom or the United States; in the United States a car horn is referred to as a car hooter (a commonly used word in the United Kingdom, South Africa, Zimbabwe and in most of the countries at a global level).

Consumption patterns or behaviour tend to vary from market to market due to a multitude of factors that constitute the external (uncontrollable) macroenvironmental imperatives such as law, differences in codes of business practices and government intervention, or regulation (such as price ceilings in the ethical pharmaceutical sector; within diverse therapeutic categories). Although it is often argued that countries that have similar levels of economic development, such as developed nations in the European Community, cultural universals, it could be argued that pan-European advertising and branding is not as popular and

EXHIBIT 3.2   OUTLINE OF CROSS-CULTURAL ANALYSIS OF
CONSUMER BEHAVIOUR

1 *Determine relevant motivations in the culture.* What needs are fulfilled
   with this product in the minds of members of the culture? How are these
   needs presently fulfilled? Do members of the culture readily recognize
   these needs?
2 *Determine characteristic behaviour patterns.* What patterns are characteristic of purchasing behaviour? What forms of division of labour exist
   within the family structure? What size packages are normally purchased?
3 *Determine what broad values are relevant to this product.* Are there strong
   values about work, morality, religion, family relations, and so on, that
   relate to this product?
4 *Determine characteristic forms of decision making.* Do members of the
   culture display a studied approach to decisions concerning innovations
   or an impulsive approach? What form of decision making?
5 *Evaluate promotion methods appropriate to the culture.* What role does
   advertising occupy in the culture? What themes, words, or illustrations
   are taboo?
6 *Determine appropriate institutions for this product in the minds of consumers.* What types of retailers and intermediary institutions are available? What services do these institutions offer that are expected by the
   consumer?

Source: Adapted from Engel et al. (1973), p. 90.

EXHIBIT 3.3   SEVEN BASIC FACTORS INFLUENCING
CROSS-CULTURAL ANALYSIS

1 Language differences.
2 Differences in consumption patterns.
3 Differences in potential market segments.
4 Differences in the way that products or services are used.
5 Differences in the criteria for economic and social conditions.
6 Differences in marketing conditions.
7 Differences in marketing research opportunities.

Source: American Marketing Association (1975), p. 295.

applicable as some proponents had envisaged during the formation of the economic alliances, and after the regional market harmonization in 1992.

   In order for international managers to apply appropriately effective advertising strategies and market specific appealing advertising campaigns, effective

cross-cultural research should be undertaken in order to reduce and avoid some of the failures as a result of the application of self-reference criterion (Cateora, 1996). Also, complications in cross-cultural advertising could be caused by differences in product usage concept as well as variations in social and economic formalities that are related to multicountry and multiculture consumer decision-making processes. However, if the factors listed in exhibit 3.3 are complied with, managers could reduce wastage of resources by developing more appropriate and effective advertising appeals, thus penetrating international market segments more profitably. Some companies could take advantage of economies of scale in advertising if cultural universals are broadly identified and defined.

Cross-Cultural Advertising

Having discussed and illustrated the inherent problems that are associated with cross-cultural studies from which cross-advertising is formulated, it is appropriate to define what cross-advertising is. For the purpose of this chapter, cross-cultural advertising refers to determining the degree to which advertising is similar or different when it is applied to consumers of two or more nations (Schiffman and Kanuk, 1978) in relation to persuading specific consumers in specific market segments or niches. It provides managers with sufficient understanding of the differences in psychological, social, cultural and broader environmental characteristics to enable them to design effective marketing strategies for each of the specific host countries in which their companies compete. The examples in exhibit 3.1 should demonstrate in practice how complex cross-advertising could be when applied without taking the necessary precautions outlined earlier. It could be generally argued that cross-cultural advertising primarily centres on the extent to which global or international corporate entities could strike a balance between taking a national responsiveness and/or standardized approach to advertising. Some of these issues are broadly discussed in Monye's chapter on global advertising (chapter 5).

Understanding and appreciation of cross-cultural studies should be the framework within which to standardize or custom make advertising campaigns. This enables managers to determine and identify cultural universals (commonalties in every nation irrespective of differences in culture) and cultural exclusives, i.e. customs or behaviour from which the foreigner is excluded. Thus, it is apparent that advertising at an international or global level is directly influenced by cultural convergence or divergence as a result of differences and similarities in phases of economic development (De Mooij, 1994). The levels of economic development influence advertising expenditure as they tend to be associated with the ability to satisfy needs and wants purchases (see tables 3.1 and 3.2).

Cross-cultural advertising is broadly influenced by diverse differences in the composition of environmental imperatives, at an international or global level, such as differences in legal requirements (Dibb et al., 1994), spatial implications, market concentration and/or fragmentation. For example, prescription drugs market segments are more susceptible to political intervention than any other

Table 3.1   Distribution of total world advertising expenditure
by region (in per cent, 1987–1995)

	Total percentage	
Region	1987	1995
North America	49.3	37.6
Europe	29.3	30.7
Asia Pacific	19.1	25.8
Latin America	1.8	4.5
Africa	0.4	0.7
Middle East	0.1	0.7

Source: *World Advertising Trends* (NTC Publications, 1997).

Table 3.2   Distribution of top five world advertising
expenditure by countries, 1995 (US$m)

Region	Country	Expenditure
America	USA	88 915
	Costa Rica	4 966
	Canada	4 142
	Argentina	3 229
	Mexico	1 092
Europe	Germany	21 992
	United Kingdom	12 803
	France	10 137
	Italy	5 221
	Spain	4 717
Asia/Pacific	Japan	39 124
	South Korea	6 077
	Australia	4 369
	Taiwan	3 207
	China	1 950
Africa	South Africa	1 259
	Nigeria	240
	Egypt	177
	Kenya	35
	Zimbabwe	29
Middle East	Israel	8 181
	Lebanon	347
	Saudi Arabia	270
	UAE	117
	Kuwait	1 167

Source: *World Advertising Trends* (NTC Publications, 1997).

industry. It could be argued that the application of global advertising is still limited even if it is often claimed that there are a growing number of global products, such as Coca-Cola, Levis blue jeans and Vaseline Petroleum Jelly or ethical drugs such as Tagamet and Zantac. There are very few 'truly global brands'. The traditional arguments that consumers buy products based on either economic emulation or distinctiveness is being eroded as there are new groups of consumers playing with an eclectic combination of tangible and intangible products to experience a series of inconsistent psychological selves (Banerjee, 1994).

As a result of this cross-cultural analysis and awareness, cross-cultural advertising will enable managers at the corporate level to deploy both tangible and intangible resources in a more efficient and effective way; as a result of understanding and appreciating the impact of self-reference criterion and cultural universals when applied to foreign markets. This suggests that managers should scan the environment in a manner that is consistent with the external environment and supplement the analysis with marketing research. Zhang and Gelb's (1996) empirical evidence on the effect of advertising appeal in the United States and China suggests that product use condition is a key component of the factors influencing the feasibility of standardizing appeals. They went on further to say that advertising standardization is feasible if a product is used in a consumption situation that matches the appeal in the ad. However, they also reinforce the argument raised earlier in this chapter that social culture plays a major role. They caution us that culture matters, but advertisers should not assume that culture's influence on responses to advertising appeal is independent of other environmental factors.

On the other hand, Anholt (1995) argues that most international corporations prefer to centralize advertising since it gives them control over the advertising message. He went on further to say: 'If all their European ads can be produced in the language they know by the agency they trust, and then simply cloned for all their overseas markets, they naturally feel secure that it is presenting their brand in the right way'. It could be noted that the concept of pan-European advertising has its limitations because there are more differences between countries than just their languages. Advertising is so intimately linked with the national culture, the social structure, regulations, business practices, consumer behaviour, ambitions, psychological selves and humour that advertising messages cannot and should not be conveyed in the exact same way in different nations.

It could be argued that advertising works more effectively when buyers are convinced that they are being spoken to by somebody who understands them, who knows their needs, and talks and feels just as they do. This suggests that beliefs, values, norms and attitudes play major roles in advertising (they trigger external cues, high and low perceived risks), and envelop all the broad variables that constitute culture, such as religion and education. Practitioners who claim to understand without appreciating the intricacies of culture will not learn much from cross-cultural similarities and differences since there is no single definition of culture. The definition by Terpstra (1991) will be used for the purposes of this chapter: culture is learned, shared, compelling, an interrelated set of symbols whose meanings provide a set of orientations for members of a society. These orientations, taken together, provide solutions to problems that all societies must solve if they are to remain viable.

Terpstra has identified components of culture in broad terms, and it is suggested that academics and marketing managers, or analysts, should be familiar with these eclectic major elements of culture as follows:

1 Culture is learned.
2 Culture is shared.
3 Culture is compelling.
4 Cultural symbols and meanings are interrelated.

The interrelationships of the four elements of culture mentioned above will vary from nation to nation since they are also influenced by other diverse external environmental imperatives such as technology, law, languages, societal, political systems and market structures. These differences and similarities will influence advertising appeals within and across cultures and subcultures. A subculture is a distinct cultural group, which exists as an identifiable segment within a larger, more complex society such as in the United States, Britain, South Africa and Nigeria. Its members possess beliefs, values and customs that set them apart from other members of the same society; at the same time, they hold to the dominant beliefs of the overall society. Such examples include religion, age groups, race, nationalities, geographical location, sex and occupation.

Each of these groups mentioned above portrays different behavioural characteristics which influence consumption patterns and need satisfaction. From a cross-cultural advertising perspective, each of these target audiences within which market segments can be identified and developed can be broken down into smaller segments which can best be reached through special copy appeals and selective media choices. In some cases, e.g. elderly people, product attributes or features can be differentiated to suit the needs of such market segments. This suggests that the messages might vary from country to country depending on the products usage concept. Overall, selective perception and retention will be broadly influenced by these market categorizations. Thus, product positioning might involve incorporating different features in order to create awareness, and to stimulate brand trial purchases. If it is an industrial product, the cues should appeal to a group of people who are directly involved in the materials acquisition decision-making process. However, it could be argued that industrial products are more standardizable than consumer products irrespective of differences in cultures, subcultures and phases of economic development at global and regional levels.

However, even if the product usage concept might be the same across nations, such as a contraceptive product, positioning such a standardized product might be influenced differently. For example, should the World Health Organization (WHO) emphasize that married and single people should use condoms in order to prevent AIDS or reduce the birth rate? The positioning is situational or market specific. A Catholic in the United States and those in Ireland or Italy might take different perspectives in relation to responding to an advertisement focusing on birth control. It is apparent that product usage concept will play a major role in terms of persuading consumers to try purchases. Because of social and economic differences, people see, understand and interpret things in their local environment differently. It could be argued that managers at corporate, business and functional levels should integrate and co-ordinate more effectively their operational activities in order to design advertising campaigns that are consistent with strategic capabilities relevant to their strategic business units, and across market segments, if they are to develop and sustain competitive leverage without risking economies of scale in advertising-cultural universals (Jain, 1993).

Market Structure and Effect on Cross-Cultural Advertising

The study for various product ranges leads one to conclude that demand for basic products is mainly influenced by underlying social and environmental imperatives that impinge on market structures at a given time, and that advertising by itself serves not so much to increase demand for a product as to speed up the expansion of demand that would come from favourable conditions, or to retard adverse demand trends due to unfavourable conditions (Borden, 1947). Borden went on further to say that demands for some products such as vegetables and professional services had grown even though the products were insignificantly advertised. The arguments raised above are true, but advertising in general or cross-advertising is determined by diverse characteristics of market structure and other uncontrollable macroenvironmental imperatives (Cateora, 1990). It could also be argued that demand for a product is dependent on whether a product fulfils a basic human felt need or a want in one country or another.

Other industries for which there has been underlying conditions favourable to demand expansion have had their demand more rapidly expanded through the use of advertising than would have occurred without such advertising. Such products include, for example, cars, radios, automatic refrigerators, camcorders and washing machines. Jain (1993) and Belch (1998) argue that global advertising plays a significant role. Jain went on further to say: 'In the case of many products/markets, a successful advertising campaign is the crucial factor in achieving sales goals. As a matter of fact more and more companies consider successful advertising to be requisite to profitable international operations'. It is important to note the tone of this quote. Jain emphasizes the word 'successful', thus it is essential that practitioners (must) understand cross-cultural universals and exclusions that tend to condition advertising appeals in different markets. This issue is broadly discussed by Monye in chapter 5 on global advertising.

Advertising does increase demand for products, but the degree to which it does varies widely and depends on the circumstances under which a company operates. Advertising's effectiveness in profitably stimulating sales for a company depends on the presence of a combination of conditions, of which the following are important (Schramm, 1975):

1   Advertising is likely to be more effective if a company is operating with a favourable primary demand trend than if it is operating with an adverse trend. With the industry's sales expanding, each concern has the opportunity to strive for part of an increasing whole.
2   Advertising is particularly helpful to individual companies in stimulating demand when their products provide chance for differentiation. Conversely, advertising is of less help if there is substitution effect.
3   The relative importance to consumers of hidden qualities of the product, as contrasted with external qualities which can be seen and appreciated, e.g. watches and cars; producers of such products find advertising helpful in building mental associations regarding the dependability of their products.
4   The presence of powerful emotional buying motives to which the concerns can appeal in their advertising. For example multivitamins have effective emotional appeal in maintaining good health.
5   Whether the company's operations provide substantial sums with which to advertise and promote their products. The pharmaceutical industry is a case in point (Simango, 1993).

Thus, it can be concluded that the effectiveness of advertising or of cross-cultural advertising in influencing selective demand depends on the extent to which the five conditions outlined above are in existence. The combination of conditions that exist, rather than any one condition, determines the effectiveness of advertising in influencing selective demand. Of the conditions, those which are particularly important in rendering advertising an effective means for increasing the demands of individual companies' products are the chance for significant product differentiation (e.g. ethical drugs), the opportunity to use strong emotional appeals (e.g. pharmaceutical products such as beauty or health care products), the existence of hidden qualities that are of importance to buyers, and the existence of circumstances favouring the accumulation of substantial sums of money to support advertising. It can be concluded that when these five conditions (listed above) are applied in cross-advertising, they vary according to the nature of the product and the countries in which companies compete.

Similarities and Differences in Cross-Cultural Advertising: A Comparative Analysis

This section discusses and summarizes the evidence of some cross-cultural advertising similarities in different countries. As can be evidenced in table 3.3, some products tend to have cultural universals in the United States, Europe and Latin America, but less similarities in China. The factors that contributed to these similarities in attitudes and interests have been fully discussed. These similarities and differences in attitudes and interests suggest that advertising appeals will have to be developed according to the specific needs of each group of markets, or standardized according to those markets that have similarities in the basis for advertising appeals. Thus, not all themes are equally applicable and useful at an international or global level because most consumers tend to buy attitudes rather than product tangibility. This tends to emphasize the psychological selves that are associated with diverse cultures. Managers will have to identify culturally universal concepts such as improved quality or product, basic everyday themes, new product or services, service to the customer and special expertise offered by a company (De Mooij, 1994).

Overall, culture has influence on the consumer as a decision maker. According to De Mooij (1994): 'The fundamental assumption in Western decision-making theory is that a decision does not happen by itself, somebody makes it. This view derives from the North American culture. The Japanese, on the other hand, let necessary action arise as a result of events, instead of controlling them by making decisions. In the USA, decisions are individual processes, whereby the decision-maker always makes his or her decisions in the context of a particular social role'. In some cultures, an individual has a significant role to play. In Japan, the individual is defined as a member of a group and, in India, this could be related to the caste system where individuals serve as examples. Individualism is valued by Americans and Swedes, but is of lesser significant value in Asian nations (De Mooij, 1994). These cross-cultural similarities and differences influence cross-cultural advertising as appeals will have to be developed according to these specific factors, suggesting a balance between decentralization and centralization in advertising. Given that culture is learned, one would expect more similarities as economies improve their levels of economic development. However, it could be argued that barriers caused by culture and language warrant some modifications to cross-cultural advertising irrespective of phases of economic development.

Within Asian countries, Tai (1997) found that more multinational corporations are transferring international advertising strategies to Asian markets than ever before, and more similar cross-cultural target groups with similar needs can be approached in the same way in Asian countries. Tai argues that this degree of homogeneity is there as a result of more educated people and rising standards of living in the Asian Newly Industrialising Countries (NIC). This finding, though regeocentric, is consistent with the argument raised earlier that effective disposable income influences the degree of cross-cultural similarities. Thus, multinational enterprises can now create similar advertising appeals to broader segments of Asian consumers. It could be argued that, in some respects, Asia is a rather unique region since it has a more tightly unified culture than most of the regions at a global level. It could also be argued that as a result of faster economic development, some of the Asian countries are also experiencing the melting pot syndrome as applied to European and American countries (the impact of individualism on society). The commonly quoted example is Japan.

Some multinational managers argue that regional approaches to the Asian market are not appropriate due to different tastes and requirements within the Asian markets. A study by Shao and Waller (1993), focusing on Singapore, Hong Kong and Taiwan, confirmed that Hong Kong has a higher level of cross-cultural advertising similarities than Singapore and Taiwan. It could be suggested that this probability of accepting and assimilating more international cultural issues is due to the effect of the past British colonial history which stimulated higher social mobility and more exposure to global products and corporate entities that invested in Hong Kong than in the other two sample countries. Hong Kong was exposed to a more diverse corporate culture and product range than Singapore and Taiwan, and its society was less insular than the latter two. On the other hand, other Asian markets, such as India, Korea, the Philippines and Malaysia, favoured regional advertising strategies with adaptations. Tai (1997) found that there are eight main barriers that restrict cross-cultural advertising standardization, which are as follows:

1   Differences in cultural background.
2   Differences in consumer tastes and habits.
3   Differences in languages used.
4   Differences in legal and regulation constraints.
5   Differences in economic development.
6   Differences in competitors' strategies.
7   Differences in marketing practices.
8   Differences in technical requirements.

It could be suggested that although most of the examples given in this section tend to have American, European and Asian focus, as case examples, it is apparent that the eight barriers listed above also apply to any market at a global level. Thus, it could be concluded that regional economic integration or economic alliances (such as the SADC, EU, NAFTA and APEC) tend to foster more similarities in cross-cultural advertising, but taking account of the eight factors listed above. It could be argued that no matter how closely linked nations are, culture is the root of national identity, national sovereignty and pride such that advertising appeals will have to be modified to some extent. Also, there are some products that are culture bound and this cannot be simply eradicated by the degree to which a nation is developed. A basic example is the difference between some EU member states which accept male nudity in ads in comparison to other member states, such as the United Kingdom and the Republic of Ireland, where it is not acceptable to the society.

Table 3.3 shows cross-cultural similarities and differences over products commonly preferred by teenagers. According to a global study by D'Arcy Masius Benton and Bowles, of New York (quoted in *Advertising Age*, 1995, p. 5), the study showed that teens around the world have very similar attitudes and interests to products shown in table 3.3. European and US teens more closely share cultural universals than their Latin American counterparts, and Chinese teens seem to be least similar in their preference for denim jackets, running shoes, jeans and T-shirts. It could be argued that differences are due to the fact that some of these products in table 3.3 are culture bound. However, since culture is not innate, it could be argued that the gap will soon be narrowed as a result of the ending of the cold war since this has fostered high social mobility between markets at a global level.

The evidence of cross-cultural similarities and differences in table 3.3 suggests that there are a multitude of factors that influence attitudes and interests as

Table 3.3 Cross-cultural comparative analysis of attitudes and interests: what teens wear

| | Product category and country | | | | |
	United States	Europe	Latin America	Asia	China
Jeans	93%	94%	86%	93%	48%
T-shirts	93	89	59	96	22
Running shoes	80	79	65	69	36
Blazer	42	43	30	27	43
Denim jackets	39	57	41	23	7

Source: Adopted from *Advertising Age* (1995), p. 3.

regards consumer behaviour. Some of these human traits are so abstract that it is not feasible to identify and quantify them. Amongst the most influential factors that contribute to need and want satisfaction are, for example, culture, social mobility, politics, levels of economic development, product usage concept, country of origin and values (all contribute to consumer preferences). The similarities and differences could mean a lot in terms of economies of scale in advertising, and how these similar products could be positioned in these markets. Strategic decision making in advertising would mean developing themes that are congruent with the Chinese perception of and usage of these products. Standardization of themes and product positioning could be more applicable to the American and European markets. It could also be noted that, overall, preferences (the psychological self) might be tied to individual effective disposable income as well as the degree and impact of the substitution effect that impinge on a particular product, and at a given time.

Global Advertising Expenditure

As more nations compete to fulfil the New International Economic Order, more countries have increased production with indigenous scientific base, and market structures in developing countries have also changed accordingly. According to a report on *World Advertising Trends* (1997), advertising expenditure reached U$247 billion in the 79 countries for which 1995 data were available. The report went on further to say: 'This is the highest figure recorded since data were first collected in 1987 and indicates the importance of advertising to the global economy. The 1995 figure represents a real terms annual increase of 8%'. As a result of the findings by the NTC report, it could be suggested that the end of the cold war has contributed to more focus on economic development, co-ordination and integration of global multinational operational activities within and across strategic business units (SBUs). Thus, the overall multinational enterprises' corporate objectives are now focused on growth, survival and creating pre-emptive barriers to sustain distinctive core competencies in order to earn above-average industry performance.

However, the report cited above cautions us by stating that 'care should be taken when analysing aggregate year-on-year growth as it can be artificially boosted by the inclusion of previously unavailable data, improved monitoring within countries and alterations in methodology by data suppliers'. It is quite apparent that comparability of international or global data is a major problem since it inflates or deflates cross-cultural research data analysis and findings.

For those countries that are registering high economic growth and are enjoying similar levels of economic growth, there is more potential cross-culturally to use standardized advertising appeals. However, this also depends on the nature of the product as to whether it is free from being culture bound. Even if the product might not be culture bound, other factors such as effective disposable income and regulation might force multinational companies to customize the strategic decisions in advertising (target segment, product positioning, objective and main advertising theme). Table 3.1 shows global advertising expenditure, and it could be noted that advertising expenditure is predominantly concentrated in the United States and European member states. Nearly 70% of advertising expenditure was spent in the American and European continents, but America is the only continent to have lost its share since 1987. Europe has maintained its share, and Asia Pacific's share has increased, while Africa and the Middle East account for 0.7% (see table 3.1) of the total global share, equivalent to US$1.7 billion. Table 3.2 shows the top five global advertising expenditure by countries in each of the five continents.

It could be argued that advertising expenditure is associated with each economy's propensity to attract competition, and the faster the economy grows, the higher the probability for cross-cultural advertising standardization. Higher effective disposal income suggests the ability to try newly introduced products, which enjoy global recognition. Within and across these regional or more affluent nations, there is high social mobility, which helps consumers not only to understand culture, but to appreciate it. It is my opinion that understanding a culture and appreciating it are two different integral issues. Thus, from the practitioner's point of view, cross-cultural advertising must be based on intelligent understanding and appreciation of cultures and subcultures too. Therefore, there is no culture that is superior or inferior if humans accept banking of education or knowledge as assets to social and economic growth!

Conclusion

This chapter has demonstrated that cross-cultural advertising is influenced by culture and subculture, which are also influenced by other diverse elements of the external environment imperatives such as law, politics, natural environment, market structure and technology. Although cultural universals are on an increase, companies must have representative cross-cultural research in order to identify similarities and differences in how advertising appeals could be standardized at a regional or global level. More research should be carried out to identify the factors that influence cultural universals and exclusions before management takes the decision to standardize or localize advertising. There is no model yet that could be used as a framework within which to understand diverse psychological selves and the relationship to business practice differences at a global or regional level. This suggests that the field of cross-cultural research and data analysis is very inconsistent because of the fluidity of the serial selves. Particular attention should be paid to product conditions and the usage concept.

More similarities are being experienced as a result of faster economic development and economic alliances such as the EU, SADC, APEC and NAFTA. This has resulted in high social mobility, more product and cultural exposure. However, due to other factors such as differences in languages and cross-national regulations, managers should be prepared to localize the strategic advertising components of advertising such as positioning and main theme development. The tactical components of advertising, such as creative execution and media buying, need a national responsiveness. However, the tactical decisions are directly influenced by the nature of market structure that prevails in a given country. In order to penetrate markets effectively, managers must not base their advertising decisions on self-reference, but should learn to understand and appreciate cultures from the international consumer's point of view. Gaining economies of scale in advertising should not be considered as a cost-effective strategy at the expense of market penetration and positive return on investment and corporate survival.

REFERENCES

Advertising Age (1995). 17 July.

Alden, D., Hoyer, W. and Lee, C. (1993) Identifying global and culture-specific dimensions of humor in advertising: a multinational analysis. *Journal of Marketing*, April.

American Marketing Association (1975) *The Marketing Book*. New York: AMA.

Anholt, S. (1995) Pan-European advertising. *Grocer*, 217(7199), 382.

Arenas, W. (1996) *Contemporary Advertising*. Irwin.

Banerjee, A. (1994) Transnational advertising development and management: an account planning approach and a process framework. *International Journal of Advertising*, 13(2), 30.

Belch, G. and Belch, M. (1998) *Advertising and Promotion*. Irwin/McGraw-Hill.

Borden, H. (1947) *The Economic Effects of Advertising*. Irwin.

Cateora, P. (1990) *International Marketing*. Irwin.

Cheron, E., Padgett, T. and Woods, W. (1987) A method for cross-cultural comparisons for global strategies. *Journal of Advertising*, Winter, 31.

Cutler, B. and Javalgi, R. (1992) A cross-cultural analysis of the visual components of print advertising: the United States and the European Community. *Journal of Advertising Research*, January/February.

Cutler, B., Javalgi, R. and Erramilli, M. (1992) A comparison of print advertising: a five-country cross-cultural analysis. *European Journal of Marketing*, 26(4).

Davis, H., Douglas, S. and Silk, A. (1981) Measuring unreliability: a hidden threat to cross-national marketing research? *Journal of Marketing*, Spring, 98.

De Mooij, M. (1994) *Advertising Worldwide*. Prentice Hall.

Deng, S., Jivan, S. and Hassan (1994) Advertising in Malaysia: a cultural perspective. *International Journal of Advertising*, 13.

Dibb, S., Simkin L. and Yuen, R. (1994) Pan-European advertising: think Europe – act local. *International Journal of Advertising*, 13(2), 125.

Encyclopedia Britannica (1991) 15th edn. USA.

Engel, J. F., Kollat, D. T. and Blackwell, R. (1973) *Consumer Behaviour*, 2nd edn. New York: Holt, Rinehart and Winston.

Ford, M. (1997) Lines of communications. *Southern African Decisions*, October–December, 89.

Greg, H. (1994) International advertising standardization: what do the multinationals actually standardize? *Journal of International Consumer Marketing*, 3(2).

Heyder, H. and Peters, K. (1992) Advertising in Europe: attitude towards advertising in certain key East and Western European countries. *Marketing and Research Today*, March.

House of Commons (1994) Trade and Industry Committee, Vol. 2. London.

Jain, S. (1993) *International Marketing Management*. PWS–Kent Publishing.

Lardy, N. (1994) *China in the World Economy*. Institute for International Economics, Washington.

Monye, S. O. (1997) *The International Business Blue Print*. Oxford: Blackwell.

Mueller, B. (1987) Reflections of culture: an analysis of Japanese and American advertising appeals. *Journal of Advertising Research*, June/July.

Mueller, B. (1992) Standardization vs specialization: an examination of westernization in Japanese advertising. *Journal of Advertising Research*, January/February.

Parameswaran, J. and Yaprak, A. (1987) A cross-national comparison of consumer research measures. *Journal of International Business Studies*, Spring, 45.

Schiffman, L. G. and Kanuk, L. (1978) *Consumer Behavior*. Prentice Hall.

Schramm, W. (1975) *Mass Communications*. Illinois: Illinois Press.

Shao, A. and Waller D. (1993) Advertising standardization in the Asia Pacific Region: what stands in the way? *Asian Pacific Journal of Marketing and Logistics*, 5(3).

Simango, C. C. B. (1992) Human resources management policy in Ireland (pharmaceutical industry). *Journal of Pharmaceutical Marketing*, 4(5).

Simango, C. C. B. (1993) Strategic locational factors influencing foreign direct investment. *European Business Review*, 93.

Southern African Decisions (1998) April–June.

Sundberg, B. (1989) *International Advertising Handbook: a user's guide to rules and regulations*. Lexington Books.

Tai, S. H. (1997) Advertising in Asia: localize or regionalize. *International Journal of Advertising*, 16(1), 48.

Terpstra, V. (1991) *The Cultural Environment of International Business*. Thompson.

World Advertising Trends (1997) London: NTC Publications.

Zhang, Y. and Gelb, B. (1996) Matching advertising appeals to culture: the influence of products' use conditions. *Journal of Advertising*, 25(3), 29.

4 American Culture and Advertising

Dag Bennett

Introduction

Why does sex feature in every advertisement for French cars? Why is British advertising humorous or ironic and American advertising so 'Hollywood'? Are consumers in these countries so different? Do they only respond to specific types of communication, even when products and brands are virtually identical from country to country? Or is it that ads are created by advertising agencies, which simply reflect their country of origin?

Twenty years ago, a discussion about the character of advertising would have centred on national culture. That is, because cultures are distinct and particular, advertising has to be distinct and particular in different countries in order to be effective.

Today it is not so clear. Marketers still feel culture is critical, but the discussion has evolved to include terms like globalization, cultural convergence, branding, tribalism and transnationalism, to name just a few. National culture is still important, but may no longer be the most important issue.

Advertising is big business, generating about $250 billion in spending worldwide in 1995 (Worldwide Summary, 1997). The United States, with about a quarter of the world's gross domestic product (GDP), has the largest and arguably most influential advertising industry. It is also home to many of the world's biggest, most global firms. American culture is pervasive because of the amount of its expression in the various media, but it is more important than size alone suggests because of the types of products and brands that American firms sell abroad (see table 4.1). The key term is brands, which are generally very heavily advertising dependent.

American here means the United States, but the focus is not purely American because, like the clients that advertising serves, American agencies are also multinational or transnational. In other words, they not only operate in, but also draw talent from, many countries. Moreover, at top levels of management, there is heavy pressure for efficiencies in marketing, and global marketing strategies veer

Table 4.1 The world's most valuable brands
(Moules, 1997)

1	Marlboro	44.6bn
2	Coca-Cola	43.4
3	McDonald's	18.9
4	IBM	18.5
5	Disney	15.4

Source: Financial World, 1996.

towards advertising that is applicable to a range of countries or cultures. Of course, different languages and ethnic typing would sometimes dictate adapted advertising that tries to appear 'local' or at least non-foreign.

And yet, ads from America generally look like American ads. General impressions of flashiness, or style, or materialism, or confidence, depending where you sit, are no less true because of exceptions or counterexamples. It must be kept in mind that discussions of culture, and of advertising, rely on very general terms and gross generalities; there will be any number of exceptions – American ads that do not look it and non-American ones that do. Generally speaking, though, American culture makes itself clear in American advertising.

Here is the rub. Views of American culture are as varied as the people who study it, and if any brilliant American culturist should happen to define who Americans really are, you can rest assured that someone else will vehemently and convincingly disagree – as well they should. The job of American culture discovery will begin again.

What follows is a brief and all too general description of American culture and its interaction with advertising – or more properly, marketing communication. It is not just about the United States, however, but also looks at how culture, marketing and business combine to shape not only America, but the rest of the world.

A Short Peculiar History

Compared to Europe or Asia, America seems a young place, lacking a long history.[1] But this lack of history, if appreciated at all, is not negatively perceived by Americans, who frequently know little about their ancestors. For many, two generations is as far as memory extends. It is not that the past is unimportant, but it is less important than the future. The country still looks like the land of opportunity to outsiders and, for Americans, the place they want to be. This is true even for those who have not lived the American dream because most still believe they will. Nor is it naive optimism; after all, America has its share of poverty and misery. Rather, it is a value built into the American psyche that says opportunity is there for the taking.

Edward Countryman in his seminal work, *Americans* (1996), describes how the American mosaic of peoples and cultures evolved in North America.

> In terms of race and class, freedom and slavery, religion and culture, gender and region, people differed enormously. Yet they faced one contradiction running through their lives. Every colonial learned about a social ideal that put enormous stress on personal autonomy. All of them lived however, within a social reality of subordination to the will and purposes of someone else. All were *subject* in some way to the will and purposes of another. (p. 32; italics in original)

Countryman goes on to describe the American revolution as a civil war, one which acted like a cauldron that boiled out much of the element that was willing to remain subject (estimates of the number of loyalists who emigrated differ wildly, but what is generally agreed is that 'establishment' figures, those with a vested interest in a connection to Britain, left). Those who remained were fiercely independent groups united almost solely by their desire for independence from Britain. After the war, they resumed pursuit of their own sectarian interests and it was only by the hardest effort at compromise that the jealous states managed to hammer out a republican framework that could accommodate the states' needs for autonomy and independence.

A Defining Moment

> English Colonel Isaac Barré, a fierce one-eyed soldier who had fought in the 7 Years War, was in parliament when debate about policy towards the rebellious American colonies was discussed. Charles Townsend, President of the Board of Trade, derided the colonists: 'Children planted by our Arms, shall they grudge to contribute their mite to relieve us from the heavy weight of that burden we lie under?'.
>
> Barré sprang to his feet, and declared: 'They planted by your Care? No! Your Oppressions planted 'em in America . . . They nourished up by *your* indulgence? They grew up by your neglect of 'em . . . They protected by your arms? They have nobly taken up arms in your defense . . . And believe me, and remember that I this day told you so, that same spirit of freedom which actuated that people at first, will accompany them still . . . They are a people jealous of their liberties and who will vindicate them if ever they should be violated – but the Subject is too delicate and I will say no more.'
>
> Parliament was stunned to silence. It was the first moment that some members of parliament began to understand the particular nature of the Americans. (Tuchman, 1984, p. 152)

America has always been a melting pot and the vast majority of Americans came from elsewhere at one time or another. The term 'Americans' covers a huge range of cultures.

As Rabin (1994) said: 'Understanding what people have in common is as vital to advertisers as understanding their differences. A person's national origin and ethnic self-identification are important, but they may not bind that person to a group as much as the attitudes and lifestyles that arise from those backgrounds. Social values, methods of communication and common interests can cross cultural boundaries.'

> Do I contradict myself?
> Very well then, I contradict myself.
> I am large.
> I contain Multitudes
> > Walt Whitman (1955) in *Song of Myself*

The American Civil War erupted over the difficulties of maintaining a federal system that subordinated the rights of states to national rights. The southern states, always economically different than the northern states, resisted what they felt were unwarranted claims to sovereignty by the national government and increasing meddling in social, political and economic affairs. Only towards the end of the third year of war, with the Emancipation Proclamation, did the central issue become slavery. While the Proclamation itself was less an act of principle than expedience – by undercutting the basis of the southern economy it prevented a compromise on matters of sovereignty – the longer term effect was to set the stage for a social revolution.

The decade after the war was one of crisis as the nation struggled to heal the wounds of war while coping with mass migration and the final settlement of the Indian issue. In many ways, the schisms remain. Garreau (1989) writes in *The Nine Nations of North America* that borders between states mean less than the economics, politics and society they share. The nation he calls Dixie, for example, stretches from Florida to East Texas, north to Indiana, south under the Appalachians and north to Maryland. This region is economically progressive though reliant on traditional industry and agriculture, and socially conservative. Ectopia on the other hand (the Pacific Northwest) is progressive on both counts and very forward thinking industrially and politically. Garreau includes Mexico, Canada and the Caribbean in his nine nations, saying that economics and culture transcend national lines. The American federal system then, is less a collection of 50 states, more a coalition of nations, none of which is fully independent. Recent agreements like the North American Free Trade Agreement (NAFTA) support this view.

The business culture of the United States reflects its fairly recent roots. The city of Chicago, for instance, was laid out in 1830 and in 1836 had 4000 residents. By 1860, the former swamp on the edge of Lake Michigan had grown to 100 000 people, 5 per cent of whom were working in industry, building such things as Cyrus McCormick's mechanical reapers (Countryman, 1996, p. 126). The city's explosive growth continued through the 1950s, making a transition from processing grain and meat to making steel and manufactured goods.

Chicago is a case study for the transition from an economy oriented towards agriculture to industry and a society motivated by wealth in land to wealth in capital. The boom times gave us the slogan: 'If you can't make it in Chicago, you can't make it anywhere'. Compare that to New York's: 'If I can make it here, I'll make it anywhere'. Making it means not only being successful in terms of wealth, but it also has an entrepreneurial or managerial flavour to it. It is not just a job that motivates people, but the dream of running one's own show.

I Gotta Be Me

Individualism is another key to American culture. It stems from a largely Protestant religious history. In many respects, the dominant values visible in advertising and other forms of popular culture are WASP (White Anglo Saxon Protestant) which esteems individual achievement. The measure of a life is what has been accomplished. It is not fatalistic, pre-ordained or excusable. At the end, each individual will be judged by his achievements. This attitude, the protestant work ethic, is religious in origin, even though many Americans, regardless of historical religion, are not actively religious.[2] Alex Weber famously used it to explain why Protestant areas of Germany and Switzerland were more successful than their Catholic counterparts.

Another cornerstone of individualism is the sense of alienation that originally drove many immigrants to leave their countries, and continues to motivate them today. Americans have been kicked out of every respectable country on earth. This is the flip-side of opportunity – the recognition that it has to be better somewhere else. American political and social values were formed and codified by an enlightened group of patricians and patriots who established a structure and organizational rationale for the country and its citizens that has proved remarkably flexible, yet firm, over time. Imperfect, yes, but less imperfect in terms of individual initiative than most other systems. The net result is that Americans feel that not only *can* individuals capitalize on opportunities, but they *should*.

With its roots in English and Protestant history, American culture tends to favour the rights of the individual over the rights of society at large. This is one of the reasons why Americans tend to have smaller nuclear families than, for example, Asian cultures which have extended families. This is less true for Black or Hispanic Americans. Witness the current controversy over making Spanish an official language in some US states. This has been opposed by a number of Hispanic groups because they feel it will keep Hispanic children out of the mainstream and deny them opportunities.

One of the most cited works on culture is Hofstede's (1980) *Culture's Consequences*, in which he looks at work-related values in forty countries. He identifies four main dimensions along which dominant value systems in the forty countries can be ordered, and which affect human thinking, organizations and institutions in predictable ways. They are: power distance, uncertainty avoidance, femininity/masculinity and individualism.[3] All have implications for the behaviour of individuals in organizations. For instance, organizations in cultures high in femininity tend to be more nurturing, while those with high masculinity are more assertive.

While the United States ranks high or low on three variables, on individualism, it takes the top position (see table 4.2). While it makes no sense to try to explain behaviour based on just one variable, as a defining characteristic, this one variable

Table 4.2 Country individualism index (IDV)

Country	IDV
United States	91
Great Britain	89
Italy	76
France	71
Germany	67
Spain	54
India	48
Japan	46

Source: Hofstede (1980, p. 158).

is characteristically American. Individualism and the drive it imparts go a long way to explaining American economic success. It is at the core of secular *laissez-faire* systems. Americans tend to eschew equality of outcome, a European idea, for equality of opportunity. Everyone should have the same opportunity to succeed. Whether the opportunity is seized is up to the individual (of course, this is only approximately true for many groups and individuals).

Push

Americans are a hard-driving people who moulded a vibrant and dominant power in a little over a century. This has not been universally popular of course; Samuel Johnson said, 'I am willing to love all mankind, except an American'. His opinion would probably not have altered much today with America having won three world wars, World War I, World War II and the Cold War, and set to enter the twenty-first century unrivalled in power. A modern commentator, the author Margaret Atwood, a Canadian nationalist, bridling against a dominant neighbour, said to a parliamentary committee:

> About the only position they have adopted toward us, country to country, has been the missionary position, and we were not on top. I guess that is why the national wisdom *vis-à-vis* Them has so often taken the form of lying still, keeping your mouth shut and pretending you like it. (Walsh, 1997)

It has not all gone America's way of course, Paul Kennedy published the *Decline and Fall of the Great Powers* in 1987 which became a surprise best seller not because people were interested in Rome's fall or the crumbling of the British Empire, but in the ultimate demise of the current 600 pound gorilla. At the time, the German and Japanese economies were much stronger and America seemed to be falling behind. But by the mid-1990s, America was back on top, as columnist Laurent Joffrin wrote in the French newspaper *Libération*: 'For five or six years the United States has obtained results on unemployment, competitiveness, growth and deficits that would make world leaders dream. They have paid the price – brutal restructuring, growing economic inequality, unbridled domination by money – but they have reduced unemployment and balanced the accounts, something that Europeans have been breaking their backs trying to do for ages' (see Walsh, 1997).

Americans can take pride in these achievements – and do, to the point that they are often criticized for arrogance. This criticism may mask an unpleasant feeling of insecurity, much as the Tory party in England complained about the arrogance of the Labour party following its unprecedented majority in 1997. Americans perceive this as being pilloried for their success. Arrogance and high-handedness aside, Americans also take a bashing on culture; a short history, naivety, no sense of irony and a lack of refinement add up to a lack of culture. This is especially true in connection with American multinationals, purveyors of fast food, rock and roll, laptops and videos. Hollywood is both a place and a pejorative.

Culture, Culture

How important is culture? Consider the opening paragraph of Bernard Lewis's history of the Middle East. A man sits at a table in a coffee house in some Middle Eastern city, drinking a cup of coffee or tea, perhaps smoking a cigarette, reading a newspaper, playing a board game, and listening with half an ear to whatever is coming out of the radio or the television in the corner. Undoubtedly Arab, probably Muslim, the man would identify himself and feel part of these cultural groups. He would probably also say Western culture was alien to him, if asked.

But looking closer, the cultural lines tend to blur. He probably wears 'Western' clothes and shoes, possibly made in the West. He smokes a Western cigarette and listens to a Japanese radio or TV. The coffee is imported, even the table and chairs are likely to be of non-Arab design. Consider also his work, he may use Western technology or work for a multinational corporation, or if in government, his bureaucratic surroundings and constitutional framework may owe their origins to Western influence.

The implication for Lewis is clear: 'In modern times, the dominating factor of consciousness of most Middle Easterners has been the image of Europe, later of the West more generally, and the transformation – some would say dislocation – which it has brought'. Lewis is talking here about cultural change, which is possibly the least understood aspect of cultural identity. While many the world over complain about change – in cultural terms such as family values – it is only recently that the debate has become focused.

Samuel Huntington writes in a new book, *The Clash of Civilizations and the Remaking of the World Order* (1997, p. 41), about how culture and cultural identities are shaping the patterns of cohesion, disintegration and conflict in the post-Cold War world. Global politics is being reconfigured along cultural lines. Huntington is writing post-Cold War, in which the demise of ideological conflict has led to the reconsideration of what upcoming conflicts will be about. He is one of many who place stress on the issues of culture as definers of identity in the confusion left in the wake of the Cold War.

On a more local level, defining culture has traditionally been left a bit vague. Most writers rely at least in part on self-definition, much as practical leaders such as Kemal Ataturk did at the birth of modern Turkey when he said that whoever says he is a Turk, speaks Turkish and lives in Turkey, is a Turk (Kaplan, 1996, p. 139). Cultures are what people think they are. A civilization or society is the broadest level of identification with which (a person) intently identifies. Huntington does not separate 'culture' from 'civilization': '. . . both refer to the overall way of life of a people, and a civilization is a culture writ large. Both involve the "values, norms, institutions and modes of thinking to which successive generations in a given society have attached primary importance"' (Huntington, 1997, p. 41, quoting Bozeman, *Civilizations under Stress*, p. 1).

But there is a problem here because most people do not identify intensely with anything too broad, and much depends on context. A group of Europeans generally do not feel European; they feel Dutch or English. Americans, on the other hand, may feel like New Yorkers, Californians or Texans. Put Europeans or Americans in a meeting with Chinese or Arabs, though, and they begin to describe themselves as European or American.

Melting pot or mosaic, the American people are diverse and ever changing in balance of numbers and background. The American culture is anything but static. Even if a culturist were able to nail it down, it would never stay nailed down for long. New people will come, new elements of culture will be imported from anywhere, and the complex mix that makes up America will continue to generate surprising results.

The Knowledge Era

The feelings people have about themselves and their identity are under tremendous pressure. The world may now be entering the 'knowledge era' or undergoing an information revolution. Like the industrial revolution, the information revolution in which the creation, storage, use and spreading of knowledge becomes the basic economic activity, is unleashing huge change. As any revolution, it emphasizes thorough, rapid and even chaotic change, and is anti-traditional, anti-authoritarian and anti-establishment.

But even in the knowledge era, culture may still be an engine of change. There is a notion of world culture, in which the boundaries between like-minded people cease to matter so much; businesspeople, doctors, computer programmers, even golfers, may have more in common with their contemporaries in other countries than they do with their next-door neighbours. This is the globalization argument applied to culture. And in many ways it can be seen not just as Western culture spreading, but more specifically American culture.

The notion of modern Westernism on a collision course with other cultures is captured by several writers. Barber (1995) argues in *Jihad versus McWorld* that the main conflicts now and in the future will be between tribal level 'cultural values (jihad) and a McWorld of technology, sameness and democracy'. He echoes Huntington's views that with the demise of ideological conflict between capitalism and communism, new divisions will emerge based on religion, culture and levels of development.

Globalization and the knowledge era do not mean cultures will coalesce. Nor does it mean that the emblems of culture, the food we eat, songs we sing, clothes we wear, will ultimately homogenize. The knowledge era is more a spreading of economic ideas. It has three main effects. The first is to cause cultures to rub up against one another, generating friction. The second effect is that they generate cooperation and tie cultures more closely together – cancelling out the first effect. Finally, it increases tensions within cultural areas as some groups accommodate themselves to the new order, others struggle and some turn their back on it. All this happens at the same time because cultures are so varied, ambiguous and ultimately so capable of dramatic change.

With a culture like the American one, characterized by change, flexibility, diversity and individuality, definitions and clear images seem transitory. Even admitting that the easily visible cultural elements are superficial (like food, language, music, clothing, etc.), they may also be a useful starting point for understanding American culture and advertising.

You Are What You Consume

American culture has become extraordinarily prominent. Kids the world over listen to the same music, see the same films, wear sneakers and eat burgers. The two biggest American export industries are aerospace, on the back of Boeing, and entertainment, e.g. Hollywood and media companies. While there is a stiff competition in aerospace from the European Airbus consortium, there is no damaging competition in the form of movies, TV, video and software. Even in new areas like the Internet, the language and look are distinctively American. This is mass culture, which is becoming world culture, and it is increasingly American.

There is resistance to this domination. The French, for instance, have erected all manners of laws and regulations to defend French language and culture. In 1993, American negotiators reluctantly agreed to some restrictions on the distribution of American films in France. While this ensures that the French film industry will remain viable, it has not kept American films from dominating the French market.

Disneyfication

At the opening of Euro Disney, Lesley Garner (1989), writing in the *Daily Telegraph*, wrote: 'Not only do I find the place sinister, I think the very concept of Disneyland is a threat to civilization as we in Europe know it.'

Since then, the amusement park has had problems dealing with weather, resistance to high prices, French eating habits, and competition from European parks like those featuring the cartoon character Asterix. Nonetheless, the park has persevered and began to be profitable in 1995. It also changed its name to Disneyland Paris.

Materialism

Fame, fortune, recognition by one's peers, acceptance at the country club, academic degrees, etc., are all yardsticks for achievement, but for Americans, the most straightforward measurement is material wealth. Call it materialism, but it is unabashed materialism, drawing on old social values that say it is right and proper to prosper from one's efforts. All cultures value material gain to varying degrees. Some are openly pro-gain, such as some Asian cultures, others seem a little embarrassed by it, European cultures for example, or at least they like to place it somewhat lower than other values. It is not that European cultures do not value material gain, but they may value social, intellectual or artistic achievement more highly. In all of which, with the possible exception of artistic achievement, wealth is assumed. Americans assume less.

The American economy is about 25 per cent of the world's total, with only 5 per cent of the world's population. Americans consume more per capita than any other country on earth. This consumption does not just happen, though, it is aided by a tremendous amount of marketing communication. The average person receives about 3000 commercial messages per day, not just from mass media, but also from outdoor advertising, transit messages, clothing labels attached on the outside. And consumption starts very young – the average child sees 40 000 commercials annually – little wonder that kids are ardent consumers and brand buyers (Shurgot, 1997).

While it is a stretch to call consumerism culture, it is clear that Americans are acculturated to tremendous spending on material goods, vast amounts of communication about stuff, and habitual shopping. For some, shopping is a sport, or at least a preferred leisure activity. But it is not without danger. Consumers may be afflicted by credit card-driven 'affluenza' which drives millions to huge debt and in severe cases results in bankruptcy. 'The number of Americans who will declare bankruptcy in 1997 is likely to be more than 1 million, more than will graduate from college' (Shurgot, 1997).

Rapacious consumption is not just an economic driver and a defining characteristic of the culture, it also shapes communication and advertising. Americans are used to split-second communication in sight and sound, massive amounts of information, and tremendous choice in goods and services. They are also litigious and demanding. Consumerism, the promotion of buyers' rights, is just one indicator of how ingrained consumption has become. Advertising, therefore, must navigate a minefield of opposites, it must be entertaining yet informative, competitive yet truthful, effective yet economical.

Countervailing Indications

The Merck Family Fund commissioned a survey[4] in the United States to assess public opinion regarding consumption in the United States and consequences for society and the environment. The survey revealed four main findings:

1 Americans believe that society's priorities are out of whack, that materialism, greed and selfishness increasingly dominate American public life and the lives of individuals. These forces are crowding out a more meaningful set of values centred on family, responsibility and community. People do not want to repudiate material gain, but they want a greater sense of balance in their lives.

2 Americans are concerned about their future. The American Dream is increasingly defined by purchasing, material gain, and by 'keeping up with the Joneses', rather than by a sense of opportunity. The children absorb the lessons of their consumer culture: 86 per cent of respondents said that 'today's youth are too focused on buying and consuming things' and 58 per cent describe most American children as 'very materialistic'.

3 People are ambivalent about making changes in their lives and society. Americans want financial security and comfort, but they also hold deep non-material aspirations for themselves and their country. Eighty-two per cent of respondents agree that 'most of us buy and consume far more than we need. It's wasteful'.

4 Americans associate the environment with these concerns, but in a general way. People have an intuitive sense that our propensity to want 'more and more' is unsustainable. Eighty-eight per cent believe that 'protecting the environment will require most of us to make major changes in the way we live'.

A New World Order and Advertising

A new order is beginning to emerge for marketing, influenced by many factors. To begin, practically every brand in the developed economies competes in a crowded market against excess supply. It is also becoming increasingly difficult to clarify where one industry begins and another ends. On top of everything, new and emerging technology is redefining how marketers and customers communicate, and creating all kinds of new opportunities.

In mature Western economies, advertising budgets are growing, but slowly. Across the board, after a period of steady growth which spanned the past several decades, ad spending in real terms is flat. The industry has matured and one obvious implication of this is that advertising growth, like growth in other sectors, will be increasingly foreign market-driven, and increasingly in less-developed markets. An indication of this can be seen in table 4.3.

Today's marketers wage huge battles for tiny incremental share gains. And in most markets share is very stable over time, only changing when there is some radical change in the marketplace. As Edward Artzt, former chairman of Procter & Gamble, says: 'About the only thing that can really alter share in a stable market is a technological discontinuity' (personal communication, 1996). In the meantime, the major marketers are shifting emphasis from home markets to foreign ones.

Of the top twenty world marketers, eight are United States based, twice as many as second-place Japan with four. In addition, while the American global marketers spend almost $7.5bn per year on advertising in the United States, they spend just over $11bn outside it.

Table 4.3   Top twenty global marketers, 1996

Rank	Company	Headquarters	US ad spending	Non-US ad spending
1	Procter & Gamble	USA	$2479mn	$2622mn
2	Unilever	UK/Netherlands	2355	948
3	Nestlé SA	Switzerland	1575	402
4	Toyota Motor	Japan	989	800
5	PSA Peugeot	France	959	0
6	Volkswagen AG	Germany	933	171
7	Nissan Motor Co.	Japan	855	557
8	Coca-Cola Co.	USA	832	612
9	Philip Morris Cos.	USA	813	2278
10	General Motors	USA	773	2273
11	Ford Motor Co.	USA	741	1179
12	Mars Inc.	USA	731	557
13	Renault SA	France	664	0
14	Kao Corp.	Japan	628	22
15	Fiat SpA	Italy	606	1
16	Ferrero SpA	Italy	580	15
17	Henkel Group	Germany	570	0
18	Colgate Palmolive	USA	561	320
19	McDonald's Corp.	USA	536	1074
20	Sony Corp.	Japan	531	653

Source: *Ad Age Dataplace*, 19 August 1996.

The situation is reversed for non-United States-based global marketers, who spend about $3.6bn on advertising in the United States and $11.2bn in the rest of the world. This shows that the United States is quite a competitive market. Notice the French car makers, both of whom used to compete in the United States, but have now withdrawn.

With the huge spending on marketing by United States-based companies, it is no surprise that not only is the United States home to a host of advertising agencies, but that these companies are also very international in their activities.

Of the world's top twenty advertising organizations, ten are based in the United States and account for about half of the top twenty's $164.5bn sales volume (see table 4.4). Looked at another way, the $86.4bn represents a market share of about 35 per cent of total worldwide ad spending of $250bn. In other words, just ten American agency groups control a third of the world's advertising spending.

Much of this advertising spending occurs in the United States, but by no means all. These agency groups contain a huge number of overseas offices. Take the number eleven company Leo Burnett, for example, it has over eighty overseas offices. Burnett reckons that about one quarter of its billings are in the United States, a figure that would probably be similar for the other agency groups. The

Table 4.4 World's top twenty advertising organizations

1996 Rank	Organization	Headquarters	1996 volume
1	WPP Group	London	$24.7bn
2	Omnicom Group	New York	23.4
3	Interpublic Group	New York	20.1
4	Dentsu	Tokyo	14.1
5	Young & Rubicam	New York	12.0
6	Cordiant	London	9.8
7	Grey Advertising	New York	6.6
8	Havas Advertising	L-Perret, France	7.3
9	Hakuhodo	Tokyo	6.7
10	True North Comm.	Chicago	7.0
11	Leo Burnett	Chicago	5.8
12	MacManus Group	New York	6.8
13	Publicis	Paris	4.6
14	Bozell Jakobs, K, E	New York	3.7
15	GGT/BDDP Group	London	3.2
16	Daiko	Osaka	1.8
17	Asatsu Inc.	Tokyo	1.9
18	Carlson Mktg Group	Minneapolis	1.9
19	Tokyu Agency	Tokyo	1.8
20	TMP Worldwide	New York	1.3

Source: *Advertising Age*, 21 April 1997.

other point the agencies have in common is that they grow faster outside the United States.

Another somewhat cloudy issue is that many of the firms are transnational in ownership. For instance, True North owns 49 per cent of Publicis, and Young & Rubicam and Dentsu each own nearly 50 per cent of Dentsu, Young & Rubicam Partnerships (Smith, 1997). This reflects the common strategy for international growth through acquisition that has been aggressively pursued by agency networks for the past 10 or 20 years. It should also be pointed out that much of the pressure for internationalization of agency networks has come from the big marketers, who, in pursuit of their global markets, have driven the expansion of their agencies.

This is not without its perils, though, because while marketing and advertising abilities are fairly abundant in the mature markets, especially the United States, they can be scarce in developing markets. Moreover, while it may be relatively straightforward for a consumer product to gain acceptance abroad, it can be very difficult to clear communication hurdles.

As a result of these developments, the role of marketing in all its forms is being heavily scrutinized by corporate marketers who want to maximize message impact and minimize waste and unfruitful spending. Today's clients want strong agency

Table 4.5   Greatest impact in promoting a positive relationship

	1996	1995
Understanding the brand	52%	46%
Mutual trust	47	51
Creative excellence	42	47
Long-term partnership	33	23
Proactive thinking	32	38

Source: Smith (1997).

partners who are at the cutting edge technologically, innovative in problem solving, effective in purchasing media and proactive against the competition. Clients are putting more emphasis on 'understanding the brand' and building 'long-term partnerships' at the expense of the other criteria (see table 4.5). It is natural that, in times of rapid change, shifting boundaries, confusing diversity and intensifying competition, advertisers would want stable, reliable agency partners.

The effect of this concentration is sometimes described as cultural imperialism. In other words, Western or American products are promoted by American agencies through their global networks, using American-owned media companies to transmit images and words of American origin (often in English).

McDonaldization

George Ritzer wrote the *McDonaldization of Society* in 1992 and brought out a second edition in 1996. He was surprised by the success of essentially a theoretically based work in social criticism. He uses McDonald's as an icon for a 'paradigm' of a wide-ranging process defined as: *the process by which the principles of the fast-food restaurant are coming to dominate more and more sectors of American society as well as the rest of the world.*

By the end of 1996, McDonald had over 21 000 restaurants in 103 countries. It is just one of many chain or franchise companies that embody McDonaldization:

- McDonald's, Burger King, Pizza Hut, Taco Bell, Subway, etc., are part of the fast-food revolution that by the end of 1993 had over $81bn in sales, a third of the total food service industry sales. In 1994, fast-food sales exceeded those of traditional full-service restaurants for the first time, and the gap between them is expected to grow (Albright, 1995).
- The McDonald's model has been extended to 'casual dining' such as Outback Steakhouse, Chi-Chi's, TGI Friday's, Red Lobster, etc.
- McDonaldization has gone global. With intense competition in the home market, McDonald's expects to build twice as many restaurants abroad as at home through the end of the decade (McDowall, 1994). The same is true of most of its competitors. Burger King operates 8900 restaurants in

56 countries (Burger King homepage) and Kentucky Fried Chicken 10 000 in 76 countries (Kentucky Fried Chicken homepage).

- Other countries have developed their own responses to McDonaldization. Fast-food croissanteries have blossomed in Paris, and spread across the continent. In India, Nirula's is a chain selling fast-food mutton burgers as well as local Indian cuisine (Reitman, 1993, pp. B1, B3).
- Other McDonaldized chains have expanded into the United States; The Body Shop, for example, with nearly 1000 shops, has over 100 in the United States (Elmer-Dewitt, 1993; Shapiro, 1991). This has spawned American imitators. Similarly, at one point Benetton had over 1000 shops in the United States.
- Other types of businesses are adapting the principles of the fast-food business to their needs. Many ambitious executives say things like: 'I want to be the McDonald's of . . .' car repair, or toys, or aerobics. Many have embarked on rapid franchising and expansion abroad, including AAMCO Transmissions, Midas Muffler, H&R Block, Charles Schwabb, Home Depot, Wal-Mart, K-Mart, Hair Plus, etc.
- Ten per cent of America's stores are franchises, which account for 40% of the nation's retail sales. It is estimated that by the year 2000, 25% of stores in the United States will be chains and account for two-thirds of retail sales (Gruchow, 1995).

The New Competition

As companies evolve, so does the marketplace for marketing communications. Historically, clients retained one multidisciplined advertising agency and gave them full rein over most, if not all, marketing communications (companies with multiple brands will generally employ several agencies). With the increased pressure for performance of the past 10 years, many companies have off-loaded increasing responsibility for brand performance to their agencies, not so much delegation as abdication.

In many firms, the marketing function has lost power relative to finance, operations and sales/service. The consulting firm McKinsey (hardly a disinterested player) talks of marketing's 'mid-life crisis', arguing that many chief executive officers believe that marketing has failed to deliver on its promises, and failed to provide evidence to justify its costs. The impetus for improved customer service, product and process innovation, and corporate re-engineering has come from other functions. Even in consumer packaged goods, resources have shifted from consumer marketing to trade marketing, and from strategic brand advertising toward more measurable, tactical activities.

McKinsey is just one of a herd of consulting firms which has spotted an opportunity to expand from their traditional areas of expertise in strategy, organization, information technology and finance into marketing strategy. In some ways, the advertising industry itself has created the opportunity by its innate conservatism, which has kept 'traditional' agencies from adapting to the new needs and structures of their clients. Although many clients have radically altered their organizational structures through delayering, decentralization, etc., both on the domestic front and internationally, most agencies are still divided into account management, creative (and sometimes planning) and media departments; the same as 50 years ago.

Imagine a constellation

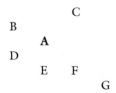

A, Full-service ad agencies.
B, Media independents.
C, Below-the-line agencies.
D, Management consultants.
E, Media owners.
F, Technology companies.
G, Film and related technologies.

The art of communication between corporations and consumers has evolved to include a host of new players who have capitalized on the opportunities created by changing consumer behaviour and new technologies. Marketing communication can be imagined as a constellation of players. At the centre are traditional full-service advertising agencies and, in some cases, their international networks. These agencies are increasingly challenged by independent media companies, some of which began their life within the womb of advertising agencies, but are now fully independent and increasingly competitive with the ad agencies.

Next come below-the-line agencies. This group encompasses both the traditional sales promotions agencies as well as the new breed of direct marketing/database marketing, plus public relations agencies. Many of these, too, once formed part of the full-service agency world. Some still do. Yet others have developed fully independent and global networks of their own. Increasingly, they are providing innovative responses to emerging customer groups. Specifically, they are succeeding in developing direct connections between clients and their customers. This breed of marketer is becoming increasingly familiar to many advertising agencies, which have already observed the trimming of ad budgets in favour of these 'below-the-line' functions.

The management consultants are new in the marketer's world – although they have had the chief executive's ear for many years. They are new because they have taken on a more expansive role in advising clients, which potentially gives them a broader influence over more aspects of the business – including, of course, marketing and advertising.

Next is a group which is sure to cause problems for the traditional agency, individually or through 'unholy' alliances. These are the 'content providers' (games, films, software, interactive creativity) and the 'distributors' (media owners, information gateways like CompuServe). Some are big. Some are tiny. The big are getting bigger. Yet even the smaller ones are joining forces to provide highly specialized, innovative, responsive solutions to many of the unique marketing challenges faced by today's clients. These alliances pose a significant threat to traditional advertising agencies, which are often perceived, accurately or not, as sluggish, layered and mired in an old way of doing business.

What Clients Will Demand in the Future

Many clients will be totally confused by the choice of technologies, relationships and roles for marketing communications which are emerging. This confusion is all the more understandable since we are witnessing not one trend, but several often countervailing trends:

- Some clients want to buy their services on a mix-and-match basis – the unbundled service offering – while others want a one-stop full-service shop.
- Some clients want a single global communications network, while others are happy to buy from the best on a local basis.
- We see a rise in huge global communications companies (News Corporation, CNN, MTV), together with a highly fragmented and local boutiquing of both creativity and software writers.
- On the one hand, global clients want global economies of scale from standardized advertising efforts across the world. On the other hand, traditional mass-marketing techniques are giving way to highly individualized communications targeted at individual consumers, and talk of the decline of traditional mass branding campaigns.

Obviously, all of these complexities will require management, and clients will seek out marketing partners who can comprehend emerging trends, be proactive in their reaction to trends, and help position their clients to excel in the dynamic market place. There is clearly a role for agencies and other advisers to clients in understanding trends, and advising their clients accordingly. Which will do so most successfully and responsively remains to be seen.

Globalization

What is a global brand? This appears to be a relatively straightforward question, but there are three distinct categories of global brand. First there are the long-term international brands, almost all American, which are exploiting a universal heritage, e.g. Ford and McDonald's. Second, there are the new products, which have been developed with a global consumer in mind, e.g. Sony Playstation. Third, there are brands which have begun life in one or more markets and then exported into others, e.g. Dove. The crucial issue is that brands hold the same values in whichever markets they are available. Consumers who travel abroad consume international media and can tell immediately if a brand stands for the same values in different markets. If it does, confidence in the product is strengthened.

Table 4.6 The world's most powerful brands

1	McDonald's	US
2	Coca-Cola	US
3	Disney	US
4	Kodak	US
5	Sony	Japan
6	Gillette	US
7	Mercedes-Benz	Germany
8	Levi's	US
9	Microsoft	US
10	Marlboro	US

Source: Interbrand Group, Information Strategy, April 1997.

The Interbrand Group (1997) rates brands on power by examining four components:

1 *Weight*. The influence of a particular brand on its market. This measure is more than mere market share.
2 *Length*. The success of the brand to reach across the market or several market-places, or its potential to do so.
3 *Breadth*. The variety of ages, consumer types and countries in which the brand is recognized.
4 *Depth*. The degree of commitment to the brand, including the intimacy con-sumers feel with the brand.

Eight of the world's ten most powerful brands are American (table 4.6), suggest-ing that the fierce domestic American competition not only helps marketers to refine their competitive strategies, but also that this process makes the brands internationally competitive.

Coca-Cola is one brand name which would undoubtedly receive a high level of spontaneous mentions in any survey which asks respondents to name global brands, even though its formulation varies from market to market, different packaging formats are available, pricing is not consistent and the name – at least for some brand extensions – is not always universal. For example, Diet Coke is well known in the United Kingdom, whereas in other parts of Europe it is known as Coca-Cola Light. Coca-Cola provides a good demonstration of a strong and consistent corporate image, providing the necessary precursor for building individual brands.

Lead Markets

Less obvious is the effect of culture. Marketers have learned that products that are successful in one market are not necessarily successful abroad. Procter & Gamble's (P&G's) disposable nappies were market leaders in the United States, but a failure in Japan. The reason was simple, Japanese nappies fit better and were more absorbent. P&G's response was also quite simple, it figured out how to make a competitive product in Japan. But their next step illustrates an approach to international competitiveness that centres on lead markets, which are those markets the company feels are most critical, competitive or trend-setting. P&G pushed Japanese product improvements through its global operations and then made The Paper Technology Center in Japan its worldwide resource for nappy technology development (E. Artzt, personal communication, 1996).

Because lead market-based strategies are used by many companies, agencies, which generally try to match their client's organizational structures, also develop lead communications markets.

Wieden and Kennedy lead Nike's communications effort in the United States and as the company expanded sales in Europe, the advertising agency went with the client and set up a headquarters in Amsterdam. In doing so, they centralized marketing for the entire European region, using marketing resources from a variety of other countries.

Microsoft and American Express are also good examples of companies which have developed single-market identities that have been transferred to their brands. If people are using the same software on the same format computers wherever you go, and if the charge card can be used in Bolivia in exactly the same way with the same level of service as in Chicago, then the symbol must be universally recognized. The role of corporate imagery is particularly effective in the marketing of corporations with common brand identities – where the corporate and brand strategies benefit from the same name, the process is made more productive because of the transfer of imagery from one to the other.

Therefore, while a clear distinction should be made between marketing the company and marketing individual products, there is a distinct benefit in the establishment of a single perception of the company among actual and potential customers across all markets. It should be pointed out, however, that it is the nature of the industry that determines the ease or difficulty of marketing across borders. Industrial products are probably easier than consumer products. Within consumer products, durables may be easier than non-durables or fast-moving consumer goods (FMCG). And within FMCG, cross-border marketing may be less difficult if the product is functional, like detergents or shampoo, or ready to use, like colas or confectionery.

The product category will clearly affect the choice of organizational structure of international companies when they move outside home territory. Once this has been established, success or failure will depend largely on how the global brand is marketed locally, and how it caters for developing marketing and consumer environments. While it is of the utmost importance that brand values are transported from market to market, consumers must feel assured that they are not dealing with an unapproachable 'big brother'. It is fine to buy a Ford in Spain, but if the infrastructure had not been established to provide assurances of customer service, buyers would become dissatisfied, followed by an inevitable decline in brand values and sales. There are assurances from buying from a large, trusted multinational organization, but only if local credentials exist.

Different parts of the world are on different steps of the evolutionary ladder of consumerism and marketing hierarchies, and these stages have to be considered for success to follow. Successful branding needs a clear understanding of consumer environments, environments that are changing at an astonishing rate.

Three New Groups of Americans

Ray (1997) has written in *American Demographics* about the emergence of new groups of American consumer types. These are based on the work of American LIVES of San Francisco.

They categorize Americans by their prevailing worldviews:

1 *Traditionalism.* A belief system for about 29 per cent of Americans (56 million adults) who could also be called Heartlanders. These Americans often appear to be rebelling against the slick city types. They have a nostalgic view of small towns and the Good Old American Way. Their icons would be the strong types portrayed by Jimmy Stewart or John Wayne.
2 *Modernism.* Modernism holds sway for about 47 per cent of Americans or 88 million adults. The antecedents of this view are the modernism that grew out of the worldview of urban middle and merchant classes and other creators of the modern economy. It defines modern politicians, military leaders, scientists and intellectuals. Modernists place high value on personal success, consumerism, materialism and technological rationality.
3 *Cultural Creatives.* The newest worldview goes beyond modernism and its adherents can be called Cultural Creatives. They comprise about 24 per cent of the population (44 million adults). The roots of this view are in nineteenth-century spiritual movement, which gained strength as Western intellectuals discovered the diversity and coherence of other religions and philosophies. It expanded greatly in the 1960s as people joined various 'movements' for human potential, civil rights, peace, jobs, social justice, ecology and women's rights.

The drivers of these changes are many. For example, by the year 2000, Asia will account for about 60 per cent of the world's population, and the growth rate will remain about four times that of Europe and the United States. Can Western marketers continue to remain Euro- or America-centric?

In the immediate decade, North America, Europe and East Asia will continue to dominate economically and will therefore have the greatest purchasing power. However, if the pace of change continues, it is estimated that China will have a larger GDP by 2003. Even if the growth rate halves, it will catch up by 2014. As another example, Singapore's GDP will soon be on a par with Germany's.

Media and its Influence

Since the launch of Telstar in the 1960s, satellite television has transformed broadcasting. With the exception of the South Pole, there is nowhere the satellite

Table 4.7 World's ten leading media companies

Rank	Company	Headquarters	1995 revenue
1	Time Warner	New York	9.8bn
2	Disney Capital Cities/ABC	Burbank, CA	7.4
3	Telecommunications Inc.	Denver	5.2
4	CBS (Westinghouse)	New York	4.4
5	Gannett Co.	Arlington, VA	4.0
6	NBC TV (GE)	New York	3.9
7	Advance Pubs	Newark, NJ	3.2
8	News Corp.	Sydney	2.9
9	Cox Ent.	Atlanta	2.7
10	Hearst Corp.	New York	2.5

Source: *Ad Age Dataplace*, 19 August 1996.

cannot beam a TV signal. Before the satellite, the media were national rather than international, and often tightly controlled. Restrictions were made possible by the simple fact that terrestrial broadcasting technology had access to only a limited range of broadcast channels. Satellite has virtually limitless channel capacity, particularly when digital compression is taken into account.

The key element for global marketing in the satellite equation is that whatever is broadcast is indiscriminate by nature – it is not and cannot be specified to a given culture. Star TV, for example, covers 43 countries and more than 3000 million people. In deregulated environments, the potential for persuasion on a wide scale is enormous, but so is the potential for mistargeted, misdirected and misunderstood communications.

Many argue that the emergence of global media is hastening the convergence of consumers and communication. One of the factors always mentioned in such arguments is the growing concentration of ownership of media companies, mostly in American hands. In fact, of the top fifty media companies, only four are non-United States based. The biggest, Time Warner of New York, has media revenue of $9.8bn (1995) (table 4.7), which is over three times the size of the largest non-United States media company, Australia's News Corp with $2.95bn. As with the marketers and agencies, the media companies have global networks, encompassing subsidiaries round the world.

Conclusion

American culture might be a mosaic of different peoples or cultures who retain a sense of ethnic identity, or it might be a melting pot in which people, regardless of where they come from, end up calling themselves American. Or perhaps it is a bit of both; a New Yorker identifies himself as Irish-American, a Minnesotan as Norwegian-American and a Texan as Tex-Mex, and all claim to be All-American.

Americans think big and that extends to their self-definition. America is a big country that has absorbed huge numbers of people from every corner of the earth in a two-century dash to maturity and now has an unchallenged position of prominence in the world.

The story is not yet finished. At the end of the 1940s, the United States accounted for half of world GDP. Today, it accounts for about one quarter. While the country continues to advance on almost all measures absolutely, relatively speaking, other countries, like Japan from the 1950s to the 1980s, the Asian tigers from the 1970s to 1980s and China from the 1970s to the present, have grown far faster. So it is only natural that the United States is decreasingly dominant economically.

On the other hand, just as culture evolves in America, so too does the economy, and the United States is firmly at the forefront of economic change, leading the way through the information revolution to the knowledge era. In addition, the United States remains the nexus of ownership and influence for the lion's share of global corporations, communications networks and media companies, all vehicles for cultural expression. On a cultural front, America remains a power to reckon with.

This does not mean that culture around the world will bend towards the American model. While there may be a convergence in the things we eat, listen to, watch and work with, these are superficialities to which cultures accommodate. After all, cultures merely reflect the people of which they are composed, and if there is one thing that all people have in common, it is an innate ability to recognize that things change. We may not always like this because with change there are always winners and losers. So change is sometimes frightening and often resisted simply because it is unsettling. But it is inevitable that the world will change, through growth, restructuring, reordering of strength, etc., and that culture will evolve with it. The American culture today is extraordinarily prominent because of American companies' strengths in leading edge industries like advertising, which provide huge opportunities for expression.

NOTES

1   This is not to ignore Native American history, but the culture that affects American advertising is generally not Native American; it tends not to reflect the values, history and culture of the peoples native to the continent.

2   There is evidence of increasing religiousness in the United States, which has many forms and is often attributed to societal confusion, apprehension of the millennium, information overload, changing family structure, etc.

3   The dimensions are defined as (A) Power distance: the basic issue involved, to which different societies have found different solutions is human inequality. Inside organizations, inequality in power is inevitable and functional. This inequality is usually formalized in hierarchical boss-subordinate relationships (p. 65). (B) Uncertainty avoidance: uncertainty about the future is a basic fact of human life with which we try to compete through the domains of technology, law and religion. In organizations these take the form of technology, rules and rituals (p. 110). (C) Individualism: describes the relationship between the individual

and the collectivity, which prevails in a given society. It is reflected in the way people live together – for example, in nuclear families, extended families or tribes; and it has all kinds of value implications (p. 148). (D) Masculinity/ femininity: the duality of the sexes is a fundamental fact with which different societies cope in different ways; the issue is whether the biological differences between the sexes should or should not have implications for their roles in social activities (p. 176).

4 In the survey, the Harwood Group surveyed 800 randomly selected individuals. For more information, contact: Merck Family Fund, 6930 Carroll Ave., Suite 500, Takoma Park, MD 20912, Tel: 301.270.2970, Fax: 301.270.2973, e-mail: merck@igc.apc.org. This survey is one of many revealing a growing concern with materialism and its effect on the society and the environment.

REFERENCES

Albright, M. (1995) Inside job: fast-food chains serve a captive audience. *St. Petersburg Times*, January 15, 1H. (As quoted in Ritzer.)

Barber, B. (1995) *Jihad versus McWorld*. Random House.

Burger King homepage, http:// .burgerking.com/company/fastfact.htm, August 29, 1997.

Countryman, E. (1996) *Americans*. Hill and Wang.

Elmer-Dewitt, P. (1993) Anita the Agitator. *Time*, January 25, 52ff.

Garner, L. (1989) A voice against Disney-fication. *The Daily Telegraph*.

Garreau, J. (1989) *The Nine Nations of North America*. Avon.

Gruchow, P. (1995) Unchaining America: communities are finding ways to keep independent entrepreneurs in business. *Utne Reader*, January–February, 17–18. (As quoted in Ritzer.)

Hofstede, G. (1980) *Culture's Consequences*. Sage.

Huntington, S. (1997) *The Clash of Civilizations and the Remaking of World Order*. Simon and Schuster

Interbrand Group (1997) *Information Strategy*, April.

Kaplan, R. (1996) *The Ends of the Earth*. Macmillan.

Kentucky Fried Chicken homepage, http:// www.kentuckyfriedchicken.com/aboutkfc. htm, August 29, 1997.

McDowall, B. (1994) The global market challenge. *Restaurants & Institutions*, 104(26), 52ff. (As quoted in Ritzer.)

Moules, J. (1997) Brand warfare. *Information Strategy*, April, 26.

Rabin, S. (1994) How to sell across cultures. *American Demographics*, March.

Ray, P. H. (1997) The emerging culture. *American Demographics*, February.

Reitman, V. (1993) India anticipates the arrival of the beefless Big Mac. *Wall Street Journal*, October 20, B1, B3. (As quoted in Ritzer.)

Shapiro, E. (1991) The sincerest form of rivalry. *New York Times*, October 19, 35, 46. (As quoted in Ritzer.)

Shurgot, M. (1997) The goods life: how much is enough? *Sierra Club*, July/August, 20.

Smith, S. (1997) How will agencies adapt to clients' changing needs? *Admap*, January.

Tuchman, B. (1984) *The March of Folly*. Random House.

Walsh, J. (1997) America the brazen. *Time*, August 4, 27.

Whitman, W. (1955) *Leaves of Grass*, ed. Gay Wilson Allen. Signet (originally published 1881).

Worldwide Summary/Total Advertising (1997) NTC Publications.

5 Global Advertising

Sylvester O. Monye

Introduction

A principal objective of an advertising campaign is to transmit information designed to persuade consumers to take a particular course of action – to buy a product or service. This simple task becomes a multidimensional and complex exercise when internationalized because it means communicating with consumers across the world. Unless a strategic approach is adopted in developing a market-sensitive campaign, there will be a gap between the intended message and what is received. Therefore, the effectiveness of a global campaign must be based on the extent to which advertisers are able to exploit cross-cultural and economic similarities without ignoring the differences (Monye, 1997).

Discussions on global advertising have evolved over the past twenty years or so around one central question: to standardize or not to standardize. The importance of the subject means that the debate goes on unabated. Onkvisit and Shaw (1987) emphasized that advertising standardization is not just another theoretical concept in search of practical application. It is a significant problem, which warrants attention and evaluation. The main thrust of this debate is the economic considerations for the globalization of marketing activities. Globalization is a term that is used perhaps glibly by both academics and practitioners. It is often presented and discussed just from the perspective of the firm – cost-driven, top-down considerations. But there are two sides to the debate. On the one hand, the argument for standardization of global advertising is often based on the premise that needs and wants of people are essentially the same everywhere, and that a carefully conceived and executed appeal can strike a common responsive chord in consumers in different countries (Peebles, 1978). Although the concept of globalization is not a new phenomenon – after all, national firms exported standardized products around the world before the advent of the new age multinational firms – it received a massive boost by Levitt's (1983) compelling and somewhat persuasive arguments in his seminal paper 'The globalization of markets'. He postulated that the worldwide market place has become so homogenized that companies can achieve real competitive advantage by pursuing a strategy that enables them to produce standardized products and services, and market them around the world with an identical approach in all the markets. To underscore his argument on globalization, he made a distinction between multinational and global companies. Levitt suggested that the latter operate in a number of countries with resolute constancy – at low relative cost – as if the entire world were a single entity, thus providing a basis for real competitive advantages and increased profitability. It is noteworthy that this strategy was embraced with a certain degree of zealousness, and success, in the 1980s by the global advertising agency, Saatchi & Saatchi.

There are those, on the other hand, who believe that the proponents of globalization of advertising have missed the point. How can the different regions and countries of the world be served with an identical marketing strategy? Banerjee (1994) suggested that those who propagate the use of standardized advertising worldwide tended to base their arguments either on the logic of standardizing advertising for 'high touch' brands (e.g. upmarket, high-fashion brands such as Gucci and Chanel) or for brands in 'high-tech' product categories (e.g. SLR cameras, personal computers, home electronics), or on the suggestiveness of piecemeal findings regarding the convergence of consumer tastes across national boundaries. But in reality, what constitutes effective and successful advertising in one country may not be suitable in another. Further, Dibb et al. (1994) pointed out that readership, viewing and listening habits differ country by country, region by region; and leisure time, spending priorities and social needs also differ.

In this chapter, we examine the contending issues in the argument under three main themes: (a) the case for standardized global advertising; (b) the arguments against standardized global advertising; (c) regulatory impediments to the strategy of standardized global advertising.

The Case for Standardized Global Advertising

The debate on standardization of advertising has a long history and centres on a simple question: should international advertising be standardized or localized? There are interesting and sometimes compelling arguments for standardization. Frequently, these arguments are founded on the issues of economies of scale. One of the earliest advocates of standardization of international advertising was Elinder (1965) who suggested that companies could become more efficient by using standardized campaigns. In the 1980s, its appeal was legitimized by the success of global advertising agencies such as Saatchi & Saatchi with this strategy.

A range of factors accounts for the attraction of this strategy to multinational firms and advertising agencies alike. Harris (1996) grouped the arguments for standardization into two broad themes:

1   Factors such as economies of scale, the need to exploit good ideas and the ability to build an international image, all of which have an explicit economic rationale in that standardization contributes to the sales and profit performance of the brands in question.
2   Factors such as the need to achieve skills transfer; concern about the abilities of the national subsidiaries and improved decision making, where the rationale

for standardization would appear to have more to do with internal organizational considerations – indicating that the international advertising practices of multinationals cannot be understood solely in terms of an econometric-based cost/benefit analysis.

There is, nonetheless, a growing realization that standardization is rather more complex than just a case of offering the same campaign in every market. Increasingly, standardization is discussed as a matter of a continuum depicting various levels of commonalties across its components (strategy, execution, language) and across regions (see, for example, Quelch and Hoff, 1986). Duncan and Ramaprasad (1995) provided very useful working definitions for the components of advertising, as follows:

1 *Strategy*. The creative selling proposition (e.g. associating Marlboro with macho-individualism).
2 *Execution*. Actual elements and their structure in an advertisement (e.g. a 6 foot 3 inch tanned cowboy smoking and driving a herd of cattle across a river with mountains in the background).
3 *Language*. Medium by which the marketer communicates with the market.
4 *Standardization*. Keeping one or more of the three basic components of a multinational campaign.

They suggest that standardization of international advertising campaigns is a matter of degree – depending on circumstances. The smaller use of standardization in execution is necessitated by cultural preferences and taboos, while the smaller use of standardization by non-Western agencies may be due to the fact that standardization is largely a Western concept.

Those observations were supported by the findings in Zhang and Gelb (1996). They found that advertising standardization is feasible if a product is used in a consumption situation that matches the appeal in the advertisement. It was also suggested that, although culture matters, advertisers need not assume that its influence on responses to advertising appeal is independent of other factors.

Available statistics tend to support the argument for use condition as a facilitating factor in standardizing advertising. Table 5.1 shows a range of industries which have maintained their drive towards a standardized global advertising campaign. It is noteworthy that the increased attraction for standardization of advertising relates more to those industries and products that exhibit universal appeal in terms of use conditions, with the airline and tobacco industries leading the way. It is significant that at the bottom of the table are products such as personal goods, disposable paper products, breakfast cereals and confectionery. Although use conditions may be the same, the appeal of these items may differ from country to country, thus offering limited scope for standardized global advertising.

This is in marked contrast with the findings in the Hite and Fraser study in table 5.2. In a survey of ninety-nine US multinational firms which advertised internationally, Hite and Fraser (1988) found that the majority of these firms (56 per cent) used a combination strategy of standardizing some portions of

Table 5.1 The use of standardized advertising by industry (top twenty) (per cent of total number of advertisements)

	1994	1996	Ranking
Airlines	70	90	1
Tobacco products	61	87	2
Cars	50	85	3
Soft drinks	79	85	4
Photographic equipment	70	76	5
Consumer electronics	58	74	6
Car hire	66	74	7
Hotels	71	73	8
Banking (corporate)	62	69	9
Computer	55	68	10
Cosmetics and toiletries	43	66	11
Office equipment	60	64	12
Corporate	62	62	13
Alcoholic drinks	45	62	14
Telecommunication	52	60	15
Personal goods	33	54	16
Clothing and footwear	31	53	17
Disposable paper products	28	50	18
Breakfast cereals	32	50	19
Confectionery	30	45	20

Source: Compiled from data provided by the Department of Advertising, University of Texas, 1995. Young and Rubicam (1977). Zenith Media Worldwide.

Table 5.2 Firms which advertise internationally (n = 99)

Using all standardized advertising	8%
Using all localized advertising	36%
Using a combination strategy	56%

Source: Hite and Fraser (1988).

advertising or localizing advertising for some markets. Interestingly, only 8 per cent of these firms used all standardized advertising. It was also found that concern over unique behavioural patterns or attitudes in foreign markets appears to encourage localized decision making. But firms that standardize international advertising apparently perceive that identical executions may be transferred successfully with modification only in language. It is noteworthy that the main demographic difference between the firms standardizing advertising and those localizing is the industry in which they operate. Thus, standardization of international advertising functions is positively associated with involvement in capital goods business, where buyers are presumably more sophisticated and homogeneous. This is consistent with the data in Table 5.1 above. It is, therefore, reasonable to conclude that global advertising will be more attractive to those companies offering capital goods whose appeal is universal.

Arguments for Localized Advertising

Buzzell (1968) questioned the wisdom of standardized global advertising in all circumstances. He pointed out that while marketing 'technology' might have universal potential, its application is limited in certain environmental circumstances. His concerns at that time remain valid today. For example, Rodwell (1996) noted that all the best advertising textbooks agree on one thing: you must know who you are talking to if you want to create truly persuasive advertising. This means not only knowing what sort of people they are, but what media they consume, what they feel about products or services on offer, and what they feel about competitive products and services. This sort of information cannot be amalgamated across a spectrum of national boundaries. It is also generally agreed that although producing a single campaign instead of local versions can save money and time in production, there is more to advertising abroad than mere translation of language – there are more differences between countries.

One of the biggest obstacles to the standardization of global advertising is the culture of the people. Understanding the role of culture in the formation of consumer behaviour is critical in the development of an effective global advertising strategy. So what is culture and how does it impact on advertising? Hofstede (1984) defines culture as the collective programming of the mind, which distinguishes the members of one category of people from another. The culture of a people derives from the totality of the components that constitute the basis for social interaction in a society, and includes factors such as language, customs, beliefs, religion, and other attributes, which provide them with distinctive characteristics, attitudes and behaviour. It is, therefore, not surprising that successful advertising campaigns are normally those that strike a chord with the culture and the things that appeal to the market.

Anholt (1995) suggests that advertising is so intimately linked with the popular culture, the social fabric, the laws, marketing traditions, buying habits, aspirations, sense of style and humour of a people that messages cannot, and should not, be communicated in precisely the same way in different countries. He argues that advertising works when consumers believe they are being spoken to by somebody who understands them. Somebody who knows their needs and talks and feels just as they do – not a foreigner speaking to them through an interpreter (see also Buzzell, 1968; Harris, 1984).

It is, therefore, essential that the message content of advertising reflects the interests and aspirations of members of a society. In their study, Zhang and Gelb (1996) confirmed the general consensus that consumers respond more positively to advertising messages that are congruent with their culture (i.e. advertising that conforms to the norms of a particular culture).

There is evidence to suggest that global marketers no longer manage international brands largely by developing ideas at headquarters then exporting them to host markets. Marketing conditions in each country are different. This may be obvious, but in the rush to standardize advertising campaigns, it can be and is often overlooked to a surprising degree. For example, one of the most significant developments in the global market in recent times is the creation of the single European market. This single political union is often misunderstood as a perfect example of a single market suitable for a standardized marketing treatment and/or strategic consideration, but in fact it would be unwise to treat it as a single market. This is illustrated by the fact that a product may be a brand leader in Sweden but unknown in Finland. It may be unique in France but a me-too in Germany. It may appeal to a social group in Britain which may not exist in Spain. It will certainly be a local product in its country of origin and a foreign product everywhere else. All these factors dictate fundamental differences in the way the product is marketed and, therefore, to claim that a mere translation of a national campaign will sell the product is patently foolish.

Further, observers point to the fact that the increasing harmonization in Europe seems to be causing a hardening of local issues, not only between countries, but also within them. It would appear that the loss of national identity in the European Union (EU) is inspiring an explosion of re-asserted regional identities. Dibb et al. (1994) noted that despite the promised harmonization of regulations across member states, advertising is still faced with sets of laws and regulations which vary significantly from country to country: what can be aired when, through which media, with what message, at what cost, and with what disclaimer. (Regulations in international advertising are discussed in detail in the latter part of this chapter.) These factors make it impossible to insist on standardization of global advertising strategy by multinational firms.

The Open Strategy Approach to Global Advertising

Although there are merits in the arguments for standardization and localization of advertising, respectively, the debate should not and must not be reduced to a matter of either/or. This calls for the application of an open strategy approach in multinational advertising. Monye (1997) suggests that an open strategy enables a firm to customize or standardize marketing communications programmes when and where it is necessary to do so. This approach recognizes sociocultural and economic differences between markets.

It is clear from the discussion in preceding sections that there is consensus that it is neither realistic nor practicable to standardize the three basic components of an advertising campaign (i.e. strategy, execution and language). Thus, the term standardization lends itself to different interpretations by both academics and practitioners. Duncan and Ramaprasad (1995) captured the consensus by defining standardization to mean keeping one or more of the three basic components of a multinational advertising campaign. Hornik (1980) classified six major propositions underlying the thinking on international advertising. He noted that:

1   Advertising standardization is not a simplistic concept and should be con-
    sidered in terms of degree of uniformity rather than in absolute terms.
2   Cross-cultural advertising is a distinct and unique form of marketing commun-
    ication, which requires special labelling, attention, instruction and methodo-
    logy. It calls for added skills: the ability to organize and develop international
    advertising programmes plus the ability to adjust to foreign market conditions
    influenced by different and varying conditions.
3   A fundamental bias in cross-cultural research arises from 'ethnocentrism' –
    from the blindness to the unique and different characteristics of another culture.
4   Cultural differences between advertisers and consumers might function as
    boundaries or barriers that must be overcome if understanding and satisfac-
    tion are to be achieved. Since the ad creator is a member of a specific culture,
    it is assumed that his ads convey messages indicative of particular dispositions
    that his culture has toward general world themes. This may be especially true
    when the marketing company instructs the creator to prepare an ad conveying
    a particular message.
5   Learning about cultural pattern is an important means of reducing uncertainty
    about the behaviour of customers of that culture. Cross-cultural diversities
    exist. These diversities and other forces may affect the reception and accept-
    ance of messages.
6   Culture is primarily a phenomenon of region or nationality; national identity
    predicts culture, but parallels between nation and culture should be carefully
    examined. It is possible to find much greater viability in a 'horizontal' analysis
    based on common occupation, socio-economic class or ethnicity (independent
    of citizenship) which will account for differences in perception. These endorse
    the logic of market segmentation abroad as well as at home.

Therefore, the application of the term standardization may not be taken literally
in the context of global advertising strategy. It is in this context that the strategy
model in exhibit 5.1 is developed. It provides a six-strategy-alternatives framework for the implementation of a global advertising campaign. These strategy
alternatives should enable multinational advertising campaigns to be standardized
or modified in accordance with market conditions and requirements without losing
the focus on the globalness of the message and strategy.

EXHIBIT 5.1   ADVERTISING STRATEGY ALTERNATIVES FRAMEWORK

Strategy alternatives

1   Standardization of strategy
2   Standardization of execution
3   Modification of strategy
4   Modification of execution
5   Standardization of strategy but modification of execution
6   Modification of strategy but standardization of execution

Regulations and Global Advertising

Is the influence of advertising on consumers just an exaggeration by those vilifying it? Can an advertisement make a consumer purchase a product for which he has no need or want? To what extent should advertisers and advertisements be regulated? These are some of the questions that have exercised the minds of academics and practitioners. Proponents of advertising often wonder whether advertising is really capable of manipulating a rational consumer against his better judgement, bearing in mind that choice behaviour is determined by a multitude of factors that include advertising. Nonetheless, the power and influence of advertising in shaping attitudes and behaviour are unquestionable. Indeed, its effectiveness is measured by its capability in causing a change of attitude and behaviour in consumers and the public alike.

However, there are also those who entertain genuine fear over the negative aspects of advertising. After all, advertisements are not just harmless entertainment. It is thought that advertising is so pervasive and powerful that it can manipulate a buyer into making a decision against his best interests in expending his resources. Indeed, the vast sums of money being spent on advertising must mean something! Table 5.3 presents an overview of the total worldwide advertising expenditure between 1987 and 1995. It shows expenditure on advertising rising steadily over the years to nearly $250 billion in 1995. It is particularly noteworthy that, in 1995, print advertising expenditure accounted for about 50 per cent of all advertising spend. A plausible explanation for the decline in television advertising expenditure is the raft of regulations on television advertising, based on its perceived power of influence on consumers.

Most religions are critical of the power and influence of advertisements. For example, Pope John Paul II (1991) insists that advertising can be, and often is, a tool of the phenomenon of consumerism, noting that:

Table 5.3 Total world advertising expenditure by the main media (US$M)

	Total	Print	TV	Radio	Cinema	Outdoor
1987	136 423	78 069	41 404	10 531	358	6 060
1988	157 198	89 083	48 531	11 923	428	7 233
1989	167 341	94 559	51 843	12 796	446	7 698
1990	183 303	102 444	57 795	13 969	549	8 547
1991	185 607	101 397	59 892	14 032	534	9 752
1992	200 162	106 360	67 944	14 864	601	10 392
1993	200 567	102 948	71 143	15 918	492	10 065
1994	222 967	112 310	80 906	17 790	517	11 444
1995	247 498	125 546	89 200	19 245	622	12 884

Source: World Advertising Trends 1997. NTC Publications, p. 5.

It is not wrong to want to live better; what is wrong is a style of life which is presumed to be better when it is directed towards 'having' rather than 'being', and which wants to have more, not in order to be more but in order to spend life in enjoyment as an end in itself. Sometimes, advertisers speak of it as part of their task to 'create' needs for products and services – that is to cause people to feel and act upon cravings for items and services they do not need. If a direct appeal is made to his instincts – while ignoring in various ways the reality of the person as intelligent and free – then consumer attitudes and lifestyles can be created which are objectively improper and often damaging to his physical and spiritual health. This is a serious abuse, an affront to the human dignity and the common good when it occurs in affluent societies. But the abuse is still more grave when consumerist attitudes and values are transmitted by communications media and advertising to developing countries, where they exacerbate socio-economic problems and harm the poor.

Some of these criticisms of advertising are based on the fact that it is highly subjective in content and style because it operates as a means to a commercial end. It is, therefore, not surprising that advertising is one of the most closely scrutinized, publicly exposed forms of marketing communication. All aspects of advertising – content, medium, audience and context – are subjected regularly to detailed scrutiny, making it essential for the industry to uphold its probity. There is also an acknowledgement on the part of advertisers, agencies and the media of the need for consumer protection and the maintenance of ethical standards. After all, it is in its long-term interest to protect the freedom of commercial speech. It is this belief that belies the industry's approach to the concept of self-regulation. This is discussed later in a separate section. Self-regulation notwithstanding, governments around the world have a responsibility to their nationals to protect them from misleading advertising claims. Consequently, every country has regulations governing the content of advertising campaigns in order to ensure that claims are decent, legal, honest and truthful. After all, the purpose of advertising is to inform and persuade people. Advertisers, agencies and media owners are increasingly recognizing that it is counterproductive to produce advertisements that offend people rather influence them favourably. It is, therefore, not surprising that the industry itself is at the vanguard of self-regulation in order to maintain its good name as responsible members of society. The extensive web of regulations imposed on the industry voluntarily and by national legislation cover all aspects of marketing communications. These regulations require that these should:

- be legal, decent, honest and truthful;
- show responsibility to the customers and the society;
- follow business principles of 'fair competition'.

In particular, these regulations tend to lay emphasis on the more contentious aspects of advertising, such as the nature and purpose of comparative advertising, the ethical issues in advertising to children, and the promotion of the consumption of alcohol and tobacco products. In the following sections, we examine the regulatory framework within which advertisers are expected to function.

Comparative Advertising

Comparative advertising is a technique that is used extensively by advertisers around the world. It is increasingly seen as an effective way for new products, especially fast-moving consumer goods, to break into new markets, or for established but 'tired' ones to regain lost market share (*The Economist*, 18 May 1991, pp. 79–80). The key question about comparative advertising is this: does it make consumers better informed or confused and worse-off? In spite of its extensive use, there is no consensus on the definition of comparative advertising. A number of researchers have focused on different aspects of the technique. For example, Barry and Tremblay (1975) defined comparative advertising as an explicit brand comparison that is obvious to the audience. Wilkie and Farris (1975) emphasized the use of specific product or service attributes for brands of the same generic product or service class as the basis of labelling advertising comparative. However, Muehling and Kangun (1985) suggest that one way of arriving at a consensus on a definition is to develop a set of criteria that define approaches to comparative advertising.

In spite of the lack of consensus in its definition, it is generally acknowledged that it is effective in advertising because it induces more positive brand attitudes for products that elicit cognitive and affective motivations. This is possible because brand comparisons facilitate an attribute-based processing style, which might otherwise succumb to the competing affective involvement (Putrevu and Lord, 1994).

Effective it may be, but criticizing a rival's products is a high-risk approach to marketing communications. There are potential pitfalls in the use of comparative advertising because it is capable of infringing on the legal rights of competitors. It is noteworthy that some countries take a positive view of comparative advertising, while others do not. For example, in the United States, comparative advertising has been commonly used since the mid-1960s and virtually no restrictions on its application exist. Nevertheless, the American Association of Advertising Agencies suggests that the intent and connotation of an advertisement should be to inform and never to discredit or unfairly attack competitors, competing products or services, and that competition should be fairly and properly identified, but never in a manner or tone of voice that degrades the competitive products or services. The reality is that advertisers rarely adhere to these guidelines. Indeed, the rough and tumble standard of American advertising has become legendary. For example, in November 1990, PepsiCo unveiled a television advertisement which featured M. C. Hammer. The campaign was designed to sneer at Pepsi's arch rival, Coca-Cola. In the advertisement, a sip of Coke turned the rap-music star into a sedate singer of sentimental songs, which he is not known for, but he was returned to his normal self, and the kind of music for which he is famous, by drinking Pepsi to counter the 'bad reaction' he suffered when he had a sip of Coca-Cola. It is particularly interesting that no eyebrows were raised by this blatant and possibly unsubstantiatable claim by the industry watchers. In a country where comparative advertisements of food-related products have been known to accuse competitors' products of causing cancer, the Pepsi versus Coke campaign seems mild by comparison. It is noteworthy that about 30 per cent of advertisements shown each year on network television in the United States are comparative (*The Economist*, 18 May 1991, pp. 79–80). Most of these are direct comparisons. It is particularly remarkable that fewer than 1 per cent of negative and direct comparative advertising is ever challenged by competitors.

In Japan, the attitude of advertisers and consumers towards comparative advertising is different. Although its use has been legalized since 1987, the Japanese frown upon it. They tend to shy away from the confrontational nature of comparative advertising. The situation in the Philippines mirrors that of Japan.

In the EU, rules and practice governing the use of comparative advertising have traditionally been member state specific, but attempts are now being made to harmonize the regulation within the EU. Prior to 1996, only Belgium, Germany, Italy and Luxembourg had either an outright prohibition on comparative advertising, or restrictions, which make its practice almost impossible. In countries where it is permitted, it is practised under very strict conditions established in voluntary codes and guidelines set out by the television watchdog. The original proposal in a directive, adopted by the Commission in September 1991, was drafted as an amendment to the Misleading Advertising Directive of 1984. It allowed comparisons in advertising provided that: '. . . only material elements were compared; the comparison should be "complete"; like should be compared with like; and the comparison should be verifiable; should not mislead or confuse customers or denigrate competitors'.

In 1996, following extensive deliberations, debates and consultations, the European Commission adopted a common position, which stipulates that comparative advertising will be allowed everywhere in the EU under the following conditions:

1 It is not misleading, and it compares only those goods or services meeting the same needs or intended for the same purposes.
2 It does not create confusion in the market between the advertiser and a competitor or between an advertiser's trade marks, trade names, other distinguishing marks, goods or services and those of a competitor.
3 It does not discredit, denigrate or take unfair advantage of the trademarks, trade names etc. of a competitor.
4 Member states are not obliged to permit comparative advertising for goods and services on which they maintain or introduce advertising bans, but comparative advertising cannot otherwise be banned.

This directive is the most serious attempt made by the European Commission, so far, to have a level playing field for advertisers in the member states. The success of the directive will be determined by the willingness of member states to enforce any sanctions where it is necessary to do so.

Tobacco Advertising

Tobacco is a product whose advertising seems to attract universal condemnation. Although the industry provides a huge opportunity for taxation income for the government and employment for the public, tobacco advertising evokes passionate debates and is perhaps the most severely regulated product advertising because of the link between smoking and cancer, and the addictive nature of the product. In the United States, the Clinton Administration is determined to regulate not just tobacco advertising and any form of promotion, but also its distribution, particularly to children. In August 1996, President Bill Clinton announced a package of measures to prevent children and adolescents from smoking cigarettes or using smokeless tobacco. Prior to the President's announcement, the Food and Drug Administration (FDA) had issued new rules to reduce the access and appeal of tobacco products for children and adolescents. The FDA rule limits its appeal by:

1 Prohibiting billboards within 1000 feet of schools and playgrounds. Other outdoor advertising is restricted to black-and-white text only; this includes all billboards, signs inside and outside of buses, and all advertising in stores. Advertising inside 'adult only' facilities such as nightclubs may have colour and imagery.
2 Permitting black-and-white text-only advertising in publications with significant youth readership (under 18). Significant youth readership means more than 15 per cent or more than 2 million readers under eighteen; there are no restrictions on print advertising below these thresholds.
3 Prohibiting the sale or give-aways of products such as caps or gym bags that carry cigarette or smokeless tobacco product brand names or logos.
4 Prohibiting brand name sponsorship of sporting or entertainment events, but permitting it in the corporate name.

The rule is based on the FDA's finding that cigarettes and smokeless tobacco products are delivery devices for nicotine, an addictive drug. It has to be said that cigarettes and smokeless tobacco products remain legal products that can be marketed and sold to adults, 18 years and over. That said, attempts by an alliance of tobacco manufacturers, convenience stores and advertising industries to fight back through the courts are ongoing. Following the announcement of the rule by the FDA, the alliance went to court to challenge the jurisdiction of the FDA to introduce such a rule. In April 1997, the Federal District Court in Greensboro, North Carolina, ruled that the FDA had jurisdiction under the Food, Drug and Cosmetic Act to regulate nicotine-containing cigarettes and smokeless tobacco products. The court, therefore, upheld all restrictions involving youth access and labelling, but delayed the implementation of some of these provisions, pending further order of the court. It ruled, however, that the FDA did not have authority under the statutory provision that it had relied on to regulate the advertising and promotion of cigarettes and smokeless tobacco products. These setbacks, notwithstanding, it is clear that the FDA will continue to pursue measures that will reduce access to and the appeal of cigarettes and tobacco products.

In the EU, the regulation of tobacco advertising is no less stringent. In May 1991, an amended proposal for a council directive on advertising for tobacco products (proposing a near-total ban on all tobacco advertising) was adopted by the European Parliament in June 1991. In February 1992, a revised commission proposal was approved by the European Parliament. The revised draft directive would have the effect of banning all forms of advertising for tobacco products throughout the EU, with minor exceptions of certain types of point-of-sale advertising, where specifically allowed by national governments. Although no formal vote has yet been taken, at least five member states (Germany, The Netherlands, Denmark, Greece and the United Kingdom) are likely to vote against the proposed ban, and thus continue to block it. Nonetheless, it is particularly noteworthy that advertising tobacco products is banned on television in all EU member states. A similar ban is in place in most countries, including Japan, Canada, Australia, New Zealand, India and China.

In addition to the EU initiatives, individual member states are pursuing unilateral control measures against the advertising of tobacco products. The situation in the United Kingdom mirrors that of the United States. In May 1994, a new voluntary agreement between the Department of Health and the tobacco manufacturers was reached. Under the new agreement (which is to last five years, but subject to review at any time), the tobacco industry agreed to reduce its expenditure on outdoor advertising by 40 per cent. Further, no poster advertising will be allowed within 200 metres of schools and the health warning area in tobacco advertisement will be increased. All permanent shop-front advertising was to be eliminated by the end of 1997. The agreement also provided for extra expenditure on the monitoring of compliance.

Alcohol Advertising

There is a universal restraint on the advertising of alcoholic beverages, particularly on television, but perhaps less stringent than those on cigarettes. The restrictions are more vigorously enforced in developed Western countries of the EU and North America. The objective of these regulations is to reduce the appeal of alcohol to children. An alcoholic beverage is defined as a drink containing more than 1.2 per cent of alcohol by volume. Most guidelines to advertisers suggest that advertisements should be socially responsible and not feature any characters, real or fictitious, likely to attract the attention of people under eighteen. People shown drinking in advertisements should appear to be over twenty-five years old. There should be no suggestion that drinking alcohol leads to social acceptance or that drinking alcohol is a special challenge. Further, suggestions that drinking is an essential attribute of masculinity should be avoided, as should any depiction of alcohol as enhancing femininity or attractiveness.

In the United Kingdom, new alcoholic drinks (such as the alcopops) marketed to a younger age group have caused renewed discussion on the codes of conduct.

In April 1996, a new code of practice on the naming, packaging and merchandizing of alcoholic drinks was adopted by the Portman Group. The new code of practice:

- bans the use of soft drink generic names such as 'lemonade' on alcohol products, unless it is made very clear that the drink is alcoholic;
- prevents the use of cartoon characters and other labelling likely to appeal to children;
- requires clear labelling of alcoholic content;
- introduces conditions on the sale of such drinks.

Other EU member states have statutory restrictions on alcohol advertising, most notably those established in the 'Loi Evin' in France. Sports events now have considerable difficulty in obtaining commercial sponsorship and many are no longer televised at all and are facing real financial difficulties. The EU restrictions on alcohol advertising on television are contained in the Broadcasting Directive of 1989. This directive stipulates that television advertising and home shopping for alcoholic beverages may not be aimed specifically at minors; advertising may not link alcohol consumption with enhanced physical performance, driving, social or sexual success; and it must not claim that alcohol has therapeutic qualities or emphasize high alcoholic content as a positive quality.

In all Muslim countries, neither the advertising of alcoholic beverages nor their consumption are allowed because of religious considerations.

Advertising to Children

Public debate about advertising to children has increased in intensity over the past few years, largely in respect of the quantity and persuasive intent of advertising. Children are considered particularly vulnerable to advertising and obviously powerless against its influence. There is an increasing amount of pressure being put on advertisers to minimize children's exposure to any form of marketing communication.

Within the EU, there are heavy statutory restrictions or bans on advertising during children's programming in Belgium, Norway, Spain, Sweden and Greece, and substantial content restrictions in other member states. In the UK, the regulations protecting children from advertising are provided for in both the 1990 Broadcasting Act and the British Codes of Advertising. In Belgium, television restrictions comprise a prohibition on all advertising for a period of five minutes before and after children's programmes. In Greece, toy advertising is prohibited on television until after 10 p.m. In Sweden, there is a general ban on all television advertising to children under the age of twelve, and it has proposed the same rule to its member state partners within the Council of Europe. In Canada, there is a similar restriction on advertising to children. Spain operates what amounts to a ban on the advertising of 'war' toys on television.

Norway does not permit any form of advertising on television to children. In a recent landmark test case in the European Free Trade Area court, Norway lost the contention that it also had the right, in pursuance of the advertising prohibition, to block trans-border broadcasting, from other member states, of material which included children's advertising. In a similar case brought against Sweden's ban on advertising aimed at children under twelve, and which was deemed to be misleading under Swedish law, the Advocate General of the European Court of Justice (ECJ) ruled on 17 September 1996 that Sweden had no right to ban advertisements broadcast from another member state. The ruling was made within the context of the European Television Without Frontiers Directive.

In the United States, the government is pushing forward with V-chip technology. The V-chip is a device that allows TV viewers the opportunity to programme their TV sets to block particular broadcasts. This technology would allow preselected parts of a programme, such as sequences of explicit sex or violence, to be 'blanked' by viewers. The development of this technology is being monitored carefully in the EU. Indeed, on 14 February 1996, the European Parliament proposed an amendment to the Commission's Television Without Frontiers Directive stating that 'any television receiver marketed for the purposes of sale or rental in the Community must be equipped with the technical device for filtering programmes by one year, at the latest, after it has been standardised by a recognised European standardisation body'.

The immediate implication of the technology is that a rating system must be devised. Such a system must identify and apply an appropriate rating methodology, which is able to indicate programmes according to portrayal of sex, violence and bad language. In which case, the rating system has to be publicized prominently in the media to advise parents and guardians about the nature and content of a broadcast.

Self-Regulation

Discussions on the true purpose and limitations of self-regulation in advertising have increased significantly over the last fifteen years or so, partly as a result of a number of celebrated cases of unethical advertising, such as Benetton's advertisement using the blood-soaked uniform of a soldier killed during the Bosnian War. The thrust of the debate is that the substitution of acts of authority by the state for acts of market exchange often generates regulatory failures. There are also those who question the extent to which state regulation can be relied upon to sustain and improve free-market performance. Boddewyn (1989) suggests that there is room for regulatory improvement in the light of new problems and experiences, but absolute faith in regulation is misplaced because there are readily observable limits to what regulation, as a form of societal control, can do. This raises the need to look beyond state regulation of the industry for the long-term good of all concerned. This is where self-regulation comes in.

The main purpose of self-regulation in advertising is to have all parts of the industry, advertisers, agencies and the media, improve and internalize higher advertising standards. It is not just about improving advertising behaviour on an industry-wide basis, but also improving a system to monitor and deal with consumers' complaints. In Europe, there is now a community-wide self-regulatory initiative, which was set up to promote effective pan-European self-regulation in advertising. This initiative was put in place as a response to the expectations of the European Commission.

In 1991, Sir Leon Brittan, the Competition Commissioner at the European Commission, challenged the advertising industry to show how the issues affecting advertising in the single market could be successfully dealt with through co-operation rather than detailed legislation. In 1992, the European Advertising Standards Alliance was formed to promote and support self-regulation in Europe. Since coming into existence, the Alliance and the industry have endeavoured to respond to the challenges of self-regulation by demonstrating their strong commitment to effective self-regulation as a means of promoting high standards in advertising across Europe and safeguarding consumer interest. Its policy objectives and priorities are to:

- study and promote the best practice in advertising self-regulation;
- bring together, on a regular basis, all those self-regulatory organizations in Europe which operate codes of practice;
- consider the possibility and desirability of convergence of the present self-regulatory systems;
- demonstrate that self-regulatory codes of practice are more efficacious than detailed legislation as a means of regulating advertising;
- promote a referral system for the speedy and effective resolution of trans-border complaints;
- act as a source of documentation, reference and advice on the subject of advertising regulation;
- encourage the setting-up of self-regulatory bodies in those European countries where none exists and the strengthening, where appropriate, of existing ones.

In its relatively short history, the Alliance has attracted members from not just the EU, but also from the Czech Republic, Slovak Republic, Slovenia, Finland and South Africa. In spite of these developments, opponents of self-regulation in advertising suggest that these efforts are a public relations gesture designed to placate critics and to fend off the threat of state regulation. They argue that enforcers are a little too kind to make any meaningful impact on errant members. To put it bluntly, trade associations sometimes put self-interest ahead of public interest. Even where there is the intention to make self-regulation effective, many factors are required to make it work. Boddewyn (1989) suggests one significant factor which limits the scope and effectiveness of self-regulation, namely the unwillingness of many of its supporters to make self-regulation as burdensome – financially, technically and morally – as regulation itself. He argued that if industry were to cope with every problem, to issue elaborate and ever-growing standards, to develop extensive pre-clearance and monitoring procedures, to solicit more complaints (which ultimately require practitioners to justify their behaviour), to publicize the wrongdoings of too many firms, and to require that such burden be willingly assumed by practitioners, then a breaking point is likely to develop.

All said, self-regulation in advertising can only be effectively developed and sustained where there are appropriate sanctions and legal back-up to punish breaches of the rules. The absence of such a back-up system undermines the true intention and effectiveness of self-regulation in advertising.

Summary

The discussions in this chapter show that advertising across cultures is a multi-dimensional and complex undertaking. The complex nature of global advertising has generated and continues to generate intense debate on how best to communicate to consumers around the world – by standardization or localization of advertising. The analysis in this chapter suggests that despite the merits in the contending views on standardization of advertising, the debate should not and must not be reduced to an either/or argument. An open strategy approach to global advertising is recommended because it enables a firm to customize or standardize marketing communications programmes when and where it is necessary to do so – recognizing sociocultural and economic differences between markets. Further, a six-strategy-alternatives framework is recommended. The strategy alternatives would facilitate standardization or modification of advertising based on specific conditions in each market without losing the globalness of the message and strategy. The chapter also discusses the economic and sociocultural imperatives underlying regulations in advertising worldwide. Regulations are imposed on advertising as a result of genuine fear over the possible negative impact of this important function on the consumers. Although the industry is committed to self-regulation as a substitute to the force of law, opponents of advertising still believe that the substitution of acts of authority by the state for the acts of market exchange often leads to failure. In conclusion, a global advertising campaign must strike a chord with the consumers and meet the regulatory requirements in each market if it is to be successful.

REFERENCES

Anholt, S. (1995) Global message – Pan-European advertising. *Grocer*, 217(7199), 38–40.

Banerjee, A. (1994) Transnational advertising development and management: an account planning approach and a process framework. *International Journal of Advertising*, 13(2), 95–125.

Barry, T. E. and Tremblay, R. L. (1975) Comparative advertising: perspectives and issues. *Journal of Advertising*, 4(4), 15–20.

Boddewyn, J. J. (1989) Advertising self-regulation: true purpose and limits. *Journal of Advertising*, 18(2), 19–28.

Buzzell, R. D. (1968) Can you standardize multinational marketing? *Harvard Business Review*, 46(November/December), 102–15.

Dibb, S., Simkin, L. and Yuen, R. (1994) Pan-European advertising: Think Europe – act local. *International Journal of Advertising*, 13(2), 125–37.

Duncan, T. and Ramaprasad, J. (1995) Standardized multinational advertising: the influencing factors. *Journal of Advertising*, 24(3), 55–68.

Elinder, E. (1965) How international can advertising be? In S. Watson Dunn (ed.),

International Handbook of Advertising. New York: McGraw-Hill.

Harris, G. (1984) The globalization of advertising. *International Journal of Advertising*, 3, 223–34.

Harris, G. (1996) Factors influencing the international practices of multinational companies. *Management Decision*, 34(6), 5–12.

Hite, R. E. and Fraser, C. (1988) International advertising strategies of multinational corporations. *Journal of Advertising Research*, 6, 9–17.

Hofstede, G. (1984) National cultures and corporate cultures. Paper presented at the LIFIM Perspective Day, Helsinki, Finland, December 4.

Hornik, J. (1980) Comparative evaluation of international vs. national advertising strategies. *Columbia Journal of World Business*, 15(Spring), 36–46.

John Paul II (1991) Centesimus Annus No 34. *AAS*, LXXXIII, 835–6.

Levitt, T. (1983) The globalization of markets. *Harvard Business Review*, April/May, 92–103.

Monye, S. O. (1997) *The International Business Blueprint*. Oxford: Blackwell.

Muehling, D. D. and Kangun, N. (1985) The multidimensionality of comparative advertising: implications for the Federal Trade Commission. *Journal of Public Policy and Marketing*, 4, 112–28.

Onkvisit, S. and Shaw, J. J. (1987) Standardized international advertising: a review and critical evaluation of the theoretical and empirical evidence. *Columbia Journal of World Business*, 22(Fall), 43–55.

Peebles, D. M. (1978) Co-ordinating international advertising. *Journal of Marketing*, 42(1), 28–34.

Putrevu, S. and Lord, K. R. (1994) Comparative and non-comparative advertising: attitudinal effects under cognitive and affective involvement conditions. *Journal of Advertising*, 23(2), 77–92.

Quelch, J. A. and Hoff, E. J. (1986) Customizing global marketing. *Harvard Business Review*, 64(May/June), 59–69.

Rodwell, T. (1996) Local flavour for a global message is common sense. *Marketing*, December 19, 16.

Wilkie, W. L. and Farris, P. W. (1975) Comparison advertising: problems and potential. *Journal of Marketing*, 39(4), 7–15.

Zhang, Y. and Gelb, B. D. (1996) Matching advertising appeal to culture: the influence of product's use conditions. *Journal of Advertising*, 25(3), 29–47.

PART 2

Aspects of International Marketing Communications

6 The Role of Packaging and Branding in International Marketing Communications

FRANCES EKWULUGO

Introduction

Branding and brand management have become centrally important in creating the basis for sustainable international competitiveness. It is now recognized that branding is an integral part of marketing management that must revolve around the basic nature of the consumer and the sort of appeal which the firm wishes to communicate. For example, brand name communicates the reputation, image and quality of the product and the manufacturer. Indeed, studies have shown that advertising rarely creates brands. Doyle (1995) argues that advertising is not the basis of a brand development. It communicates and positions it. This chapter examines the concept of branding and its interface with other elements of the marketing mix, particularly the product management. It goes on to discuss the impact of societal marketing and brand management, and the overall impact of branding and packaging on the marketing communication.

The Concept of Branding

A brand is a name, term, sign, symbol or design, or a combination of them, which is intended to identify the goods or services of one seller or group of sellers, and to differentiate them from those of competitors (Kotler et al., 1996). Brand name represents product image, company image and corporate identity (Levitt, 1983(a); Doyle, 1995). Branding enables consumers to recall memories, thereby facilitating the initial buying action or perhaps more frequent buying, adding to customers' loyalty. It enhances the effectiveness of advertising because of the built-in advantage of product recognition and appeal. Doyle argues that successful branding could only be achieved through advertising because of the exposure of the product to strong media coverage. Doyle's position needs to be questioned; Marks & Spencer, for example, have succeeded in establishing their brand using only small-scale advertising.

As part of a product's physical element, brand is a very important component of product development strategy. Motorola, facing strong competition from Japanese companies, concentrated on quality to establish a brand image that made them leaders in the cellular telephone market. Motorola achieved this success by dedicated quality control and manufacturing improvement. Furthermore, Motorola also extended its quality control to its suppliers, knowing that a product is only as good as the components that it is made of. They gained credibility from one product area of the business which they extended to the other products. Today, Motorola is known for its brand image.

Adam Smith, in his deeply influential book, *The Wealth of Nations*, stated that 'The customer is king'. To satisfy a customer's needs and wants, in providing products or services, firms sometimes have to convert latent demand to attract effective demand from consumers.

Many customers are quite knowledgeable in terms of what they are expecting from products or services, and expectation varies from individual to individual, country to country, and culture to culture. Sophistication and the affluent society have played a great part in shaping the expectations of customers. Thus, a basic product could be made more complex; hence, firms carry various product ranges and many product portfolios, and are continuously trying to establish what customers could easily spend their money on to meet their needs and wants. Levitt (1983(b)) explains in his total product concept that the expectation of customers has gone beyond the basic satisfaction of core benefit, that a product is more than a physical entity. He then identifies other factors that play a part in whether a consumer would lift a product off the shelf or not. He describes the physical product as features, styling, quality, brand name and packaging. He states that firms now compete on augmented products, taking into account such factors as installation, after-sales service, warranty, delivery and credit terms. It could be concluded that a product is a web of benefit and attributes, which could be compiled in different ways to meet the different customers' needs.

Branding creates image. To create an image, firms often spend large sums of money trying to establish reputation and credibility. Reputation is an offshoot of quality, without product there will be no acquired value of reputation, and reputation is experience built over a long period of time. When a product is bought and it has served its purpose satisfactorily, the customer will perceive the product to be of good quality. To achieve credibility for high quality, a company must first develop a reputation for producing and delivering quality products (Bell, 1994; Fitzgerald, 1988). Herbig and Milowicz (1993) stated that 'Credibility is the believability of the current intention; reputation is a historical notion based on the sum of the past behaviours of the entity. Both credibility and reputation are dynamic in nature – both are prone to change over time and are a function of time'. To maintain credibility and reputation, firms must embark on a developing brand management. To what extent a company is able to satisfy the customers and maintain brand loyalty depends on the firm's capabilities in terms of finance, management and quality of employees – these, to an extent, are controllable factors, but there are also wider issues such as the macro environment, which plays a major part in international branding.

A brand could be said to represent the totality of a product, including the company's image. Image is described by Semiotics at University of Bologna as 'a beautiful thing'. The brand of a product is related to the image of the company or the country of origin. Many writers have contributed to the concept of 'made in'. Made in a given country could conjure a negative or positive image of a product. Products made in Taiwan and Japan have conjured a poor image in the past. It gave the connotation of inferior quality. If image is beautiful, it could be said that beauty is in the eyes of the beholder. If beauty varies from person to person and from nation to nation, obviously there is bound to be stereotyping of products depending on the country of origin. For four decades, Japan was known as a producer of poor-quality products. Japan, however, worked continuously to have the world's strongest economy through quality production. Now other countries are striving to emulate Japan. The Taiwanese make many world-market clothes and electronics, but these are not sold under Taiwanese brand names. These products are produced for internationally famous brand names and sold all over the world. Therefore, it could be concluded that consumers are loyal to the brand, not to the producers. Powerful brand names have consumers' loyalty.

In recent research into food products, it has been established that compared with the North American consumer, the African is much more concerned about the taste and the fragrance of the product, and less concerned about its nutritional and health characteristics.

Brand names must describe the product's function (e.g. Rex bathing soap). The stereotyping of brands does not stop only with individuals or countries, but also with the channels of distribution. Branded products are easily acceptable by channels of distribution because a branded product will tend to sell itself, and it is easier for customers to find and select. For branded goods, price differentials are not of significance. It is an uphill task to gain acceptance of an unbranded product in most retail outlets. Virgin Cola had considerable problems getting the product to the outlets.

Segmentation

Branding is a key way to segmentation. For example, umbrella brands could be formed with layers of segments. Nike and Reebok serve mainly male and sports segments. A brand name increases the value of the product in the eyes of the customer. Consumers associate with the name, symbol, device or packaging and some other factors of value, which are beyond the core product. A brand conveys something about the buyers' values – Mercedes buyers value high performance, safety and prestige. Cadbury, as an organization, has deliberately developed a strong image for the Cadbury corporate name to act as an umbrella for their entire product brands. Hence, their products benefit both from the affection that consumers hold for the corporate name and from the individual character developed by, for example, Cadbury's Flake, Cadbury's Dairy Milk, Cadbury's Drinking Chocolate and all their other products. In the car market, Ford similarly use their corporate name in conjunction with individual identities for their models (Ford Escort, Ford Fiesta, Ford Mondeo, etc.), whereas both Volvo and Peugeot rely more on the company name and so do not try to build character through model names. Thus, Volvo have produced the Volvo 440 series, while Peugeot also label their individual models by numbers, such as 106, 309 and 405. These brand names represent many things to the consumer. The best brands often stand for quality, value and product satisfaction. Organizations develop brands as a way to attract and keep customers by promoting value, image, prestige or lifestyle.

Social Issues and Branding

The company's history, style and dynamism are often determining factors in the creation of a brand image. The company image encompasses a broader set of factors that contribute to its formation and diffusion (e.g. retailers, shareholders, employees, trade unions) and thus expands the range of rational and emotional elements that are part of the brand image and, companies with high brand equity have more leverage in bargaining power.

In some markets, customers have strong bargaining power and these influence the way companies offer their products. The saying that the consumer is 'king' still prevails; therefore, if manufacturers do not cater for consumers' complex sets of needs and expectations, they will lose business. It is suggested that what is underneath the label should be in line with the personal values of today's consumer and firms should reposition their brands to reflect those values.

Brands are not static and need to change with their environment. The thrust for companies in the 1990s has not been towards new brands, but towards strengthening and expanding those which already exist. Consumers are continually evaluating goods and services not just on the basis of how they will satisfy their immediate material needs, but also on how they will satisfy their deeper moral needs. Not only are customers' wants inadequately considered, but also there is much reason for fearing that the goods and services of many organizations are against the long-term interests of customers and society as a whole (e.g. harmful food and drugs). Marketing should be aimed to maximize customer satisfaction, but within the constraints that all firms have a responsibility to society as a whole and to the environment. For instance, Body Shop gained fame through ecological friendliness. Indeed, a customer may purchase a brand of goods not because of its quality, but because the manufacturer supports a good cause which the consumer approves of. The Co-operative Bank does not invest money in areas that do not support environmental causes. Barclays Bank was boycotted by many customers and countries for their support of apartheid for many years.

It is difficult to reconcile the needs of internal stakeholders with marketing needs. Satisfying the needs of internal stakeholders boosts the marketing effort, as enlightened work policies secure greater commitment and loyalty from workers, and therefore better output. Communication of a company's values is a key part of internal marketing. Being a good employer, a profitable company and a caring company, especially for the environment where the company operates, count considerably in the eyes of customers. Oil companies have met customer requirements for a range of energy products, but there has been a cost in terms of environmental damage even to those societies who have not directly benefited from the cheap, accessible energy sources. This created a bad reputation that is transferable to the brand image, e.g. Shell in Africa.

Societal marketing has an endowment effect, the benefit derived could be cumulative and matures late in the process.

In the past, marketing has to some extent disregarded the wider needs of society. These needs could be communicated through branding. The wider needs of customers vary greatly owing to culture, nationality and the environment where the company operates. Marketing may bring together suppliers and customers whose needs are both met, but at the expense of other members of society.

Branding and the General Product

Major brand manufacturers have recognized the opportunities offered by own-label manufacture. Shops like Body Shop, Benetton and Marks & Spencer carry their own brands. In the United Kingdom, one of the largest supermarkets, Sainsbury, carries 50 per cent of its stock as own-brand items. This is due to aggressive competition in the sector and also to overcapacity at the manufacturing plant. For example, Heinz produces own brands for UK supermarkets and is now looking for customers in Europe. Some brand owners have refused to supply products for retailers' own-label items; companies like Kellogg's advertise the fact that they do not make goods for anyone else. Despite this, many own brands are thriving in the market and challenging the popular brands. When manufacturers produce for other companies, they may be in danger of sending the wrong signals to consumers – consumers believe that if a major brand manufacturer produces an own brand for another company, then the own brand is as good as the popular brand. Retailers invest in their own brands to the extent that their quality levels are often on a par with leading brands. In Europe, the European partners have established legislation on intellectual property and the bill has been made to prevent own-label brands from imitating the 'distinctive signs' of brands. The group wanted to strengthen this to 'overall appearance' and to have look-alikes treated as unfair competition, as they are in other countries.

Own-label brands tend to be localized and this tendency has grown from 34 per cent to almost 40 per cent of supermarket sales in the United Kingdom in just three years. The trend is spreading across Europe.

The threat of own labels should not be ignored. Mars announced that it has to move into own-label manufacture of 'wet cooking sauces' (e.g. Dolmio bolognese sauce in a jar) after sixty years of resistance to such supply. The reason for such a move is the existence of aggressive competition in the sector.

Indeed, it is suggested that retailer brands are increasingly perceived as equal to or superior to traditional brands (de Jonquieres, 1993) and customers may increasingly question whether or not manufacturers' brands possess additional values which qualify them for premium prices. Retailers are themselves more actively engaged in internationalization and their established domestic brands will in most cases accompany them. In addition, their own brand could be globalized.

International Brand Development/ Market Developments

Universally, branding has become a central issue in product management strategy because companies with high brand equity have more leverage in bargaining power in the marketplace. Firms are desperate to increase their market share and attain economies of scale, especially where the market is very competitive. There is a need to attain cost leadership and the use of differentiation strategy. Many multinationals have turned to the newly growing market economies of Central and Eastern Europe mainly as a way of increasing their market share and partly as a way of escaping from the highly competitive market in which they operate. Developing a brand in a country like Russia has proved to be difficult. In the confectionery market, Mars went to Russia first, followed by Cadbury, Nestle, etc., but they have all suffered economic setbacks, such as devaluation of the rouble, and high duties and taxes. The main problem is lack of marketing infrastructure and market information which is fundamental to brand management and adoption. Brands depend on mass distribution, but Russia's retail industry is still in a state of transition. There was no means of measuring targeted TV audiences, and alternative means of promotion and evaluation are not feasible (Teather, 1995).

To develop a brand, the firm needs to define the benefits to the consumer and the attributes of the product. These benefits and attributes go a long way to meet the consumers' needs and wants, and must be communicated by the products. In branding services, augmentation plays a major part. Brands could succeed if marketers get closer to their customers and identify the services they appreciate. In buying financial services, augmented elements could be the quality of the cashier that served customers, and the quality of advice received; hence, brands take the image and the corporate culture of the company.

International branding development facilitates the adaptation process and acceptance of new products, because users assume new products have the same quality level as existing ones; the established firm will incur a minimal cost because they already have a well-established presence. Also, since name research will not be needed, extensive advertising for brand name awareness and preference will not be necessary, and user response will tend to be faster, thereby reducing the introduction stage in the product cycle, creating early profits recovery. In addition, another advantage often obtained is greater ease in gaining distribution (particularly shelf space) due to the familiar name. The reputation of the established brand name can facilitate the introduction of a new product. Any problems with the new product can, conversely, affect the saleability of all items bearing the same name. If consistency in new product quality is not maintained, user dissatisfaction may result, which may carry over to older successful brands in the line. Family branding, therefore, places high demands on quality control because every single item is considered representative of the entire line. A lower quality item may hurt sales of the better quality product. This may result in credibility gaps among potential buyers. A new product failure may well tarnish the reputation of related products carrying the same brand name.

Brand positioning is one of the techniques that is critical in developing a brand. This is done through a series of activities in which the key elements of product perception are examined and subsequently tested in relation to key ideas that may be used in the brand communication strategy. It is essential that the brand has a distinct position in the eyes of the customer. Each brand should have a unique niche, independent of the similarity of the substance of the products with which it competes. Discovering a niche in the market can be the first step in developing an effective brand. This niche could also include an international market. There might be a need to reposition an established brand in the market for many reasons. Perhaps a competitor has launched a rival brand next to the company brand and cut into its market share. Customers' needs and wants may have changed, creating less demand in the market. In this case, repositioning may require changing the image and adapting the product. For example, Kentucky Fried Chicken changed its menu, adding lower fat skinless chicken and non-fried items such as broiled chicken and chicken salad sandwiches to reposition itself toward more health-conscious fast-food consumers. It also changed its name to KFC.

Global Branding

In the past, many companies went international with national products. Products were exported to countries where there are demands for them.

Brand owners have the opportunity to take advantage of world markets. When extending a brand beyond its national borders, companies can choose from a number of branding strategies. They may want to standardize all aspects of the marketing mix, standardize the name or the product only, or they may vary both the name and the product to fit local needs. It is difficult to classify a totally globalized product with any form of adaptation, in terms of packaging, language, colour, etc.

When the firm uses the same name for essentially the same product worldwide, it is said to have a global branding strategy. A global brand is more than a single name for an identical or similar product. It also has the basic personality, strategy and positioning in world markets. Coca-Cola, Levi Strauss, Mercedes-Benz and Sony are examples of brands that have made the transition from national to global brand. Many global brands adapt the product or positioning in such a way as to meet local market needs. For example, Avon carries different types of skin products, formulas and colours based on the various skin types of women around the world. Likewise, Time Magazine publishes 257 weekly editions around the world. McDonald's adapted its products in India, and has made changes to its menu to cater to local tastes elsewhere in the world. In 1996, McDonald's launched its first restaurants in India; to respect local custom, the menu there did not include beef. Instead, there was a novel item: the Maharaja Mac, made with mutton, but served in the McDonald's sesame-seed bun.

There is strong evidence in favour of the continued internationalization of brands, but the international brand, with similar market positioning and communication strategies in different markets, has been limited to selective product categories, such as soft drinks, jeans and perfumes. The argument is: can the concept be applied more generally? Does the ill-defined concept of 'globalization', when applied to the international marketing of standard brands (Levitt, 1983(b)), inevitably lead, at the extreme, to a bland appeal that would then open up areas for exploitation by international companies. It has, however, been argued that the truly global brand does not exist and is unlikely to. As Clark (1987, p. 36) wrote: 'Consumers do not see them (global brands), do not expect or want them and so not respond to them in any meaningful way.' Clark suggests that the focus on global brands is supply driven, affected by the manner in which businesses view the world. Brands could be adopted differently in different geographical areas and economic environments. Value, perception and usage could vary widely. Heineken beer, for example, is viewed as a high-quality beer in the United States and France, a grocery beer in the United Kingdom and cheap beer in Belgium.

It is also evident that even well-quoted examples of so-called global brands have been adapted in some way to take account of local conditions. It may be an essential requirement to acknowledge cultural dissimilarities and adjust marketing strategies to suit specific requirements. Generally, those who question the feasibility of a global standardized branding strategy argue that the dissimilarities from language alone far outweigh any similarities, and that adaptability and variation in marketing strategies across geographical markets are likely to be the norm.

When the same product has different brand names in different countries, it is a world product. World products are quite common, evolving naturally in companies that have been multinational in orientation. The multinational firm focuses on adapting to local conditions, and typically finds a good reason to choose a local 'invented here' name for a product sold worldwide. Almost every company that has operated as a multinational has world products. Lever Brothers, for example, manufactures the same formula of detergent in several European countries. It is sold under different brand names, like If, Viss or Cif. Many companies are re-evaluating their world product policies and converting to global brands. Mars, until recently a US confectionery company, marketed the Snickers chocolate bar as a world product with a different name in every major market. For example, it was called Marathon in Britain because Mars felt that 'Snickers' was too close to the word 'knickers', a British word for a woman's undergarment and a style of men's shorts.

In response to the rapidly emerging single market in Europe, however, Mars recently decided to switch from a world product strategy to a global brand strategy for their chocolate bar; they took advantage of the efficiency and leverage of a single block of a global brand. Mars now uses a single, common name and Marathon is known as Snickers worldwide. To create a global brand, a firm will also have worked towards creating the same personality, image and positioning for the brand in all world markets.

Implementing a global brand strategy is complicated by different language, different customs and different marketing tactics in different nations. For example, Vauxhall thought it would be simple to extend its Nova as a global product. Unfortunately, the words 'no va' in Spanish mean does not go – a misconception of words – wrong brand name.

The word diet also poses problems, even when correctly translated. In the United States, the term has come to mean 'low-calorie', but in some foreign countries diet connotes a medicinal or therapeutic product that must conform with local laws for pharmaceuticals.

Another challenge facing marketers as they try to create global brands is the development of a global brand personality. If a personality is based on a single country or culture, it may or may not be extended. The Jolly Green Giant may be seen as intimidating in some nations, for example. Despite the many difficulties of developing global brands, the rewards of achieving such branding can make the effort very worthwhile.

Companies could, by skilful branding, build, develop and sustain an advantage over their competitors, and thereby maintain or increase their sales or market share. The development of competitive advantage is particularly crucial in mature, low-tech, markets. Turning to specific instances, it is difficult to develop competitive advantage in the food and drink market because companies can easily imitate product developments or packaging improvements, using different brand name labels, packaging and advertising.

Brand Extension

Brand extension is when a company introduces a product under a new category or under the same brand name. Honda uses its company name for all its products. Reckitt and Colman established the Dettol brand name in 1933 and has since used the name for all its products very successfully.

Reasons for brand extension are to utilize excess manufacturing capacity, meet new consumer needs, match a competitor's new offering or gain more shelf space. It gives new products instant recognition, and enables the company to enter new product categories more easily. For instance, Sony puts its name on all its electrical products. New products are easily recognized and accepted. Brand extension reduces advertising to establish awareness. It could be argued that brand extension has its limitations. It may lead to loss of meaning, especially where the subsequent lines are not as good as the original. It could cause confusion, especially where the original brand product is too strong in the market.

Branding and Advertising

Marketing communication is the process of both informing and educating users and dealers about the company and its objectives, and influencing attitudes. It has been established that firms communicate through personal and non-personal means, and branding is one of the very powerful ways of communicating the characteristics of the product. The brand name is sometimes the name of the product, i.e. the 'language' is taken as meaning the product itself and whoever makes it. A good example of this is the classic case of the name Hoover, the name of the American company manufacturing vacuum cleaners. People refer to all vacuum cleaners as a 'Hoover', when they actually mean a vacuum cleaner, and when the vacuum cleaner is used people say they are hoovering. There are many products which have given rise to the use of a generic name, e.g. Bic, Coke.

Careful brand management is necessary in order to generate successful brands. The generation of successful brands involves the building up of image, instilling distinctiveness into customers' minds. After spending resources on naming a product, it is imperative to support it through advertising and communication. The first job of advertising is to build brand awareness and corporate brand approval. There may be a correlation between the level of advertising investment and the level of brand awareness achieved. For many decades, the famous brand names were Hovis bread, Kellogg's cornflakes, Cadbury's chocolate, Schweppes mineral water, Brooke Bond tea, Colgate toothpaste, Kodak film, Heinz beans, Mars bars. It is worthwhile evaluating these brands as to where they are now. They are still brand leaders in their various markets. The success of these brands is a result of continually maintaining the quality of their output and its relevance to consumers over a long period. Success has resulted from putting through the right communication message to the customers. Coca-Cola has continuously used this approach. The strength of advertising depends on affordability; for example, a small business with limited finance might find it extremely difficult to communicate its message, therefore it could be difficult to build a brand image.

John S. Bowen, chairman emeritus of D'Arcy Mesius Benton and Bowles once said: 'Brands that offer consumers a consistent advertising message and regularly updated product will lead their industries'. He goes on to say that companies that believe in outstanding advertising are those which will build leadership brands. The commitment to the brand's success is encompassed in its advertising. In the increasingly competitive marketplace, advertising, marketing and promotion may be the only things that differentiate extremely similar products. To set against this view, as mentioned earlier, Marks & Spencer built up their brand image without intensive advertising. They rely on high street presence and customer experience, although it takes a longer time. Anita Roddick, who believes that advertising is wasteful, has made her alternative brand-building methods the basis of her company's strategy. However, advertising positions the product through creative messages communicating brand values that meet the requirements of the targeted audience.

Packaging

Advertising does not happen inside the shops, therefore packaging and design sell the pack, and advertising supports the brand's design.

The impression of a product upon a consumer is influenced by the physical contact made with the package, hence an effective and efficient packaging will increase sales. For example, when Sunkist packaging was changed to an attractive blue colour, the sales increased. Kotler defined packaging as: 'The activities of designing and producing the container or wrapper for a product'. Therefore, packaging serves two main functions: it protects the contents from high/low temperatures, insects, damp, light, and other highly perfumed and flavoured products; it also protects the product during transit and distribution so that it arrives in a satisfactory condition. It promotes the products and therefore should be persuasive and have a strong identity. Packaging, although it serves as a functional element, may and if possible should enhance the product image and competitiveness. It communicates product image positioning and it is a powerful communicator at the point of sale. The quality of a package plays an important role in providing satisfaction to customers' needs, hence packaging is part of a product. An article in *Packaging News* (June 1995, p. 41) states that good packaging empties shelves, and that branding and eye-catching presentation are very important factors in generating sales. For example, the Cadbury confectionery group differentiates its products by using innovative packaging techniques, as well as quality materials and strong branding.

Packaging is an important element of the promotional mix complementing advertising, sales promotion, public relations, exhibitions, direct mailing and so on. When a consumer is faced with a confusing number of products, it is often the packaging, and the information it contains, which can influence the final decision on what to buy. Luxury perfumes are sold by brand names and packaging, the consumer is rewarded by using the brand that accords with their lifestyle. Some products sell in different countries for different reasons; for example, packaging expresses a product in different ways to meet the customers' needs within the environment they operate. For instance, the colour of a product could convey different messages to different customers. White could mean purity, cleanliness and honesty; black – strength, darkness and death; red – heat, extravagance, mystery and seriousness. In addition to this, colour attracts buyers' attention and enables them to identify the product, and provides a reason to buy. Pringle (1994) suggests that packs need a strong individual presence to be noticed in the current retail environment. For example, Coca-Cola, Toilet Duck, Radion and J Cloth are products combining good quality with individual packaging. Internationally, a packaging decision has to be made about whether to standardize or adapt to specific needs of the market. In making this decision, the protectional and promotional aspects of packaging need to be considered. In some countries, especially countries with low levels of literacy, language may be a problem, depending on the extent of compatibility with the country of origin; for example, the use of the French language could be perfectly acceptable in Canada. English is acceptable in the United States. Some companies use two or more languages on their packaging, making it easy to sell in many countries, e.g. pan-European products. Low levels of literacy may require more emphasis on pictorial design. For example, pharmaceutical companies use pictorial signs to communicate dosage or target audience. Cans have proved to be good marketing tools. They have been used for novelty packs ranging from tennis balls to personalized gifts, have served to carry mail to remote islands and have been used as greetings cards. Light-sensitive microchips, UV-sensitive printing inks and holographic images have enabled the production of talking cans and active promotional designs. Examples of promotional cans are cash-in-can promotions, Sterogram images on Pepsi-Cola cans and graphics appearing in bright sunlight. Giant inflatable cans and cans used to construct buildings have served to promote drinks cans (*Canner*, September 1994, pp. 26–30).

Protectional considerations must be taken account of both in the marketplace and in transit to the marketplace. For example, the handling that the product is likely to receive depends on the length of time the product will spend within the international distribution chain, considering that the chain may be longer than that for the domestic country. The consumer usage rate and consequent storage time must also be taken into consideration. With these in mind, the packaging, wrapping or case in which the product is offered for sale can consist of a variety of materials, such as glass, paper, metal or plastic. In the soft drinks market, a variety of packaging materials are used.

Japan is a leader in world consumer packaging for many reasons: greater spending on research and development than in Europe, a more advanced consumer market and a more even distribution of wealth. The quality of packaging is a function of the cost of packaging. Packaging costs are very often included in production costs and are not added to the advertising budget. Therefore, many companies do not see packaging as a major part of a promotional budget. In some cases, packaging constitutes the major part of the total cost of the product. 'The cost associated with package design – direct and indirect cost for materials, labour, and overheads – must be capitalised rather than deducted as an advertising expense under UK Internal Revenue Code (IRC Section 162. Under Revenue Ruling 89–23)'. Package design is defined as 'an asset that is created by a specific graphic arrangement or design of shapes, colours, words, pictures, lettering, and so forth on a given product package, or the design of a container with respect to its shape or function'. Classic examples of this are expensive cosmetics and Teachers Whisky. For instance, in spite of stringent control, and purchasing materials at the lowest possible cost consistent with quality, the value of the packaging material exceeds that of a bottle of whisky.

Manufacturers also need to consider package size very carefully. For example, a high level of car ownership and a developed supermarket retail system are highly likely to indicate large packs. By contrast, in developing countries, a very low per capita income may suggest small packs. A good example of this is cigarettes, which in many developing countries are sold singly. Internationally marketed products, perhaps especially those used by tourists, should be immediately recognizable. Kodak films provide a well-known example of a product which is instantly recognizable because of a distinctively designed internationally standard package. Packaging is an important link between advertising and the buying decision about a product. A package could become the focus of brand advertising – using the same logo or colour stripe makes packaging a differentiating element. Packaging helps to identify products, e.g. Coca-Cola, and promotes brand visibility, familiarity and consistency.

In considering packaging, there is a need to consider the environmental issues, as responsible packaging is important for the preservation of life and health and of the complicated environment where the firms operate. In the United Kingdom, Tesco has opened several centres to recycle tonnes of cardboard outer packaging and plastic shrink-wrap.

In Europe, the European Commission introduced a directive stipulating that a minimum of half of all waste packaging must be recovered, and many countries have taken a stringent approach to the issue of recycling. Under Germany's packaging law, 60–70 per cent of each material must be recycled, except that which is incinerated, used in land fill or returned for re-use. Between 1991 and 1995, packaging use by householders and small businesses fell by 900 000 tonnes to 6.7 million tonnes, or 12 per cent. More than 5 million tonnes (79 per cent) of this was dropped in Grune Punkt collection bags and containers, about 65 kg per person. In the European Union, additional requirements have been designed to protect or inform the consumer and attempts have been made to standardize units or quantities. Prices could be compared using standardized size or weight.

Labelling is part of packaging, all products must be labelled. This could vary from a simple tag to more complicated information. Labels may carry only the brand name and, depending on legal requirements, more information relating to the product. Labels have many functions: they identify the product or brand, e.g. the Coca-Cola logo identifies the product whether it is packaged in plastic, a can, a box, etc. It gives the product international recognition.

There is a long history of legal concerns surrounding labels, as well as packaging and products in general. In 1914, the Federal Trade Commission Act held that false, misleading or deceptive labels or packages constitute unfair competition. The Fair Packaging and Labeling Act, passed by Congress in 1967, set mandatory labelling requirements, encouraged voluntary industry packaging standards, and allowed federal agencies to set packaging regulations in specific industries. The Food and Drug Administration (FDA) has required processed food producers to include nutritional labelling that clearly states the amounts of protein, fat, carbohydrates and calories contained in the product, as well as vitamin and mineral content as a percentage of the daily allowance. The FDA recently launched a drive to control health claims in food labelling by taking action against the potentially misleading use of such descriptions as 'light', 'high fiber' and 'no cholesterol'. Consumerists have lobbied for additional labelling laws to require open dating (to describe product freshness), unit pricing (to state the product cost in standard measurement units) and grade labelling (to rate the quality level of certain consumer goods).

Some segments of the market are frequently ignored. Throughout the world, there are millions of people who are registered blind or partially sighted, and others who have problems with reading and opening packages. To a large extent, this area has not been fully addressed by manufacturers. It would seem that it is very much in manufacturers' best interests to look at this issue very carefully, because bad packaging will fail to communicate with the consumer, and poor communication probably means a lost sale.

REFERENCES

Bell, C. (1994) Building a reputation for training effectiveness. Training and Development. *Journal of Marketing Research*, 28(February), 16–28.

Chung, K. K. (1995) Brand popularity and country image in global competition: managerial implications. *Journal of Product and Brand Management*, 4(5), 21–33.

Clark, H. (1987) Consumer and corporate values: yet another view on global marketing. *International Journal of Advertising*, 6(1), 29–42.

de Chernatony, L. (1992) Brand pricing in a recession. *European Journal of Marketing*, 26(3), 5–14.

de Chernatony, L. (1993) Categorising brands: evolutionary processes underpinned by two key dimensions. *Journal of Marketing Management*, 9, 173–88.

de Jonquieres, G. (1993) Not just a question of price. *Financial Times*, 9 September, 8.

Doyle, P. and Baker, M. J. (1995) *The Marketing Book*, 3rd edn. Butterworth-Heinemann.

Dubois, B. (1993) The market for luxury goods: income versus culture. *European Journal of Marketing*, 27(1), 36–44.

Fitzerald, T. J. (1988) Understanding the differences and similarities between services and products to exploit your competitive advantage. *Journal of Services Marketing*, 2(Winter), 25–30.

Herbig, P. and Milowicz, J. (1993) The relationship of reputation and credibility to brand success. *Journal of Consumer Marketing*, 10(3).

Kotler, P., Armstrong, G., Saunders, J. and Wong, V. (1996) *Principles of Marketing*. The European Edition. Prentice Hall.

Levitt, T. (1983a) The globalisation of markets. *Harvard Business Review*, 83(3).

Levitt, T. (1983b) *The Marketing Imagination*. New York: Collier Macmillan.

Pringle, D. (1994) *Packaging Week*. 10(26), 12.

Saurudin, A. A. (1993) Cross-national evaluation of mae-in concept using multiple cues. *European Journal of Marketing*, 27(7), 39–52.

Teather, D. (1995) Out of the gold. *Marketing*, 2 November, 26–9.

7 International Public Relations Management

SAM BLACK

Introduction

The expanding development of satellite communication and the rapid growth of international trade have helped to speed up the process of globalization, which has been such a strong feature of world affairs and international relations during the last two decades.

In parallel with the growth of international relations, there has been rapidly growing interest in international public relations. Until comparatively recently, public relations texts made little or no mention of this branch of the subject. This is not true of more recent texts, but even these make only passing reference to the ways in which 'international' public relations differs from professional work carried out in one's own country.

Agreeing Definitions

Perhaps the best way to consider this subject is by trying to establish accept-able definitions. A useful definition of international public relations is 'achieving mutual understanding and good relations where it is necessary to bridge a cul-tural, geographical or linguistic gap'. Stressing that it denotes public relations programmes or activities that have, or are likely to have, effects or significance outside the country of origin can extend this definition.

Expressed in basic terms, it implies planning globally, but acting locally. An American professor, James Anderson of the University of Florida at Gainesville, has commented: 'Communication innovations combined with information and public relations initiatives have shrunk our planet. Historical developments of momentous importance since World War II make it imperative for everyone in public relations to acquire a global perspective on behalf of employers and clients.'

To quote Ellis Kopel, a British practitioner with extensive international experi-ence, 'After many years when everyone paid lip service to globalization and internationalization of trade, and therefore the need for public relations to be able to work efficiently across borders, the need itself has now actually arrived.'

Ironically, as political and trading blocs become bigger, it becomes more and more difficult for an individual citizen to identify on a wide canvas, and indeed the result may be a narrower point of view. It is difficult, for example, for people to think of themselves as Europeans, and much easier to remain as Britons, Irish, Spaniards or Catalans.

Since public relations is conditioned by reputation, credibility, confidence, harmony and mutual understanding, it is essential to study and to take into account the subtle relationships which result from national feelings.

It is only necessary to consider recent developments in the former Soviet Union or Yugoslavia to realize how difficult it is for even close neighbours to relate positively to each other or to agree on almost anything.

The Influence of the International Public Relations Association

While the modern practice of public relations has flourished in the United States since 1923 when Doctor Edward L. Bernays published the first textbook and taught the first university course in public relations at New York University, the professional activity made little progress in Europe and other parts of the world until after the end of World War II. Until his death in March 1995, at the age of 103, Bernays continued to have a positive influence on the development of professional public relations practice.

In Britain, men and women who have been carrying out public relations duties in the services naturally wish to use their experience in civilian life. This led to the formation of the (British) Institute of Public Relations in February 1948. Its membership has grown from less than 100 to over 5000.

This example was followed in other European countries, and in 1951 a few leading practitioners from Britain, France, The Netherlands, Norway and the United States started informal discussions about ways in which public relations could be encouraged worldwide and particularly in those countries where few, if any, professionals were operating.

History records how these negotiations led to the formation of the International Public Relations Association (IPRA) in May 1955. The initial five countries were soon joined in membership of the IPRA by practitioners from other countries where public relations was developing as a management discipline. The membership today is over 1000 and the members are senior practitioners from over sixty countries. The Association celebrated its fortieth anniversary on 1 May 1995 and this occasion was marked by the publication of a commemorative book: *A Commitment to Excellence – IPRA, the first 40 years*.

Public relations world congresses were instituted in 1958, during the World Expo in Brussels, and have been held every three years in different parts of the world. The IPRA has encouraged the formation of public relations associations and its members have exerted a powerful influence on the spread of public relations as an international function.

Since the break-up of the Soviet Union, the importance of public relations has become recognized in the former communist countries. For example, active public relations associations have been formed in Russia and Hungary, and others are planned in several countries in Eastern Europe. One of the author's books, *Introduction to Public Relations*, has been published in Russian and its 57 000 copies sold out quickly.

China, too, has shown great interest in public relations, encouraged by the spread of industrial joint ventures between China and the West, and the China International Public Relations Association was formed in Beijing in 1991. The author has carried out extensive lecture tours in China and can vouch from personal knowledge of the keen interest now shown in public relations in both public and private sectors in China.

Organizational Responsibilities

Professor Melvin Sharpe, of Ball State University, Muncie, Indiana, has emphasized that public relations can be explained in terms of ethnic social behaviour that achieves and maintains human relationships. He has postulated that before an organization can perform effective public relations, four simple principles must be accepted by the management. They are:

1 Management must recognize that in a global communications society, an organization's stability is based on favourable public opinion and support.
2 All men and women have the right to information about planned decisions that may affect their lives and have the right to voice their opinions in relation to the planned actions.
3 Organizations must manage their communications in such a manner as to ensure that adequate accurate feedback is continually received so that the organization is capable of keeping up with changes in the social system.
4 Organizations that cannot change will inevitably die.

Social stability and ethical behaviour are the essential underpinning of public relations, and this is particularly applicable to the planning and implementation of public relations in the international context.

The late Kerryn King, a prominent US consultant, was once asked by a student at Ball State University: 'What do you consider the greatest public relations campaign of this century and what made it great'. King replied that he could not identify a specific campaign but he could mention one of the most significant contributions. This was his statement:

> Somewhere out there is a fellow who is serving as an adviser to a chief executive officer who said 'Don't do that'. The reasons he gave were that it would be self-serving . . . It would make us look great for the time being . . . We would make a few

bucks . . . But in the long run we will alienate our customers; we're going to bring the legislature down on our heads; we're going to have some discriminatory taxes passed against us. And all the great profit we could make is going to be taken away because people aren't going to like us for doing it.

One of the problems in practising public relations across frontiers is the necessity to appreciate the sensitivities in unfamiliar organizations and individuals that need to be harmonized.

Some Inconsistencies

Some companies and some individuals appear to be hypnotized by the concept of 'international' public relations. An example of this is a true story told by Ellis Kopel. Some years ago, his agency was asked to pitch for a public relations contract with the Cake and Biscuits Industries Trade Federation. The specification for the contract was the requirement to demonstrate an ability to work internationally. Kopel was able to show experience of working successfully and won the contract. Having won the contract, Kopel held it for ten years, but at no time during that period was he called upon to do any work outside Britain.

Potential Problems of Linguistic Differences

It is always necessary to watch out for ambiguity or *double entendre*. This can be difficult sometimes when using your own language, but becomes a veritable minefield when it comes to composing messages in a foreign language. Even using the services of a national may not avoid problems unless they are familiar with the subject of the message.

A few examples will emphasize this point. A motor car did not sell in one country because its name, when translated, meant 'coffin'. An airline produced an advertisement publicising its 'rendezvous lounges' only to find out too late that in the local language it meant 'a place to have sex'. These are only two examples of the kind of embarrassing mistakes which can happen so easily when working overseas.

Methods of Organizing International Public Relations

In the period immediately following World War II, many American corporations tried to conduct their overseas public relations operations from their headquarters in the United States. In most instances, these attempts were unsatisfactory because of the difficulties of understanding and conforming to national customs and susceptibilities.

The results of this experience, which was mirrored by that of other large companies endeavouring to carry out public relations from far away in another continent, have led to the acceptance of four main methods of organizing international public relations.

1 There are few large international public relations consultancies which can provide the services of their own subsidiaries in all the major industrial centres. The two best-known examples of this are Hill & Knowlton and Burson-Marsteller.
2 Another choice is to employ the services of a large international group with fully or partly owned offices and affiliates worldwide. The leading example of such a network is Shandwick.
3 There are several groups which bring together independent public relations consultancies in the major industrial centres. Two well-known examples are the Pinnacle and Worldcom groups, which have members throughout the world.
4 Other networks operate on a very informal basis, without regular meetings, and which refer clients to each other and work together as appropriate.

The major difference between using these four different methods of securing support in different countries is the question of control. Overall control should always rest with the employer, but inevitably questions of choice between alternative possibilities will arise and must be dealt with quickly.

Some Diverse Examples of Public Relations Working Internationally

Even within one country, the type of challenge and opportunities for creative public relations is very diverse. From an international viewpoint, the variety is almost infinite.

This fact has been emphasized by the results of the IPRA Golden World Awards for Excellence, which commenced in 1990 and are held annually.

A selection of case studies from this competition has been published recently by Kogan Page. *International Public Relations Case Studies*, edited by Sam Black, includes forty cases from fifteen countries.

The book groups the forty cases into nine chapters: corporate and business; public affairs; protecting the environment; employee relations; community relations; health care and medical; business to business; art and culture; international public relations. The diversity of subjects is quite remarkable and illustrates the wide range of situations, which are met in public relations.

A few examples are worth quoting.

1 A medium-sized management consultancy with world headquarters in Chicago wished to achieve dramatic growth in size and reputation. The strategy adopted was to position the chairman of the consultancy as a

thought leader on a very important issue to the day – the competitiveness of US companies against foreign competitors.

2   How a comparatively small company in the UK travel industry made a planned attempt to be taken seriously by the City as an important player in the travel industry. The dynamic investors relations campaign, which featured a direct approach to the financial media, analysts and institutional investors, achieved notable results. The company's share price increased 863 per cent and the share was acknowledged as the best performing share on the London stock exchange in 1991.

3   The desirability of adopting a cautious low-profile approach instead of a brash high-level profile was shown by the success of Lasmo in securing permission to drill for oil off the Nova Scotia coast in Canada, where Texaco had failed dismally only a few years previously. This report emphasizes the value in this instance of taking informed local advice and considering strategy and tactics carefully, instead of rushing in with a high profile.

4   A high-level industry initiative brought together a number of public and private organizations in the United States to protect the global environment and to reduce damage to the ozone layer. The methodology adopted was to seek a global partnership of industry and government to identify alternative technologies, and to promote their transfer to countries and companies, which need them. This partnership was named ICOLP. It has met all its initial objectives and its work will continue and expand.

5   'Communication 2000' was the title adopted by a large French chemical company, Rhône Poulenc, which had a very large subsidiary in the United States. Aware of the need to improve internal communication in order to avoid friction and to encourage a better environment, which would encourage employees to be more productive and creative, a very imaginative programme was adopted. It included a number of projects, which introduced the stolid American workers to the traditions of France.

6   A report from India describes an ambitious successful project, 'the Magic Train', which brought medical attention and surgery to outlying areas of the country. This was one example of IMPACT India which co-ordinated available resources from the public and private sectors to prevent and treat disabilities. Voltas Ltd, the largest Indian engineering and manufacturing enterprise, had been very generous in providing resources and had allowed the general manager of its corporate relations department, Mrs Zelma Lazarus, to direct IMPACT India. She was also the moving spirit behind the Magic Train programme.

7   For twelve years, ICI Paints had administered an ambitious community relations programme. Each year, the company presents supplies of paints for selected community projects. Since the scheme began, 4500 organizations have been given supplies of paint to the value of £500 000 for painting many different kinds of communal and charitable projects.

8   The serious effect of the Gulf crisis on air traffic in 1991 led to British Airways introducing 'the world's biggest offer' in which every one of the 50 000 seats in their route system would be given away free on 23 April.

This scheme was carried out very satisfactorily despite the immense logistic problems involved in carrying out the programme on a worldwide scale.

9   A very different programme was the Prostate Awareness Week in the United States. This condition is the second largest cancer killer in that country and over 32 000 men have died of it during the last few years. The programme's objective was to encourage men to take part voluntarily in a national screening programme, which would definitely save many lives. More than fifty clinics co-operated and over 40 000 men inquired for information about the screening.

10   A somewhat similar campaign in Australia, but for breast cancer screening, was very successfully carried out in Sydney. The idea was to use Rembrandt's famous portrait of Bathsheba reading her letter from King David as the main focus of the public relations and advertising campaigns. Dr Joan Croll, head of the Sydney Square Breast Clinic, realized the significance of the dimpling round the nipple of the model posing for Rembrandt's painting. It was summed up in the phrase: 'to an art lover the painting is a classic example of Rembrandt's mastery but to a doctor it is a classic example of incipient breast cancer'. The programme was very successful and was copied in other parts of Australia. This is an example of using a gimmick as a focus for a public relations programme. Normally, gimmicks have no part to play in public relations, but this is permissible when the gimmick is so closely related to the subject. This case study won a top award in the IPRA Golden World Awards for Excellence.

11   Most people believe that leprosy is a scourge of the past. Unfortunately, leprosy is still a problem in many parts of the world despite the fact that it is now curable by drugs. It is estimated that over 13 000 people suffer from leprosy in Europe. It is particularly a problem in Turkey and a leading Turkish magazine commissioned a public relations campaign to alert the Turkish people to the magnitude of the problem and how it could be ameliorated.

12   Great benefit can be brought to sufferers of many serious conditions by organ transplants. The problem is securing enough donors. This case study described the European Donor Hospital Education Programme, which had as its objective the establishment of a pan-European medical education programme to address the problem of the growing shortage of donor organs and tissues in Europe.

13   The British toy industry was becoming increasingly worried by the bad publicity in the press about 'dangerous' toys. The industry was convinced that most, if not all, of these substandard products were cheap imports. The solution adopted was to inaugurate a scheme with a Lion Mark logo, which would guarantee the quality and safety of the toys possessing the mark. This Lion Mark scheme was supported by the majority of British manufacturers and has done much to banish the previous bad publicity.

14   An example from the consumer goods field was the campaign to persuade British housewives to buy unusual species of fish. With the co-operation of most fishmongers in Britain, the campaign was very successful. The

programme was backed up by an active media relations campaign and the provision of suggested recipes for cooking these unfamiliar types of fish to best advantage.

15   An example of 'opportunist' public relations came from Chicago in the USA. Dean Foods, a leading dairy and food processor in the United States that is based in Chicago, wished to change the poster on a high sign in the centre of Chicago. When the workmen climbed up, they found that the sign had been appropriated by a family of hawks, a protected species of bird in the United States. Moreover, the mother hawk was sitting on her eggs. Under the Migratory Bird Treaty Act, the birds could not be disturbed until after the birth of the chicks. Deans Foods accepted the advice of its public relations advisers and set out to achieve as much good publicity as they could from this unusual situation. The results were quite outstanding and this is a striking example of how a crisis can be turned into an opportunity.

16   Another example from the food industry was the programme carried out by the Idaho State Commission to promote the sale of Idaho potatoes, usually regarded as the best available. The problem was that the term Idaho potato had become regarded by American housewives as a generic term for potatoes. A widespread media campaign and an imaginative publicity programme achieved a considerable improvement in the sale of 'real' Idaho potatoes.

17   A leading South African insurance company, Santam, has been promoting a child art project for the last thirty years. It affords an opportunity for children of all races to enter an annual art competition. Thousands of schools participate and the winning entries, which are always of a very high standard, are shown in exhibitions in South Africa and overseas. In recent years, the scheme has been extended to cover bursaries for school leavers and students at university.

18   Another noteworthy public relations programme in the field of art and community relations is from Tokyo. A leading manufacturer of shutters for shop fronts commissioned research to ascertain how the blank metal shutters which come down when shops close could be transformed into a living street art exhibition. With the help of the local university art department, a method was found of depositing colour pictures directly onto the metal shutters. The result has been a resounding success, transforming the street into a blaze of colour and beauty at night. It has helped to transform an area which was becoming rather run down into a very popular shopping district again and a magnet for foreign tourists.

19   Hungary is one of the countries in Eastern Europe which is actively replacing the straitjacket of decades of communism with a market economy. Effective public relations has been accepted as one of the factors that will be helpful in achieving this objective. Most Hungarian journalists speak little English and operate quite differently from Western reporters. For this reason, Pratt & Whitney, who were involved with a case of breach of contract with Malev, the Hungarian airline, found great difficulty in

securing a fair exposure of their point of view. However, with the assistance of a Hungarian public relations consultancy, a satisfactory resolution to their problem was achieved within a comparatively short period.

The Great Diversity of International Public Relations

These nineteen case histories are a representative ten-nation sample of the forty case studies from fifteen countries, which are described in considerable detail in the IPRA casebook. Each case analyses the background, the necessary research, the planning and implementation, and the final assessment and evaluation. This points to the need for any public relations programme to be planned logically and systematically. Dr Edward Bernays has described public relations as an art applied to a science. The art indicates the scope for initiative, creativity and imagination. The allusion to science in the definition emphasizes that even the best idea must be carried out comprehensively and efficiently if it is to achieve worthwhile results.

International Media of Communication

Using the media is one of the usual means of communicating as a part of a public relations programme. When working within your own country, there is little difficulty in drawing up a suitable media list according to the type of media in which it is hoped to secure publication. When it is desired to carry out media relations at a distance, it may be difficult to prepare an appropriate media list.

In such circumstances, it is often decided to concentrate on the increasing number of international business newspapers. The *Financial Times* now has twenty-nine fully manned bureaux overseas and international editions are printed in the United States, Germany, France and Japan. The paper claims a circulation of over 100 000. The European edition of the *Wall Street Journal* is now selling over 50 000 and also has an Asian edition of about 40 000 sales. Another international newspaper, which circulates widely among businessmen, is the *International Herald Tribune*. A new international medium which is becoming increasingly significant is the MBC satellite programme, which was founded in Saudi Arabia and broadcasts news, views and features to 100 million Arab viewers in the Middle East, Africa and Europe. It rivals in importance the BBC World Programme and CNN International.

In dealing with local and national media, local knowledge is essential as the culture and methods of journalists and editors vary considerably from one country to another.

When dealing with financial news internationally, it is necessary to bear in mind the rules of the local stock exchanges and the different time zones, which can be very important when price-sensitive subjects are being handled.

International Sponsorship

Sponsorship has become well established as one of the useful methods of communicating with selected publics and audiences. Sponsorship has been described as 'an international calling card' which can be used effectively as a tool of global communication.

Sponsorship has certain advantages over other methods of communicating worldwide. It can be associated with sport, art, music or other cultural events that have universal appeal, and usually presents few translation problems. It is an excellent way of promoting a name or a brand image. A large signboard at an international sport occasion will be seen by millions through national television and global satellite links.

An outstanding exponent of this form of publicity is the Coca-Cola Company. For more than 20 years, Coca-Cola has supported sport and music events at both national and international levels. The company attributes much of its success to this widespread use of sponsorship.

Some International Case Histories

It is very difficult to describe all the different types of programmes which come under the description of international public relations, but the following case studies will illustrate a few interesting projects, which have been carried out successfully in different countries.

For American Telephone and Telegraph (AT&T), who work worldwide, international public affairs and public relations are an everyday fact of life. This is well illustrated by three recent reports.

The installation of an AT&T international gateway switch and satellite earth station made Armenia the first of the former Soviet republics, other than Russia, to have a direct telecommunications link with the United States. Such an event was obviously a good opportunity for public relations and the company made this technical achievement a remarkable event for Armenia and the thousands of expatriate Armenians in the United States.

The main thrust of the public relations programme to celebrate this special occasion was to be a huge Armenian-style barbecue beneath the huge new satellite dish for 200 officials, media representatives and AT&T executives. Such an event would be simple in an advanced country, but in Armenia the logistic difficulties were great.

It was planned for the event to be linked by conference call to New York and Los Angeles, despite the time discrepancy. In New York, 600 Armenian church, academic, business and community leaders and envoys were to have breakfast with a senior AT&T executive. In Los Angeles, the main speaker was the Armenian Minister of Culture, a successful author who happened to be in the United States, participating in an AT&T-sponsored international writers programme.

He hosted a group of local schoolchildren of Armenian descent, who had created artwork which would be faxed to Yerevan in Armenia. So at 4 p.m. in

Yerevan, 9 a.m. in New York and a sleepy 6 a.m. in Los Angeles, direct satellite contact was made. Seldom has any public relations event achieved such an emotional and rapturous reception. In Armenia, they published the republic's first postage stamp since the 1920s, combining the icons of Mount Ararat, a satellite dish and the AT&T name.

A quite different problem presented itself in the relations of AT&T with Mexico. The long-standing suspicion between Mexico and its big brother, the United States, has hitherto encouraged AT&T to adopt a very low profile in its Mexican operations, until recently confining itself to providing a long-distance service through its Mexican subsidiary.

The top management of AT&T decided that an intensive public relations campaign was an essential prelude to a successful development of AT&T activities in Mexico. Otherwise, prejudice and suspicion could have led to political intervention or guerrilla action.

There were four main business objectives, which the public relations programme was expected to support:

1 To establish the AT&T brand in Mexico and to achieve consistent brand management.
2 To establish AT&T's identity in Mexico as an industry leader who could solve Mexico's serious telecommunications problems.
3 To use AT&T Bell's laboratories to spearpoint technological innovation in Mexico.
4 To stimulate the sale of goods and products through trade shows and co-ordinated marketing and publicity.

The full case study has been published in *International Public Relations Case Studies*, edited by Sam Black, but the purpose of referring to it here is to emphasize the vital part played by public relations in helping to counter such deep-rooted antagonism between neighbouring countries.

A different example of AT&T's public relations programmes is illustrated by its daily electronic newspaper for employees worldwide. The objective was to devise a method of informing simultaneously all its employees about company activities, and to provide a means of effective two-way communication between employees and management through a lively letters section. This ambitious objective was possible because of the widespread availability of e-mail throughout the company in all the countries where it operates. The newspaper was started experimentally in January 1990 and has proved very successful.

Sea Containers Ltd decided to introduce a new service across the English Channel using the new type of large hovercraft known as the SeaCat. The first SeaCat, *Hoverspeed Great Britain*, was built in Tasmania and it was decided to use its delivery voyage to Britain to secure international media coverage by challenging for the Hales Trophy for the Blue Riband of the Atlantic. The existing record was made by the ocean-going liner, *SS United States*, in 1952. Under the Hales Trophy regulations, the craft must be a passenger-carrying vessel and must not refuel between Ambrose Light and Bishop's Rock.

Having decided to make this record attempt, the company's public relations department adopted a very active media programme. Sea Containers Ltd commissioned a series of five video news releases (VNRs) to provide attractive footage for television stations in America, Europe and Australia. The first VNR covered the sea trials in Tasmania. The second VNR showed its arrival in New York and the third VNR filmed the start of the challenge voyage from the Ambrose Light off the US East Coast. The fourth VNR included coverage of the SeaCat completing its record attempt at Bishop's Rock, off the Isles of Scilly. The final VNR covered the SeaCat's triumphal arrival at Falmouth. The VNRs were widely used on television and were part of the wide media coverage of the voyage in the United States, Europe and Australia. The use of VNRs was only one aspect of the imaginative public relations programme planned and carried out by Sea Containers' in-house public relations department in London, supplemented by public relations consultancies in Australia, the United States and France.

After its first spectacular record-breaking appearance, the Hoverspeed SeaCat has become established as a safe means of marine transport. In addition to operating across the English Channel, it operates from Scotland to Northern Ireland and from the Italian mainland to the island of Sardinia.

The Common Thread

These case histories illustrate different ways in which public relations were used to support different objectives. By their intrinsic nature, public relations programmes or projects are likely to be as diverse as industry itself. Like any other management discipline, however, it is not an isolated activity, but supports and enhances the strategy and objectives of its company or organisation.

Speaking the Right Language

Even though we find today that computers can talk directly to other computers, this does not detract in any way from the importance of the spoken word and the written word.

Within a country or a culture, it is likely that words will mean the same thing, thus avoiding misunderstandings. Unfortunately, this is not universally true. It has, for example, been said that 'America and the United Kingdom are two nations divided by a common language'.

When using a foreign language, it is always necessary to appreciate the potential differences between correct speech and the language as it is used in current practice. This danger dictates great caution in the choice of translators and interpreters.

Those of us who are not good linguists view with satisfaction the increasing adoption of English as the common language of international public relations. This fact facilitates general communication between countries, but does not help when working inside a country where English is not the first language.

Non-Verbal Communication

There is another 'language' that can cause difficulties. Non-verbal communication, or body language as it is often referred to, can be used advantageously or can give serious offence.

There are four different types of actions, which can be identified:

1 Symbolic gestures, such as a salute or thumbs up.
2 Emphasis while speaking, such as arms waving or pointing.
3 Facial movements of emotion, such as smile, a grimace or a grin.
4 Nervous reactions, possibly indicating stress or nervousness, such as blinking, fidgeting or swaying backwards and forwards.

When controlled, these gestures can be used effectively to give emphasis to a speech or a delicate negotiation. When used unconsciously, or at wrong moments, they can prove counterproductive or even harmful.

Cultural Differences

Apart from gestures and other body movements, there are many customs restricted to certain countries or races. These may relate to kinds of food, or how they are eaten, or to ways in which it is permissible to sit, or how to greet friends or strangers. Sometimes faults of etiquette may be laughed away, but at other times they may cause serious offence or result in lost business.

This sector of human relations is a veritable minefield and it is necessary for those in public relations to be fully cognizant of these dangers so that they can help to prevent their colleagues from giving unnecessary offence.

Summing Up

The case histories that have been described point to the problems that can arise when working beyond national frontiers, but also the many opportunities for using imagination and creativity to prepare public relations programmes which can achieve ambitious objectives.

The theory and philosophy of public relations practice are similar whether the field of activity is at home or abroad. This means that the four stages of research, planning, implementation and monitoring and evaluation apply equally. But immediately the detailed planning and budgeting starts, it is necessary to take into account the logistics and practical aspects peculiar to the territory being considered.

The axiom that it is possible to plan globally, but action must take place locally, is the one feature of international public relations that cannot be denied. Anyone trying to ignore this fact does so at his or her peril.

8 The Role of Trade Fairs and Exhibitions in International Marketing Communications

Lakhdar Boukersi

Introduction

Marketing, as a subject area, owes its modern origin to economists' inquiries into the nature of the distributive process, at the end of the nineteenth century (Baker, 1991). One can also suggest that its ancient origins go back to the era of the Pharaohs. The concept of organizing business activities at the crossroads of major Egyptian cities seems as culturally familiar as the pyramids. As far as Europe is concerned, the Romans founded their Gallic capital, Lugdunum, in 43 BC at the confluence of the Rhone and the Saone rivers. This capital, which then became known as Lyon during the Renaissance, experienced its second golden age when it hosted the first trade fair for printing and publishing equipment (Laushway, 1993/94).

The study of trade fairs and exhibitions remains the poor relative of marketing communications. The European Business ASAP CD-ROM shows 168 entries associated with trade fairs, the majority of which are small articles published in professional journals or magazines, and only a very few in refereed journals.[1] Marketing textbooks are all too laconic about the subject. At best it is covered in one or two pages (Keegan, 1989; Bradley, 1991; Kotler, 1994; Terpstra and Sarathy, 1994; Czinkota and Ronkainen, 1998); at worst it is totally neglected. Despite some recent academic research interest in trade fairs in recent years, academics do scant justice to this oldest aspect of marketing. Paradoxically, they recognize, tacitly, that trade fairs are one of the most powerful forms of international media. However, due to a lack of empirical evidence, they have yet to be convinced of their effectiveness in enhancing organizational performance.

Trade fairs and exhibitions do not, however, suffer from the same research deficiency on the part of practitioners. The press abounds with publications on the subject. More importantly, there is a common agreement amongst these that trade fairs, when used in combination with other marketing efforts, can have significant benefits for a company's market exposure (McDermott, 1993). The importance of this medium is reflected in the organization, in 1994, of more than 1100 events in over 200 cities across fourteen European countries.[2] In addition, over 80 per cent of these European shows were international. Hence, aside from global advertising, it is hard to think of a more visible and high-profile marketing communication medium than trade fairs and exhibitions. In the United Kingdom, between 1991 and 1996, an average of 670 trade fairs and exhibitions were organized annually, attracting an estimated actual attendance of 9 700 000 visitors, including 121 000 from abroad (Exhibition Industry Federation, 1997).

This chapter is designed to compensate for the lack of attention to this topic in the academic literature. It sets out to demonstrate the importance of trade fairs as a marketing communication medium, and to give some insight into the exhibition industry both in Europe and the United Kingdom.

Trade Fair Defined

To prevent semantic difficulties, the terms 'fair' and 'show' are used interchangeably in this chapter. Also, the expression 'trade fairs/shows' is used, unless stated otherwise, in its general meaning, designating all categories of fairs. According to Banting and Blenkhorn (1974), trade shows can be defined as follows:

> A facilitating marketing event in the form of an exposition, fair, exhibition or mart, which takes place at periodically recurring intervals, ranging from quarterly to triennially; having pre-established hours of operation during a period lasting one day or several weeks whose primary objective is to disseminate information about, and display the goods and services of competing and complementary sellers who have rented specially allocated and demarcated space or 'booths' clustered within a particular building(s) of bounded grounds; and whose audience is a selected concentration of customers, potential buyers, decision influencers, and middlemen.

Notwithstanding its significant age, this definition still maintains its relevance, accuracy and comprehensiveness. It puts forward the four major characteristics of a trade show, i.e. its nature, purpose, structure and constituents. First, the authors recognized trade fairs as an integral part of the marketing mix, not just a mere element of sales promotion, an aspect that is recurrent throughout several textbooks. Second, they placed emphasis upon its primary objective, which is first and foremost communication, without denying the existence of other objectives. Third, they showed the structural dimensions of trade fairs. Finally, they identified the high variety of participants, who are basically the same players found in the marketplace.

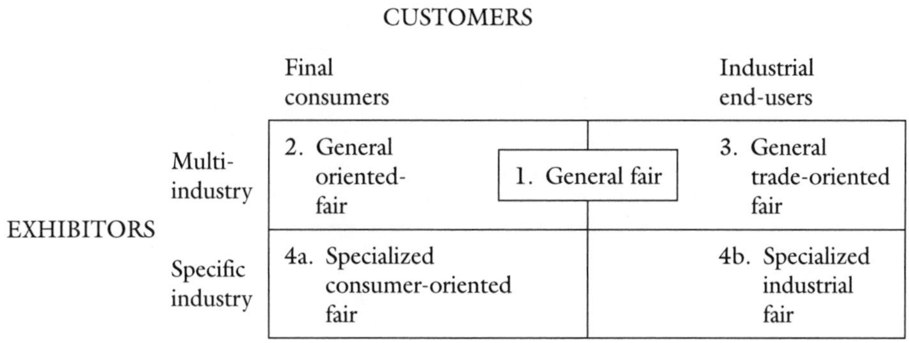

CUSTOMERS

Final
consumers

Industrial
end-users

Figure 8.1   Types of trade fairs.

Classification of Trade Fairs

Today, most practitioners and industry associations consider trade shows as a 'marketplace' in microcosm. This must be understood in its conceptual sense without geographical connotation. Therefore, these events are, like other strands of the global economy, heavily influenced by the international market and marketing trends. As markets become more individualized and sophisticated in terms of customers' requirements, so visitors to trade fairs are more selective in deciding which trade show(s) to attend. Consequently, it is safe to say that even trade fair organizers must embark upon a strategy of market segmentation.

In general, the classification of trade fairs follows closely that of markets. The most basic scheme classifies trade shows into two broad categories: (1) the consumer-orientated fair and (2) the industrial trade fair. In addition, both categories can, in most cases, be endowed with an international dimension. Perhaps the most useful system to classify trade fairs is to take into consideration the two major participants involved in these events, namely the customers/visitors and the exhibitors. Basically, trade fairs attract two groups of visitors: (1) the final consumer or the public at large and (2) the industrial end-users. Likewise, exhibitors can further be broken down into two subgroups: (1) exhibitors taking part in multi-industry shows and (2) exhibitors interested in specific-industry shows. These categories of participants in combination produce four types of trade fairs (as shown in figure 8.1).

Type 1: general trade fairs/horizontal

This category of trade fairs has, as its name suggests, a highly diversified nature. It hosts a wide range of exhibitors right across markets. Both consumer and industrial goods are displayed in one single location. Similarly, such fairs attract a cross-section of domestic and foreign visitors. As indicated in table 8.1, in Europe, France has a reputation for organizing general fairs, followed by Italy and Spain.

Table 8.1   European trade fairs and exhibitions per country/per type

Countries	Multi-industry fairs/consumer and industrial goods or general fairs	Multi-industry trade/business fairs or general trade/business-oriented fairs	Multi-industry consumer-oriented fairs or general consumer-oriented fairs	Specialized fairs (11 industrial sectors) both consumer and business
Austria	4		6	49
Belgium	2		2	18
Finland			1	42
France	58			122
Germany	2	2	62	285
Great Britain			4	47
Italy	11		6	137
Luxembourg		1	1	7
The Netherlands		2	5	82
Norway				32
Portugal	2			69
Spain	9		10	236
Sweden			3	106
Switzerland	1		1	30
Total	90	5	101	1262

Source: Compiled by the author from *European Trade Fair & Exhibition Statistics*, 1994.

However, general fairs are not popular in other European countries. Because of their horizontal orientation, general trade fairs are perceived as countries' 'shop windows', the main objective of which is to promote their exports, especially in less developed countries. General trade fairs are also distinctive by their sheer size, long duration – on average 10 days – and annual cycles. According to *European Trade Fair & Exhibition Statistics*, ninety general trade fairs have taken place in the fourteen European countries that provided data in 1994. Undoubtedly, the annual Paris Fair is the largest of its kind in Europe. In 1996, it attracted a total of 3027 exhibitors, 739 of whom came from overseas, representing seventy-six countries. Some 950 000 tickets were sold, including 2852 to foreign visitors (see table 8.2).

Type 2: general consumer-oriented fairs/horizontal

General consumer-oriented fairs host a diversified range of consumer products. The primary objective of firms participating in this type of fair is to interact with existing customers and to meet new ones. Although their main aim is promotional, consumer fairs can also be considered as selling opportunities. Type 2 fairs, like general fairs, are also organized on a yearly basis, but for a shorter period. As shown in table 8.1, with sixty-two consumer fairs reported in 1994, Germany is the leading country in respect to organizing this type of fair in Europe.

Table 8.2 Examples of general trade fairs

Event	Country	Duration	No. of foreign countries	Exhibitors		Visitors[a]	
				Total	Foreign	Total	Foreign
Paris Fair	France	11	76	3027	739	950 000	2 852
Marseille Fair	France	11	50	1332	178	404 921	1 885
Bordeaux Fair	France	10	54	1462	183	312 726	5 677
Palermo International Fair	Italy	16	30	519	86	232 591	261
Messina	Italy	14	15	467	71	127 770	9 150
Munich IHM	Germany	9	26	1650	354	263 643	18 455
Graz Spring Fair	Austria	9	18	1232	161	231 704	5 746
Berne Fair BEA	Switzerland	9	7	1096	21	295 492	NA

[a] Based on numbers of tickets sold.
Source: Compiled by the author from *European Trade Fair & Exhibition Statistics*, 1996.

Moreover, table 8.3 highlights the importance of German consumer fairs both in terms of the number of foreign countries taking part and the number of exhibitors and visitors attracted. For example, in 1996, the Frankfurt Ambient Fair, with participants from seventy-seven foreign countries, hosted 4861 exhibitors and attracted 123 629 visitors.

Type 3: general trade/business-oriented fairs/horizontal

This type refers to multi-industry trade/business fairs designed to host a wide range of industrial products only. In this particular case, the term 'trade' connotes 'business' or 'industry' orientation, as opposed to consumer orientation. Organizing general trade-oriented fairs requires a larger space and extensive preparatory work. Difficult logistics have to be faced in organizing construction and product display. This is probably one of the main reasons why this type of fair is the least popular in Europe. According to table 8.1, only five trade-oriented fairs were organized in 1994. With a total of 6928 exhibitors, including 2557 from abroad representing sixty-two countries, Hanover Fair is by far the largest of its kind (see table 8.4). Another reason for its lack of popularity can be attributed to the fact that very few business people show interest in wide displays of industrial products. On the contrary, it is an area where management interest is focused upon a rather small and specific number of products or industrial sectors.

Table 8.3 Examples of general consumer-oriented fairs

Event	Country	Duration	No. of foreign countries	Exhibitors Total	Exhibitors Foreign	Visitors Total	Visitors Foreign
Frankfurt Ambient	Germany	5	77	4861	2359	123 629	29 582
Berlin Import Fair	Germany	4	71	666	571	36 593	1482
Dusseldorf Aktiv Leben	Germany	9	18	674	62	100 329	1104
Hamburg Du Und Deine Welt	Germany	10	50	1049	152	218 687	4374
Birmingham Forecourt	UK	3	NA	142	NA	5992	NA
Harrogate Craft Fair	UK	5	NA	745	NA	14 220	NA
Luxembourg International Spring Fair	Luxembourg	9	15	524	259	108 169	NA
Milan Chibuca	Italy	4	24	997	303	162 619	NA
Najaarsbeurs Consumer Goods Fair	NL	4	5	99	10	37 033	305
Palma de Mallorca BALEART	Spain	20	2	125	11	32 579	NA
Bilbao (E) Expoconsumo	Spain	5	9	113	7	24 665	NA

Table 8.4 Examples of general trade-oriented fairs

Event	Country	Space occupied (m)	No. of foreign countries	Exhibitors Total	Exhibitors Foreign	Visitors Total	Visitors Foreign
Hanover Fair	Germany	348 476	62	6928	2557	396 032	73 662
Luxembourg International Fair Autumn	Luxembourg	35 251	12	428	219	61 000	NA
Utrecht Technishow	The Netherlands	21 000	5	522	39	59 817	3910

Table 8.5 Specialized fairs per industrial sector

Industrial sectors	No. of specialized fairs in 14 European countries for 1994[a]	No. of specialized fairs in the UK for 1995
Agriculture, Forestry, Viticulture, Horticulture, Landscaping and their equipment	87	23
Foodstuff, Restaurant and Hotel, Catering and their equipment	110	17
Textile, Clothing, Shoes, Leather, Jewellery and their equipment	95	23
Public works, Building, Completion and Extension and their equipment	106	15
Furnishing, Household and their equipment	81	35
Health, Hygiene, Environment, Safety and their equipment	128	33
Transport, Traffic and their equipment	51	22
Information, Communication, Office organization and their equipment	117	24
Sport, Leisure, Travel, Game and their equipment	196	98[b]
Other Industries, Service & Technology, Science & Technology	257	86
Arts and Antiques	34	
Total	1262	376

[a] Based on the data provided by fourteen European countries. Not all events organized in these countries are covered.
[b] Including Arts and Antiques.
Source: Compiled by the author from the *European Trade Fairs & Exhibition Statistics*, 1994 and the *UK Exhibition Industry, The Facts*, vol. 7, 1995.

Type 4: specialized trade fairs/vertical

Specialized trade fairs can either host exhibitors of consumer goods (cell 4, figure 8.1) or those of industrial products (cell 5). Whatever the case, specialized trade fairs are targeted at specialist visitors, in one or few related industrial sectors. Specialized trade fairs are characterized by their very high number, specific focus and shorter duration. Because of its industry-specific orientation, the specialized fair is the most predominant type in the world. Currently, the trend is a movement away from large multi-industry fairs to smaller and more focused events dealing with a single industry or even a single product. For 1994 alone, table 8.5 shows that 1262 specialized fairs, covering eleven industrial sectors, have been organized across fourteen European countries. The primary objectives of this type are to recruit distributors and possibly take orders in the case of consumer goods. They also provide information and get competitor intelligence in the case of industrial products. As mentioned earlier, as industries become more sophisticated, specialized trade shows are one way to attract a good-quality audience. Also, as visitors' requirements become more and more individualized, organizers are increasingly opting to run tailor-made events that attract the right kind of visitor in the right numbers. Hence, this type of show is set to proliferate even more rapidly in the future.

Benefits of Trade Fairs

Trade shows reflect the 'marketplace' in miniature. Almost all market forces are at play in one single location. In addition, these events offer the best opportunity to interact directly, in a very short span of time, with a large number of people – customers (existing and potential), competitors, suppliers, decision makers/ influencers, service providers – all important to the company. This underlines the primary reason why participating organizations perceive more benefits than do their non-participating counterparts.

A comprehensive literature survey has identified twenty reasons for organizations to participate in trade fairs and exhibitions (Carman, 1968; Banting and Blenkhorn, 1975; Cavanaugh, 1976; Bonoma, 1983; Bellizzi and Lipps, 1984; Kerin and Cron, 1987; Alfred, 1988; Gopalakrishna et al., 1995; Dekimpe et al., 1997; Herbig et al., 1997; Dwek, 1997). These are classified into four major groups: (i) selling; (ii) promotional; (iii) research; (iv) strategic benefits. In the academic literature, selling and non-selling taxonomy has been widely used (Bonoma, 1983; Kerin and Cron, 1987).

Selling benefits

- To interact with existing customers.
- To make direct sales.
- To take sales orders.
- To meet new customers and build up a prospect list.
- To meet new distributors, suppliers and buying decision makers/influencers.

Perhaps the two most common benefits cited by the majority of participants in general trade shows are the opportunity to maintain contact with regular customers and to meet potential ones. The former is seen as a way to consolidate existing relationships and ensure customer satisfaction. The latter is perceived as a method of developing new customer links and to build up a prospective list. In addition, trade fairs are used in several cases as a golden occasion to recruit high-quality sales representatives, dealers and franchising agents. Equally important is the fact that buyers are on neutral ground. They can express themselves and discuss freely and directly with salespeople.

In Europe, almost all of the businesspeople at international trade fairs are buyers or distributors ready to do business. According to Golob (1988), first-time participants from the United States have sold as much as 25–33 per cent of their annual production in a few days.

Overseas trade shows can be an effective channel through which small and medium-sized firms develop new customers and launch new products. For instance, in 1995, 90 per cent of exhibitors at Electronica, an international electronics fair organized in Munich, Germany, reported establishing concrete new export contracts (Thorne, 1996). In 1996, it was also reported that new cosmetic products – such as 'Oh! de Mischino', a new, light, fragrance – were successfully introduced at the twenty-ninth edition of Cosmoprof, one of the world's largest cosmetics trade shows (Barone, 1996). Furthermore, one major benefit of the German specialized trade fairs in information technology industries is to bring together US suppliers with potential business partners from all of Europe.

Promotional benefits

- To re-enforce the communication mix.
- To promote existing products.
- To introduce/launch new products.
- To build up brand name.
- To provide technical information through demonstrations.

To consider trade shows as only selling opportunities is a myopic view. On the contrary, they should be viewed in a broader network sense since they have profound implications for the overall company's marketing mix. Particularly in the case of industrial products, these events can constitute a significant source of information and communications (see figure 8.2). At trade fairs, exhibitors bring into play all of their policies on products, pricing, distribution and communication. Nowhere else are participating companies able to bring together, in one location, all the integrated elements of the marketing mix programme, than at trade fairs. The hallmark of trade fairs lies in the fact that they provide a platform for the company's marketing package to be in direct contact with prospective customers who can, at best, experiment with the desired product(s) and at worst acquire technical information. In addition, the face-to-face contact dramatically shortens the communication process between exhibitors and visitors. Thus, the major instruments of this process can be integrated together to form an effective promotional programme. Staff manning the stand can provide all sorts of valuable

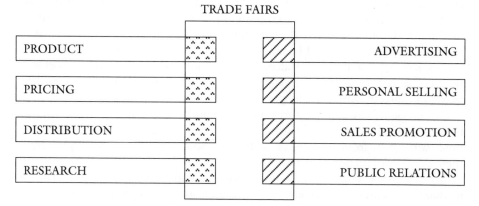

Figure 8.2 Trade fairs as an integral part of the marketing mix.

information and services: videos and short films can be shown; leaflets, catalogues and samples may be distributed; and national/local media – patronizing the show – can generate positive press on the event in general and on the company in particular, especially if the latter is nominated for a particular prize or award. Zanussi Ltd provides a good illustration of how trade shows can be an extremely effective technique of promotion. In 1993, this company commissioned Park Avenue, a trade show specialist, to create a no-expense-spared extravaganza at Birmingham's NEC in order to 'educate' around 2500 white goods retailers of the new Zanussi positioning, and to speed up the implementation of its brand-building strategy. The company took this decision after heavily reducing its TV advertising. By doing so, Zanussi increased its share of the total UK white goods market to 11.7 per cent, closing the gap with the market leader Hotpoint, on 16 per cent (Dwek, 1993).

Research benefits

- To get competitor intelligence.
- To collect general market and marketing data.
- To test market receptiveness for new products.
- To test entry into new markets.

Trade fairs are also occasions for low-cost market research. They offer particip-ants valuable first-hand information and in-depth feedback can be obtained that would normally be beyond the firm's reach. In addition, since industrial shows are seen to attract visitors who influence purchasing decisions, they provide an ideal environment for market testing. The case in point is the 'CeBIT' trade fair in Hanover, Germany, which is regarded as an excellent occasion for company managers and executives to see a broad range of the latest automatic identification and data collection (AIDC) technology on display with other corporate information systems. Also, American companies are notable for using European trade fairs as testing grounds before they finalize their market entry decisions.

Strategic benefits

- To establish presence in the market.
- To keep up with competitors.
- To keep abreast of new market and industry trends.
- To enhance personnel morale.
- To raise company profile/image.
- To develop a particular location as a trading centre.

In today's global marketplace, attending trade shows is one of the most effective ways of understanding international competition and keeping abreast of relevant technologies and new trends. Many large businesses are motivated by the 'we cannot afford not to be there' syndrome. In other words, they adopt the so-called 'follow the herd' strategy in the same fashion as expanding their marketing operations into international markets. Most of the specialized fairs, especially in high-tech industries, are considered as corporate summit meetings attended by top-level management. A great deal of strategic arrangements related to such fields as product diversification, foreign market entry and international alliances are being made at these meetings. For many years, trade fairs have offered exporters in less-developed countries an extremely cost-effective marketing tool to meet foreign buyers and representatives, display their products and determine whether they have a chance of succeeding in international markets. Moreover, visiting trade fairs in Eastern European countries, before and after their economic reforms, remains one of the best channels through which to explore new commercial opportunities and find suitable business partners.

Furthermore, the Hong Kong Trade Development Council (HKTDC) signed an agreement, in 1992, with the Shenzhen Special Economic Zone in China to organize international trade fairs there as part of its strategy of helping Hong Kong joint ventures promote their products (Baldinger, 1992). Similarly, in 1993, Samsung Co., Korea's largest trading company, extended its travelling trade fairs in Qingdao, China, to strengthen its long-term marketing activities in the Shandong province. France provides another example of how trade fairs are used to develop strategic trading centres in specific industries. In 1996, instead of selling machinery and supplies to wood processors, exhibitors at Carrefour International du Bois, in Nantes, were selling logs, lumber and other wood products. A consortium of French public agencies at the local and national levels contributed to the trade fair's costs in order to strengthen the city's position as a major wood-trading centre (Blackman, 1996).

Trade Fair Evaluation

The rapid growth of the exhibition industry, together with increasingly tighter budgets, has put greater pressure on businesses to justify their promotional expenditures. Ideally, companies should rely on how well their organizational goals have been met in determining the effectiveness of their promotional investments. Measuring effectiveness is a topic that concerns all managers in all organizations. Yet, despite its importance, the characteristics of an effective trade show are neither universally recognized nor readily apparent. Effectiveness is commonly defined as the degree to which predetermined goals/objectives are achieved. As far as trade shows are concerned, to translate such a simple definition into practice is a very difficult task.

Measuring the impact of trade shows on corporate marketing objectives is more complex than that of other communication mix components such as advertising, personal selling and public relations. It is not so much that the problem is more difficult, rather, it is because of the integrative and interactive nature of this communication medium. As well as heavy cost requirements, such complexity arises from a number of factors.

First, effective evaluation requires systematic research, the first step of which is a clear definition of objectives. Unfortunately, setting clear objectives is a painful exercise for many companies, let alone specifying which objective(s) needs to be evaluated. Second, the non-existence of clear measurable criteria and numerical data prevent meaningful evaluation. These criteria used to evaluate advertising – reach, response, commercial results and recall, product awareness, intent to purchase – are not easily measurable from trade fairs and exhibitions. Third, the quasi non-existence of performance standards/benchmarks is another major hindrance in determining the success of a trade show. Trade fair expenditures are not recorded separately from other promotional mix elements. Very often, they interact with other promotions to produce higher sales than an equivalent investment in either individual activities. Finally, it is vital to establish effective and proper monitoring mechanisms without which meaningful and timely data cannot be tracked nor stored.

Individual cases of effective trade shows are legion throughout the business literature. Nevertheless, experts in the field do recommend caution, as there is no conclusive evidence that participation, *per se*, makes a positive impact. Companies are, therefore, advised to prioritize their needs and select events that best coincide with their particular objectives. Hence, participation without proper planning and clear objectives may prove to be a costly activity with little communication effects.

Early attempts to evaluate trade shows go back to the beginning of the 1960s (Harris, 1961; The Industrial Advertising Institute, 1960; Simpson, 1961). Academic research has yet to demonstrate whether trade show investments do generate positive economic returns to the participants. Even if the cost of exhibiting can easily be estimated, future economic benefits remain difficult to establish with any degree of certainty. A recent American Express survey revealed that most exhibitors still rely on 'rules of thumb' when assessing the success or otherwise of their participation (Dwek, 1993). This confirms the conclusion of Gopalakrishna et al. (1995) that the area of trade show effectiveness has been a matter of faith with little scientific evidence.

Since trade show investments are too important not to be justified, in the absence of acceptable value measurements, empirical studies rely on 'proxy' variables to evaluate trade show performance. Basically, four groups of studies have been identified in the academic literature, which we cluster in the following way:

- Audience-orientated studies.
- Objective/benefit-orientated studies.
- Comparative studies.
- Outcome-orientated studies.

Audience-orientated studies

This group focused mainly on trade shows' audience-related factors as proxy measures to evaluate trade show performance (Carman, 1968; Cavanaugh, 1976; Bellizzi and Lipps, 1984). Extensive surveys were conducted to ascertain whether trade shows have a positive impact on such variables as audience activity, proportion of target audience visiting the stand, number of new accounts opened, sales leads generated at the show and inquiry cards left by visitors at the booth. However, these studies were criticized as being weak, unsophisticated and too exploratory. Furthermore, they are unidimensional in that they attempted to assess only one single factor – the audience – in an environment where a multitude of influencing factors, such as those related to the organizer(s), the exhibitor(s), the industry(ies) and the trade show(s), interact simultaneously in one single location. Finally, these audience-orientated techniques of evaluation were seen as providing more benefits to organizers than to exhibitors.

Objective/benefit-orientated studies

This group placed the emphasis on qualitative research by asking marketing executives to rate their firm's trade show performance based upon a certain number of benefits, such as those listed in the section Classification of Trade Fairs (Bonoma, 1981; Kerin and Cron, 1987; Shipley et al., 1983). Each dimension was rated on a given scale of importance, then benefits are ranked on the basis of their degree of perceived importance. The scope of these studies was very limited given their exploratory nature and the fact that no attempt was made to account for the effect of other marketing mix elements. However, their results suggested areas where trade shows provided practical benefits to exhibiting companies. Another positive contribution of this group is the fact that they started to gear research on trade show effectiveness towards exhibitors' objectives and benefits.

Comparative studies

The purpose of the comparative group was to examine trade show performance by comparing this medium to other promotional techniques (Banting and Blenkhorn, 1974; The UK Exhibition Industry, 1997). Participants were asked to judge the importance of trade exhibitions, by means of a given measuring scale, in relation to advertising, personal selling, sales promotion and public relations. Mean scores are then used to rank order these communication media and to determine the specific rank order of trade shows. This comparative approach was deemed too simplistic and produced inconsistent results/ranking across trade shows as the performance of each element of the communication mix is perceived differently across industry sectors. In a few industries, however, the results were seen as useful in that they serve as guidelines for apportioning and allocating promotion expenditures.

Outcome-orientated studies

This group of studies has, undoubtedly, generated the most powerful results to date (Gopalakrisna et al., 1995; Dekimpe et al., 1997). In addition to minimizing many of the deficiencies of previous research, this group is unique in the way they have addressed directly the question of whether the trade show can demonstrate positive economic returns. This could be through incremental sales and profits by associating costs (exhibition expenditures) to outcomes (sales effects). Their analysis relied on a technique used to evaluate advertising effectiveness. Based on a set of specific conditions, they were the first authors to report direct positive returns on trade show investment. Furthermore, their study has generalized and extended the previous research findings in three ways:

1 They have tested and extended findings from a single US show to a large sample of US shows.
2 They have augmented previous US benchmark results with show- and industry-specific variables by considering multiple shows.
3 They have attempted to describe and explain the extent to which US-based findings are extended to trade shows in the United Kingdom.

In the United Kingdom, organizers and exhibitors alike believe that evaluation of trade fairs and exhibitions is set to be the major focus in the late 1990s, similar to advertising in the 1960s and public relations in the early 1980s. Also, the advent of such technical developments as the Internet, digital technology and multimedia will dramatically facilitate trade show evaluation. The interactive characteristics of these innovations will enable quantitative and qualitative research to take place at a relatively low cost.

Furthermore, new evaluation instruments are being developed. For example, Coventry Data Services has already introduced two new evaluation tools. The first is a light pen, which is designed to scan the bar code on visitors' badges. This is a

revolutionary way to track and store demographic data about the audience by converting the information into disk format. The second pen, called Compulead, also
enables the visitors' demographic information to be uploaded directly into a PC
or printed out. The major advantage of the latter tool is its convenience of use and
adaptability to computer technology. Such a characteristic facilitates post-show
surveys by printing letters or other follow-up material as soon as the show is closed.

The Exhibition Industry in the United Kingdom

In 1995, British companies spent a total of £1016 million on domestic exhibitions,
an increase of 10 per cent over the previous year with a total of £929 million. The
total spent on international trade fair participation grew by almost 6 per cent
in the same period, in real terms from £328 million in 1994 to £347 million in
1995 (Exhibition Expenditure Survey, 1995). In addition, the total number of
trade shows increased by 6 per cent: from 691 exhibitions in 1994 to 733 in
1995. With an estimated actual attendance of 10.392 million in 1996, the total
number of visitors rose by 7 per cent compared to 1995 with 9.705 million
visitors (Exhibition Industry Federation, 1997).

Compared to other advertising media, trade fairs and exhibitions have experienced the most dynamic growth in terms of expenditure. Between 1985 and 1995,
the total advertising expenditure rose from £5161 million to £11 462 million, an
increase of 122 per cent. In the same period, the total exhibition expenditure
(private exhibitions not included) grew in real terms by £559 million: from
£191 million in 1985 to £750 million in 1995; a growth rate of 336 per cent.
(Incorporated Society of British Advertisers, 1996).

This dynamic growth is also reflected in the proportion spent on exhibitions
compared to that on other media. The share of the total advertising expenditure
accounted for by exhibitions (excluding private exhibitions) rose from 4.88 per
cent in 1985 to 8.9 per cent in 1995. With such a significant increase, exhibitions
rose from sixth position in 1985, outstripping the medium of magazines and
periodicals, to fifth position in 1995, behind TV (27 per cent), regional newspapers (17.1 per cent), national newspapers (12.5 per cent) and direct mail (9.9 per
cent) (Incorporated Society of British Advertisers, 1996). This rapid development
in exhibition expenditure is attributed to two major factors. First, it is caused by
the shift in focus on the part of organizers promoting more vertical and specialized shows which are in increasing demand for reasons already mentioned in the
section Classification of Trade Fairs. Second, the trend in advertising expenditure
indicates that TV and newspapers start to produce diminishing returns as these
two media are entering the maturity stage in their life cycle.

Generally speaking, the exhibition industry is examined from a short-sighted
perspective. Although the above-mentioned statistics are related mainly to the
exhibitors, the boundaries of this industry as a whole go beyond those of the
exhibiting companies. As shown in figure 8.3, other key players with direct
involvement in the organization, promotion and servicing of these exhibitions
need to be examined, namely the organizers, the contractors and the hall owners.

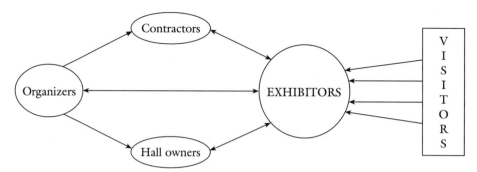

Figure 8.3 Global view of the exhibition industry.

Organizers

Organizing companies, also called sponsors or promoters, are responsible for the overall management of a trade show. They may include private entrepreneurs, subsidiaries of publishing houses or trade/professional associations. Their role ranges from planning to the implementation and operation of the event. They attract exhibitors, draw attendance, select sites and hire venues. In addition, they are involved in various activities such as promoting the show, attracting the national/local media and ensuring editorial coverage. They also deal with contractors, hall owners, publishers and local authorities. Their primary aim is to meet the needs of the exhibitors in terms of the quality of audience, the venue and aesthetics. Furthermore, they collect information on traffic, demographics and attendees' lists, which can later help evaluate the show.

Organizing trade shows is a multi-billion market. In 1991, the British market was estimated to be worth some £600 million, the German £1.3 billion, the French £1 billion and the US market £5 billion.

According to the Association of Exhibition Organizers (AEO), there are between 300 and 400 organizers operating in the United Kingdom. Miller Freeman, the product of a recent mega-merger incorporating what was Blenheim Exhibitions, organizes over 300 events in many foreign countries, in industry sectors ranging from building construction to hotel and catering, and information technology. It is the world's leading independent exhibitions organizer, with shows in the United Kingdom, France, Germany, Switzerland, Spain, Belgium, Italy and the United States. This is followed by Reed Exhibitions, a division of Reed Elsevier, an Anglo-Dutch firm.

Contractors

Exhibitions comprise a series of displays of 'stands' or 'booths' built by the contractors. These are provided in different sizes, shapes and designs. In most cases, they take the form of a 'modular unit' or 'shell scheme'.

Table 8.6 Exhibition services category classification

1	Audio visual
2	Builders/rubbish removers
3	Carpets/floorcoverings/carpet tiles/platforms
4	Cleaning contractors/exhibition stand cleaners
5	Computerized registration/badging & entry systems/computers
6	Display fabric suppliers/upholsterers/cloth ceiling/walldrapes
7	Electrical contractors/special lighting effects
8	Exhibition employment agencies/labour suppliers
9	Exhibition materials suppliers
10	Exhibition stand designers/interior stand design/stand dressing
11	Floral decorators/landscape contractors
12	Furniture & furnishing
13	Tents/mobile trailers & display vehicles/PVC & plastic welding
14	Metal work – exhibition & display
15	Painting & decorating
16	Photographic printing, exhibition & display/electro static printing
17	Project management & technical consultants/exhibition organizers
18	Security/traffic control
19	Shell scheme suppliers
20	Signwriting/graphics/silk screen printing/banners/lettering
21	Standfitters/custom build traditional/modular
22	System manufacturers & suppliers
23	Transport/lifting/forwarding agents

Contractors serve the needs of organizers and exhibitors from original designs to stand construction, landscape gardening, standfitting, flooring, furniture and furnishings. They also carry out mechanical engineering, photographic printing and provide cleaning services. According to the British Exhibition Contractors Association (BECA), there are approximately 400 exhibition contractors in the United Kingdom. These are classified into twenty-three categories on the basis of services provided (table 8.6).

Hall owners

The role of hall owners, also called 'landlords', is to provide covered space, visitor reception and catering facilities, and a range of ancillary services ranging from car parking to security. These facilities are usually commissioned by exhibition organisers.

In the United Kingdom, according to the Exhibition Liaison Committee, there are forty-four qualifying venues with a total capacity of 536 047 square metres, across twenty-seven cities. While London accounts for the highest number of venues (Incorporated Society of British Advertisers, 1996), Birmingham offers the largest capacity, with 158 949 square metres. The National Exhibition Centre (NEC) alone covers 155 949 square metres. Apart from the case of the NEC, hall owners, in the United Kingdom, are independent organizations.

The Exhibition Industry in Germany

Germany is the largest organizer of international trade fairs and exhibitions in Europe. The reason why Germans views trade fairs as more important may be a matter of history. The rapid development and proliferation of trade fairs started after World War II as an integral part of the public policy to attract more foreign companies to be involved in the reconstruction of Germany. Once the reconstruction was achieved, the authorities geared these trade shows towards other objectives, *inter alia*, the promotion of domestic and foreign trade. Today, every big city in Germany is endowed with at least one well-developed and modern exhibition centre. This development is also the result of the close rivalry that exists between German cities for trade fair organization. Germany possesses three of the world's five biggest fairgrounds and hosts two-thirds of the 150 leading international fairs.

The country has fifty-three major exhibition venues with a total gross capacity of 2.54 million square metres in hall space and 1.5 million square metres in open-air space. In 1995, Germany hosted 879 trade fairs, attracting 223 000 exhibitors, including 79 000 from abroad. It attracted 22.6 million visitors, of whom 1.9 million came from overseas. Furthermore, around 100 companies are involved in trade fair organization, generating a total turnover of DM 3.2 billion in 1995 (Confederation of German Trade Fair & Exhibition Industries, 1995).

According to the Incorporated Society of British Advertisers, in 1991 German companies spent around 25 per cent of the total advertising budget on exhibitions, compared to only 8 per cent spent by their British counterparts. One major trait of the German exhibition industry is the fact that most fairgrounds are owned by the local authorities. The city and state governments subsidize most of the property costs and recruit their own organizing firms. Compared to their British or French counterparts, German organizers are not expected to make lucrative profits. The emphasis is not so much on short-term profits as on stimulating the long-term development of the local economy. As a result, the industry has enjoyed steady investments despite recent economic recessions. Rentable space has risen by 17 per cent since 1990 and experts forecast another increase of at least 7 per cent over the next five years. In real terms, more than DM 5 billion will be invested in new exhibition venues and a modernization programme (*The Economist*, 20 January 1996, p. 67). Today, it is safe to suggest that, after the car and machine tools industries, promoting trade fairs is another domain where Germany enjoys competitive advantages.

Finally, another interesting aspect of German exhibitions, which is not common elsewhere, is the fact that, due to the German Data Protection Law, visitors are not required to provide personal information on registration. As a result, organizers find it very difficult to collect accurate statistical information.

Summary

Trade shows can be traced back to the pre-biblical era. Despite their extensive use, these events have drawn little academic attention. Today, however, this medium is beginning to come out of oblivion as both academics and practitioners recognize its importance as an integral component of the marketing mix in general and the communication mix in particular. From the mid-1980s onwards, the exhibition industry began to gather momentum, not only in the United Kingdom, but throughout the world. The increasing number of specialized shows in recent years, compounded by a steady flow of investments into the industry, bear testimony to the perceived importance of trade fairs and exhibitions. However, measuring the economic returns of this medium remains a challenging issue. Advances in computer applications, digital technology and multimedia techniques, however, are expected to remedy the problem of trade fair evaluation in the future.

As far as Europe is concerned, Germany plays a leading role in organizing trade fairs. The hallmark of Germany lies in the way these events are planned and organized as an integral part of the public policy. In the United Kingdom, the exhibitions industry has experienced the fastest proportional increase in expenditure since 1991, and with TV and print advertising entering into their maturity stage, trade shows are expected to be one of the most significant communication media in the next millennium.

NOTES

1 Browsing through the 243 410 articles of the European Business ASAP CD-ROM showed that 1341 published articles were associated with advertising; 304 with sales promotion; 432 with public relations; and only 168 with trade fairs and exhibitions.

2 European Trade Fair and Exhibition Statistics (1994). Fourteen countries only had provided data. These countries did not provide data on all events taking place in their territories. For many other trade fairs, taking place in 1994, data were not available.

REFERENCES

Baker, M. J. (1991) *Marketing: An Introductory Text*, 5th edn. Macmillan.

Baldinger, P. (1992) Selling Hong Kong. *China Business Review*, 19(3), 37–9.

Banting, P. M. and Blenkhorn, D. L. (1974) The role of industrial trade shows. *Industrial Marketing Management*, 3, 285–95.

Barone, A. B. (1996) Cosmoprof 96. *Journal of Drug and Cosmetic Industry*, 158(6), 16–32.

Bellizzi, J. A. and Lipps, D. J. (1984) Managerial guidelines for trade show effectiveness. *Industrial Marketing Management*, 13, 49–52.

Bello, D. C. and Barksdale, H. C., Jr. (1986) Exporting at industrial trade shows. *Industrial Marketing Management*, 15, 197–206.

Bendow, B. (1992) Evaluating trade promotions. *Journal of International Trade Forum*, 3(July–Sept).

Blackman, T. (1996) French timber crossroad takes a different path. *Journal of Wood Technology*, 123(7), 22–4.

Bonoma, T. (1983) Get more out of your trade show. *Harvard Business Review*, Jan/Feb, 75–83.

Bradley, F. (1991) *International Marketing Strategy*, 2nd edn. Prentice-Hall.

British Exhibition Contractors Association: *Members Directory 1997–1998*.

Carman, J. M. (1968) Evaluation of trade show exhibitions. *California Management Review*, 11(Winter), 35–44.

Cavanaugh, S. (1976) Setting objectives and evaluating trade show effectiveness. *Journal of Marketing*, 40(October), 100–3.

Confederation of German Trade Fair and Exhibitions (1996/97) Trade fairs made in Germany. *Exhibition Facts*.

Czinkota, M. and Ronkainen, I (1998) *International Marketing*, 5th edn. Dryden.

Dekimpe, M. G., Francois, P., Gopalakrishna, S., Lilien, G. L. and Van den Bulte, C. (1997) Generalising about trade show effectiveness: a cross-national comparison. *Journal of Marketing*, 61 (October), 55–64.

Dwek, R. (1993) Zanussi trade show to boost new range. *Marketing*, January, 13. *European Trade Fair and Exhibition Statistics*, 1994 and 1996.

Exhibition Industry Association. The facts. *The UK Exhibition Industry*, Vol. 7 (1995) and Vol. 9 (1997).

Exhibition Liaison Committee (1995) *Exhibition Industry Explained*.

Gabb, A. (1991) Blenheim's traveling show: Has the fast-growing international organiser got what it takes to survive? *Management Today*, February.

Golob, S. (1998) Sell overseas at trade fairs. *Nation's Business*, 3(March), 57–9.

Gopalakrishna, S., Lilien, G. L., Williams, J. D. and Sequeira, I. K. (1995) Do trade shows pay off? *Journal of Marketing*, 59(3), 75.

Exhibition Expenditure Survey (1995) Incorporated Society of British Advertisers, November 1996.

Harris, M. (1961) *How to Evaluate Your Trade Show Program Scientifically*. Association of National Advertisers, Inc.

Keegan, W. (1989) *Global Marketing Management*, 4th edn. Prentice-Hall International Editions.

Kerin, R. A. and Cron, W. L. (1987) Assessing trade show functions and performance: an exploratory study. *Journal of Marketing*, 51(July), 87–94.

Kotler, P. (1994) *Marketing Management*, 8th ed. Prentice-Hall International Editions.

Kresse, H. Exhibitors continue to take advantage of German Trade Fairs. Confederation of German Trade Fair and Exhibitions.

Laushway, E. (1993/94) Lyon: profiling France's seductive other city. *European Journal*, 332(Dec/Jan), 32–4.

McDermott, K. (1993) Making the most of trade fairs. *D&B Reports*, 42(4).

Millman, A. F. and Spencer, R. A. (1987) Industrial exhibitions and trade shows. *Quarterly Review of Marketing*, Spring, 20–6.

Rosson, P. J. and Seringhaus, F. H. R. (1995) Visitor and exhibitor interaction at industrial trade show. *Journal of Business Research*, 32(1), 81–90.

Schafer, J., Hage, W. and Dowd, D. (1988) Overseas trade shows. *Business America*, 109(15).

Simpson, V. L. (1961) *How to Get True Value from Your Trade Shows*. Association of National Advertisers, Inc.

Terpstra, V. and Sarathy, R. (1994) *International Marketing*, 6th ed. Dryden International Editions.

Thorne, P. (1996) International trade fair for components & assemblies. *Journal of Canadian Electronics*, 11(3), 38.

9 The Role of Personal Selling in International Marketing Communications

EUGENE M. JOHNSON AND JAMES M. CURRAN

Bud Abbott and Lou Costello, well-known American entertainers in the 1940s and 1950s, had a comedy routine about sales and salespeople that exemplified the attitude many people had towards salespeople at the time and which is still common today. Costello needed a job and, because he had no skills to do anything else, it was decided that he would get a job in sales. The sales job he obtained was selling electric vacuum cleaners to housewives by going house to house. His training consisted of being given a sample vacuum cleaner, which he would use for demonstrations, and the advice not to take 'no' for an answer.

As the routine progressed, Costello was getting frustrated with the rejection of having virtually every door shut in his face. He finally decided that he would not take 'no' for an answer on his next sales call. He strode up to the door with his vacuum cleaner under one arm and a bucket of dirt in his other hand. When a woman opened the door, Costello stuck his foot in the doorway so that she would not be able to close the door until his sales pitch was completed. Then, to the woman's surprise, he managed to throw the bucket of dirt through the door and onto her floor. Costello then made the promise that if the vacuum cleaner that he was selling did not clean up all of the dirt that he had just thrown onto the floor, he would eat all of the dirt.

At this point, the woman disappeared into the house and returned with a sugar bowl. She asked Costello if he would like sugar on his dirt because she had no electricity in the house to run his vacuum cleaner. As always, Costello failed in his mission, which means success in comedy. Failures, such as this, due to lack of skill, preparation and training of salespeople are not uncommon in the business world, and are certainly not funny in the real world.

Personal Selling in Promotion

Personal selling, advertising, sales promotion and public relations are the tools available for the promotion of a company's products and services. The tools used and the extent to which they are used are a reflection of a company's customer base and marketing strategies. For example, a mass marketer of soaps and detergents would use advertising and sales promotion extensively, while a producer of industrial machine tools would place its emphasis on personal selling.

As a promotional technique, personal selling is dependent on the successful interpersonal interaction between the representative of the company and the customer. Unlike the other promotion options, which involve a mass appeal to a general customer base, personal selling is geared toward providing more individualized attention to each customer and the customer's needs. This individual attention is usually more expensive than other promotional methods, but for expensive and complex products it is the most effective tool available. As a result, personal selling, either in person or by telephone, is a substantial part of the promotional mix for many companies.

What is Personal Selling?

Personal selling has evolved over time, reflecting the attitudes of companies toward their products and customers. Early in the twentieth century, attitudes such as that of Henry Ford, who would sell his customers any colour of car they wanted as long as it was black, were common. This was a time when the 'selling concept' in business prevailed and the focus of business organizations was to manufacture products according to their own plans, without regard for their customers' needs. Once a product was produced, promotion and selling efforts would find the customers necessary to consume all of the production. The 'if we build it, they will come' mentality fostered the stereotypical salesperson ridiculed by Abbott and Costello and so many others. Relics of this 'hard sell' mentality still exist today, but progressive companies and their salespeople have moved beyond this to the level of the 'marketing concept'.

The marketing concept is defined as a 'marketing management philosophy that holds that achieving organizational goals depends on determining the needs and wants of target markets and delivering the desired satisfactions more effectively and efficiently than competitors do'. To be successful using the marketing concept, businesses must have trained and skilled people interfacing with their customers to identify appropriate opportunities for mutual benefit. The emphasis for sales professionals must be problem solving, relationship building and creativity. Salespeople need to listen to their customers, assess their needs, and relate all relevant information back to the company so that all necessary steps can be taken to preserve and develop relationships with customers.

Who Sells?

In reality, every member of a company or organization who comes in contact with any member of the customer's organization is performing a part of the sales function. Impressions made on the customer by management, salespeople, engineers, manufacturing, clerical, delivery, security and even janitorial personnel can be lasting. It is critical that everyone in an organization, not only those whose formal function is sales, be aware that they represent the company.

The formal structure of sales organizations can vary widely according to the preferences of management and the dictates of the competitive environment of the company. Sales responsibilities can be divided by geographical territory, by product line sold, by industry served, by specific customers, or combinations of the above. Sales functions can be divided into inside sales, where business is transacted primarily by telephone, and outside sales, where face-to-face contact with the customer is predominant.

Team selling, where sales calls are made by a group of several product and service experts, has become popular in industries where complex products are sold because it is difficult for any one individual to be expert in every aspect of the product. Another version of team selling that has been used successfully for years involves inside and outside salespeople working together to identify and qualify prospects, determine customer needs, offer product solutions and provide ongoing customer service.

Sales tasks can be divided into categories according to the work being done: development, missionary, maintenance and support. Developmental sales has the identification and cultivation of new customers as its primary focus. Missionary salespeople help retailers and distributors sell their products through incentive and training programmes, demonstrations and other sales support activities. Maintenance and support salespeople are basically concerned with servicing existing customers. They take and expedite orders, handle inquiries from existing customers, and generally provide assistance to and promote goodwill among the company's customer base.

No matter how sales functions are structured, the mission of the sales team is to achieve the organization's sales goals, as established by management. To accomplish these goals, salespeople must understand the selling process and prepare as best they can to meet the challenges they will face.

The Selling Process

Whether done in person, by telephone, or electronically, the process of selling must follow the same sequence if it is to be successful. The following are the steps which all sales encounters will follow to some degree. It is rare that all will occur on the same occasion, but eventually the salesperson will move through each stage if a prospective customer is to become a customer.

Prospecting is the first step in the selling process. This is the task of identifying potential customers. Prospecting can be done using a vast array of sources. These sources include industry directories, existing customers, telephone books, government listings, mailing lists, which can be personally developed or bought, cold calling and promotional campaigns. Once identified, prospects must be evaluated or qualified. Separating those prospects with real potential from those who are not likely to buy and will consume a salesperson's time and energy unprofitably is the challenge of qualifying. A salesperson must make sure that a prospect has a definite need for the product, the ability to pay for the product and the authority to make the purchase.

Preapproach is the groundwork that needs to be done to give the salesperson the greatest possibility for success in the sales effort to be undertaken. It is here that Costello failed, because he could have discovered, before the sales call, that there was no electricity in the house that he was about to approach. If there was no electricity in the entire neighbourhood, the failure would be in the qualification stage. In the preapproach, the salesperson must accumulate all relevant information about the potential customer and the environment in which that customer exists. This preparation will be useful throughout the rest of the selling process. It is here that the salesperson will form ideas of what the prospect's needs may be, so that the basics of the sales presentation can be developed.

The *approach* is when the prospect is actually contacted either in person or by telephone. It is critical to make a favourable impression on the prospective customer at this stage so that there will be interest in the product and the person and company selling it. Building on initial interest, further development work can be done later. A poor first impression will be very difficult to overcome if this customer is to be pursued. Therefore, it is important to be prepared to answer initial questions, to be knowledgeable about the prospect and his or her business, and to listen to the prospect's reactions to the approach. An effective approach will stimulate a prospect's interest in knowing more about the product. However, salespeople must be careful to avoid a 'hard sell' during the approach. The easiest way to lose customers at the beginning of a sales effort is to be too pushy and not give them the respect that they feel they deserve. Listening to customers and understanding their position is the key to a successful beginning as well as to a successful relationship later on. In many cases, the approach step must be repeated a number of times before the prospect will allow the salesperson the opportunity to move on to the presentation.

Presentation follows a successful approach. To reach this stage, the salesperson has been successful in sparking interest from the customer in the product or service. Now the salesperson will use the information learned about the customer from the preapproach and approach steps to develop a presentation tailored to the target buyer's specific needs. By demonstrating how the product will meet the buyer's needs, the salesperson can build on the buyer's initial interest to create actual orders. For complex products, the presentation stage is often handled as a team project. Experts from different operational areas within the selling company join the salesperson in a team selling effort. The benefits of team selling can be numerous: bringing product and company expertise to the customer, showing commitment to the customer and giving non-salespeople first-hand knowledge of the customer's needs. There can be drawbacks to the team concept as well, in that a customer can be overwhelmed by the size and good intentions of the team. Thus, it is important to plan the team sales call and the procedures to be followed.

At an appropriate point toward the end of the sales presentation, the salesperson will solicit questions abut the product being sold or ask for an order. If there is any real interest on the part of the customer in making a purchase, it should be obvious at this point. Rarely, however, will a sales presentation be so effective that the customer will agree to buy the product without some resistance. So *handling objections* now becomes the function of the salesperson. An effective salesperson will welcome the customer's objections and questions because they allow the salesperson to identify the areas of customer concern and deal with those issues specifically. This is a critical time in the sales effort. If the salesperson is well prepared, the objections can be turned into a positive exchange of information which should lead to a sale. If the objections are handled poorly, they become an excuse for the customer not to buy. Once again, preparation by the salesperson becomes the key to a successful sales effort.

Having dealt with a customer's questions and objections, the salesperson will then attempt to *close* the sale. It is critical that the salesperson knows when to close and how to close. Signs that a customer is ready to close might include enthusiasm on the part of the customer for the product, or the customer asking questions about price, delivery or credit terms. The salesperson must be astute in observing the customer and be able to read these signs. Once the time appears right, the salesperson can try to close in a number of ways. It is common to ask for an order directly. Some situations may, however, require the salesperson to be less direct, so then the options may be to review the main points of the presentation, soliciting the customer's opinion, preferences and agreement on each point, discuss a delivery schedule or credit terms, or offer the customer incentives to purchase now.

In many cases, having the customer commit to a purchase is only the beginning of the work needed to satisfy that customer. At the time of the close, the salesperson should make sure that details such as delivery schedule, pricing, payment terms and customer specifications are clearly agreed to by all involved parties. Once the details have been resolved, *follow-up* is needed to ensure that all of the promises made are kept and that the customer is indeed satisfied with the purchase experience. It takes a great deal of effort to have reached this point in the sales process, but if the delivery of the first order is not handled properly, the order that was won through hard work may be the last from that customer. On the other hand, a satisfied customer is likely to become a repeat customer.

Repeat business from existing customers takes less of a sales effort than the initial order. This means that future business will be more profitable to the salesperson and company because they are reaping the benefit of efforts already expended. Relationships can be built on the satisfactory treatment of customers and the mutual trust which can be developed between the buyer and seller. *Building relationships* is key to the ongoing flow of business which companies need to succeed and prosper.

International Selling

Much of what is written above holds true for selling in most countries throughout the world. As Kevin Corcoran, the Vice President of Marketing for an international training company, puts it: 'Selling skills are pretty much the same across all cultures. The abilities to listen, ask the right questions, and probe for needs are necessary in any country' (quoted by Cohen, 1996, p. 70). While selling skills may remain constant, the strategies under which they are practised can vary widely.

There are several levels of commitment to international markets which a given company may have. At one extreme are companies that dabble in international markets. These companies do not have a large-scale commitment to foreign markets. They sell to foreign customers to reduce excess inventories or simply fill orders from foreign customers who have sought to initiate the relationship. At another level are companies that are committed to selling their products aggressively in international markets. Often, these firms view their many markets as having individual characteristics requiring tailored marketing and selling plans to accommodate the circumstances of the countries in which they find their customers. The company's production levels and profit goals include these foreign markets as an integral part of the business. Some companies move beyond this stage to a global strategy for marketing and selling. A global marketing strategy is one where all of the world is treated as though it is one large market, and, whenever possible, standardized products, services and sales approaches are used.

Globalization Versus Customization

Levitt (1983) distinguishes between global corporations and multinational corporations. He defines multinationals as companies which operate in a number of countries and adjust their products and practices in each at high relative cost. In contrast, global corporations are companies which operate with 'resolute constancy' and relatively lower costs, selling the same things in the same way everywhere (Levitt, 1983, p. 92). Although there are cost savings to be realized by using a standardized approach, standardizing sales techniques may be a questionable practice.

Some companies have been very successful in using a global approach to business. David Whitwam, the chief executive officer of Whirlpool, attributes his success in building Whirlpool into a world leader in the 'fabric care' business to standardizing production processes and integrating the best features required for local operation into Whirlpool's global products. To accomplish this type of integration, it is necessary to understand fully the markets you hope to serve. As Whitwam puts it: 'When you enter a new market, your sales organization, your knowledge of the local consumer, and your overall capabilities have to develop to a certain level before your business can hope to become a full-fledged, participating member of the global organization' (quoted by Maruca, 1994).

While the concept of complete globalization has its appeal, there is a growing realization that a one-product and one-market strategy may not be realistic.

Although companies have discovered that many product attributes and marketing practices are accepted internationally, there are also attributes which will vary across boundaries. This presents a challenge to sales and marketing managers. Kustin (1994) found that multinational corporations have adopted modified strategic plans in diverse global markets and standardized strategic plans in homogeneous global markets. So it would seem that globalization has led to a new segmentation of markets in which national boundaries may be overcome to take advantage of commonalities among consumers from different countries. Marketers have also realized that national boundaries do exist in many instances and must be respected for the different challenges they present.

The Challenges

It does not matter whether it is a multinational corporation attempting to implement a global strategy or a small firm making its first foray into an international market, the challenges which must be met for international success are essentially the same. They fall into three distinct areas: economic, legal/political and cultural.

Economic

The economies of the world have changed dramatically over the last century. Industrialized nations, such as the United States, Japan and the members of the European Community, have raised their standards of living to unprecedented heights. With high disposable incomes, relatively easy access to credit and a willingness to consume, these markets are the prime target for many marketing campaigns. It is easy to implement a one product for one market strategy within these countries because buyers are used to international products and are more than willing to accept them. Many similarities can be found among the consumers across these markets because of their shared knowledge and experiences. Middle-class consumers from one industrialized country are likely to have as much in common with middle-class consumers in another country as with their own countrymen.

These markets have enjoyed prosperity for many years and they will continue to be a major factor in the world's economy. However, there will be significant shifts in market emphasis as developing nations follow similar paths to a more prosperous lifestyle, and the population growth in the industrialized nations stabilizes or, in some countries, declines. The combination of the need for affordable labour, the willingness of some countries to open up to industry and the exploitation of natural resources has led to a newfound wealth in these developing nations.

Examples of developing nations can be found throughout the world. Taiwan and South Korea in the Pacific Rim have willingly accepted manufacturing operations from multinational corporations and have developed the infrastructure needed to support them. Arab nations in the Middle East have exploited the value of their natural resources, largely oil, to establish economies which should remain strong even when their oil reserves are diminished. Eastern European countries, such as Poland and Hungary, have been industrialized for many years, but have been limited by communist influences. Now free, they represent opportunities for improvement of production as well as new consumer markets. South American countries, such as Brazil and Venezuela, have begun to develop their easy access and available labour pools into strong business assets.

Even though many countries have begun the process of industrialization, there are many that have remained underdeveloped and perpetuate a lifestyle which is considered primitive compared to more developed nations. In underdeveloped economies, there is often little opportunity for economic growth, very little disposable income, low living standards, unstable currencies and restrictive governments. These countries also lack the transportation, communication and financial systems necessary to become active members of international trade. In some of these countries, the populations are growing at alarming rates, a situation which will further tax their economies. These growing populations may represent viable markets in the future, but not until a sound business policy and infrastructure are established.

Legal/political

A major obstacle to the one-world philosophy that global marketers face is the territorialism fostered by years of governments and businesses serving only national interests and markets. Governments have created a number of methods meant to bolster business efforts in their own countries and promote exports while protecting domestic markets from foreign competition. Some of the common methods used to protect domestic markets include tariffs, quotas, local ownership requirements, product standards and currency restrictions. Each of these methods deals with a different aspect of conducting business, but all are used for the same basic purpose: to protect domestic businesses. These restrictions are a two-edged sword; when they are applied by other nations, international trade is restricted and all businesses suffer lost opportunities. Never before have the economies of the world been so interdependent, although it is taking a long time for individual governments to remove their barriers to trade.

In recent years, the international community has recognized the need to ease restrictions on trade, and steps have been taken to open borders to business. The General Agreement on Tariffs and Trade (GATT) is an agreement among member nations to reduce tariffs and other measures that hinder the free flow of goods and services among markets. Ratification of the GATT treaty resulted in the formation of the World Trade Organization as an independent organization to review trade practices among member nations and to settle disputes regarding those trade practices. Although this was an unprecedented step in international trade, it was adopted reluctantly by some countries which feel that submitting their international trade practices to outside scrutiny and influence is counter to their national interests.

Governments make the rules by which multinational corporations must live, and one potential detriment to attracting business is the stability of the government itself. It is not uncommon to have the government and the rules of business change frequently, particularly in underdeveloped countries. History tells us that fragile governments have expropriated operations, seized assets and changed tax rules. If the political environment is not stable, business executives will be reluctant to invest in a country.

Exchange rates, the value of currencies and the flow of money are crucial to an ongoing international business. The International Monetary Fund (IMF) functions as a safeguard for businesses that are concerned about the stability of their trading partner's currencies. In addition, trading partners in developed countries have a number of means to protect themselves. For instance, they may buy the currency of their trading partner at the time of agreement. This will protect them from any fluctuation in exchange rates. Companies trading in lesser developed countries, whose currency is not commonly traded on open markets, may be unable to find a favourable exchange rate between their own currency and the currencies accepted by their trading partners. This is where the IMF can mediate an acceptable agreement which will allow the trade to happen.

Cultural

Perhaps the most obvious differences among trading partners, and most difficult challenge to international salespeople and marketers, are cultural differences. Culture can be defined as the way in which a group of people has agreed to conduct themselves as a society. Key differences between cultures which are critical to sales and marketing people are language and communication, values and attitudes, customs and etiquette, social structure, religion and concept of time. Although some of the differences between cultures are obvious to an outside observer, many others are more subtle. International salespeople must be as well prepared for the cultural differences between buyers as they are to present product benefits and advantages to prospective buyers.

Language is the first obstacle which must be overcome when selling in a new country. It is difficult enough to sell when a salesperson can understand the inferences made during a conversation or presentation, but it becomes much more difficult when key meanings can be lost in the translation from one language to another. English is accepted as the international language of business, but it is not uncommon for prospective buyers in a foreign country to revert to their native tongue while discussing issues among themselves. Even if English is the only language used, words and terms may have different meanings for buyers and sellers from different countries.

Non-verbal communication, such as body language and gestures, is another important aspect of the culture of the buyer which must be considered by the salesperson. An experienced salesperson may sometimes be able to tell when to close by the actions or reactions of the buyer. If such signals are missed in an encounter with someone from another culture, the sales opportunity may be postponed or lost. Gestures may have one meaning in one culture and a completely different meaning in another. What is acceptable in one country may be misunderstood or considered offensive or rude in another. For example, the American gesture for 'OK' is to form a circle with the thumb and forefinger while holding the other fingers straight out. In France, this gesture signifies zero or worthless, in Japan it signifies money, in parts of South America and Germany it is a vulgar gesture, while in Russia and Greece it is only impolite. A nod of the head means 'yes' in most countries, but actually means 'no' in Bulgaria and Greece. In Arab countries, using your left hand to exchange documents is considered rude and exposing the sole of a shoe is interpreted as a sign of disrespect.

An understanding of cultural values and attitudes can give a salesperson insights into the customs and business etiquette which may be encountered in foreign markets. Cultural values are the beliefs or sentiments 'that some activities, relationships, feelings, or goals are important to the community's identity or well being'. Attitudes are an individual's 'positive or negative evaluations of objects, situations, or behaviors, which predispose the individual to respond in some manner'. In other words, attitudes are very specific to a situation, where values are more general standards used as a basis for attitudes. Values are developed by the culture and passed on through generations. Values, just as cultures themselves, can change over time, but neither will change quickly. Salespeople and marketers must understand that buyers from a different culture may sample and eventually adopt a new product, but they will do so on their own terms.

Values reflect the way that people of a culture choose to live their lives. The introduction of products which are counter to their beliefs may not be warmly received. For instance, when EuroDisney, located outside of Paris, opened its doors, it followed the same rules that were used in the Disney parks in the United States and alcohol was banned from the park. Little thought had been given to the reality that it is common for the French to drink wine with their meals. This lack of consideration for local customs was not well received by the French, became one of a myriad of problems for the start-up operation, and was eventually changed.

Religious beliefs can play a large part in the development of many business relationships. Accommodations must be made for the emphasis that many potential business partners put on their religious beliefs. Muslims must pray five times every day and their religion prohibits charging interest. When entertaining business partners, one must be aware of the restrictions that their religion may place on what they may eat. Sikhs and Hindus do not eat beef. Muslims do not eat pork or drink alcohol, and Orthodox Jews eat kosher food. The Sabbath is on Friday for Muslims, Saturday for Jews and Sunday for Christians, so the working week will vary according to religious customs. Holidays differ among religions and must be considered when dealing with members of another religion.

People's concepts of time, schedules and deadlines can vary widely throughout the world. Salespeople should be aware of the differences in perceptions of time and use them to their advantage. While travelling internationally, it is always wise to schedule appointments in advance. The courtesy of scheduling the appointment is never incorrect and often required. Beyond the appointment, the idea of the business meeting is subject to local customs. In the United States, Germany and Venezuela, it is expected that a salesperson will be punctual, that the meeting will get directly to the point of the discussions and then end on time. In France and China, meetings will start at the appointed time, but last longer as time is taken to establish a comfortable relationship. Still other countries, such as Italy, Brazil and South Korea, look upon appointments as approximate meeting times and will often keep salespeople waiting. Even if this is known, it is still wise for the person making the appointment to be punctual.

Researching the Markets

There has never been a time when the access to information throughout the world has been easier than it is now. Information technology has connected the world in unprecedented ways, and further development of technology will make it easier for sales organizations to gather the information they require. The Internet or world wide web provides salespeople with access to databases from all countries throughout the world. It also provides them with an opportunity to establish relationships with potential buyers from the targeted countries, prior to establishing business ties, to learn first hand their customs and culture. Some companies are using the web as a tool to gain entry into new markets, but it is unlikely that technology will replace personal contact in the foreseeable future.

Long-established information sources such as government agencies, chambers of commerce, industry trade associations and local consultants remain valuable providers of information on local situations. Local libraries, universities and publications can now be accessed on-line as well. The access provided by new technologies augments well-established sources of marketing information, such as trade shows, public databases, conferences, and existing sales and distributor networks.

Existing information exists in many places and forms, but its accuracy must be validated in some fashion. Salespeople familiar with the target market are the ideal sources of information relevant to the successful implementation of an international sales strategy. There is no substitute for experience, and researching secondary sources, while valuable, will only augment first-hand knowledge.

Entering a Foreign Market

Once it has been determined that a foreign market presents a profitable opportunity, there are a number of options a company may choose to enter that market. At the most basic level, a company may choose to export products from existing production facilities directly to customers in other countries. This is an attractive option if existing production capabilities are less than fully utilized and the target market has the needed distribution networks to bring the product to the desired markets. This last point is crucial, because a lack of understanding of realities of distribution may lead to excessive delays in products reaching their destination, costing valuable time and money. To export directly, a company must be able to establish contact with the ultimate customer, which is not always an easy thing to do.

At times, it is beneficial to have a local partner who is familiar with local business practices and can lend instant credibility to a product or company which is new to the market. Indirect exporting, or the use of local intermediaries to facilitate the delivery of products to foreign markets, has its advantages. Similar in nature to using manufacturer's representatives, indirect exporting involves a local importing firm that will act on the manufacturer's behalf, interact with the customer, and take responsibility for the delivery of the product once it reaches the destination market.

Other options which a company can consider as methods to enter new markets include licensing, joint ventures and subsidiaries. Licensing is a contractual arrangement between companies allowing a local company in the target country the right to use the industrial property rights of the licenser, such as trademarks, patents and proprietary processes, for a royalty or fee. Usually, a licensing agreement will be for a specific period of time and a specific geographical territory. The advantages of licensing are local production of products and a minimum of investment and risk in doing business in the target country. Fees and royalties are collectable for as long as the agreement remains in place, while management of the local business is left to others. The major drawback to licensing is the lack of input or control over local management that is common to other business arrangements. The producing company controls all production, which can create quality issues, and sales efforts, which can create strategic difficulties in accomplishing worldwide goals. Although licensing presents a relatively risk-free entry into a foreign market, it is often an unattractive option due to the inherent loss of management input it often entails.

A joint venture is a common alternative to licensing in which some management control is maintained, but shared with another local partner. In a joint venture, a new company is set up by the partners and is jointly managed by the partners. In some countries, this type of arrangement with a local partner is a requirement for a foreign company to transact business within that country's borders. The advantages of a joint venture are the connections of the local partner within the new market and the shared responsibilities for the new operation. The disadvantages relate to the shared management responsibilities between two partners who may have different expectations for the business. While it is impossible to anticipate or control all of a partner's actions, it is wise to know as much as possible about a prospective partner before entering a joint venture to avoid management conflicts detrimental to the venture's success.

Another option is to start a local operation in a foreign market as a wholly owned subsidiary company. This requires investment in plant, warehouse and personnel, and would only be appropriate if a major commitment on the part of the parent company is being made to that foreign market. A subsidiary gives the parent complete control of the new operation without any interference from partners, but this also leaves the parent to assume all of the risks involved with doing business in a new market. A thorough knowledge of the business conditions in the market is required before taking a step as large as setting up a subsidiary.

Often, the subsidiary company can result from buying a local company or buying out a partner in a joint venture once local knowledge has been gained.

The International Sales Organization

Once a company has settled on its overall approach to a foreign market and the type of organization it will use to service that market, it must organize its selling efforts to achieve the goals it sets. The sales function may be developed in several ways.

One common method for companies desiring direct control of the sales force is to have a home-based sales force travel internationally and set up international sales territories. This type of strategy requires that salespeople become experts in many countries and cultures as well as the product lines being sold. International territories also require a great deal of travel time and expense, which may limit the number of sales calls that can be made by the sales representatives. The approach of using a globe-trotting sales force may be effective for smaller operations or those not fully committed to international markets. Once full commitment is made, other sales organizational structures may prove to be more fruitful.

Another option open to sales managers is to hire agents, or manufacturer's representatives, in the targeted country. They will be expert in the business practices of that country and have existing connections which are needed for a new endeavour. While having a local salesperson can bring instant credibility, it also poses a danger in that the exporting company loses direct control of its sales efforts. Manufacturer's representatives are independent business people whose business is to sell products for contracting firms. Their interests and goals are to make money selling the products which are most profitable to them. Therefore, the performance a company can expect from these independent contractors will depend largely on how much money the agent makes from selling the products. This can be a problem when a product is being introduced to a market and the immediate sales potential is limited. The manufacturer needs some missionary work to be done to develop interest in the product and the agent needs to sell volume to make money. It is common that these agents also represent other companies doing business in their country, and they will naturally emphasize the products which yield them the highest commissions. Another potential drawback to using agents is the potential for them to offer their services to a competitor at a later date, taking sales training, insights and product expertise with them.

Distributors, or intermediaries, provide another alternative to companies entering new markets. This type of sales structure requires more effort and commitment from the company entering a new market. At this level, the company will establish and serve its own dealer network within the territories it seeks to enter. This type of arrangement allows the company greater control over sales efforts than using manufacturer's representatives. The distributor network will provide salespeople to sell the products, but it is up to the new company to train and motivate the employees of their distributors. The advantage to having distributors is gaining an instant sales force familiar with the market. Potential problems stem from the quality of the distributors that are selected. Good distributors will expand the market for their products, while poor distribution will hinder any sales in the new market.

If control is important and there is a high level of confidence in the new market, a company may opt to establish its own sales force in the new country by hiring salespeople directly. Using a dedicated sales force provides the company with complete control over training, sales methods being utilized and time allocated to service its customers. However, finding the right people to work in an unfamiliar market is a challenge to even the most experienced international business people. For this reason, establishing a company sales force is usually a step taken after some presence in the market has been established using one of the other sales organizations discussed above. Hiring direct employees for the company will increase overheads and may limit the flexibility of the company to change directions at a later date. In some countries, it is unacceptable to fire employees for non-performance so selection of the new salespeople becomes very important.

Managing International Sales

As is the case in managing a domestic sales force, the international sales manager must recruit the best people for the job. In addition to the usual unknowns in hiring the right individuals to represent the company, the variables of language, culture and local knowledge present the sales manager with a much more complex task. Once the right people are found, they must be trained properly and given an incentive and compensation package appropriate for their situation.

It is often preferable to hire native salespeople to take advantage of their local connections and their knowledge of business customs and practices. However, these locals will require a complete indoctrination into the company's products and procedures. They may be unfamiliar with sales methods used by the company and possibly with the entire product line as well. Patience with their progress will be important in bringing new hires up to speed.

An alternative to hiring local talent is to send expatriates from other markets, usually the company's home market, into the new market to sell. Training of a different sort will be needed to be successful with this strategy. These people already know the company and its products, but they must be schooled on the intricacies of the new market. A third option is to utilize a team approach, combining the talents of local hires with expatriates and allowing them to learn from each other as they progress. This option also requires extensive training as all involved must be taught the policies under which they will operate.

As the discussion on hiring indicates, there is a distinct need for the sales management team of any international venture to invest in an appropriate training programme which will provide the sales force with the needed tools for success. An unforgivable mistake in sales is to approach the customer unprepared. Management must provide its salespeople with adequate knowledge of the company, its products, its procedures and its markets. Allowing the sales representative to contact customers without full knowledge of each of these areas is dooming them to failure. Knowledge is the critical input that a salesperson must bring to any sales encounter. Personality and experience can occasionally cover for a lack of knowledge in some areas, but a lack of overall knowledge will reflect poorly on the salesperson and the company.

Appropriate incentives and compensation are other complicated issues in international sales. In the United States, it is common to compensate salespeople with a salary and incentives based on individual performance. In other countries, such as Japan, the idea of reward based on individual performance is unacceptable. Japanese workers are very proud of their association with their company and only wish to be rewarded for the company's success. Therefore, it is wise for the sales manager to know the local customs and formulate an incentive plan utilizing salary, commissions, bonuses, travel allowances, non-monetary rewards and perks that fit the country and circumstances of the individual salesperson.

Selling to Foreign Markets

The selling process in most international markets is similar to that described earlier in this chapter. However, some of the steps need to be adjusted to account for the differences in the market places being served. In many countries, cold calling a potential account will be unsuccessful. In these countries, it is important to have a personal reference from a mutual associate to gain access to a potential customer. This is because the emphasis on personal relationships is of the utmost importance. For example, in China, it would be difficult, if not impossible, to meet a new customer without a reference. In many countries, the courtship of a new customer may be a lengthy process as the buyer will want to know the salesperson and the company before committing to any business dealings.

Sometimes, participation in trade shows throughout the world will spark interest from a customer in establishing a business relationship. Trade shows provide both sides with a neutral place in which to get to know one another. In this atmosphere, new relationships can develop. International sellers should use trade shows to promote their products and create goodwill for their companies, but not to close sales with all customers who show interest. International buyers are shopping for information and will rarely be interested in buying at a trade show. As long as salespeople understand these rules and are thoroughly prepared to demonstrate the advantages of their products, trade shows can provide an opportunity to cultivate new customers.

Once a salesperson has established the initial contact with the customer and has been able to set up the first meeting, it is important to proceed at an appropriate pace for that customer. As already discussed, the customer may have an agenda to which the salesperson must become sensitive. This agenda may include a great deal of time to get to know the salesperson and the company being represented.

A meeting which involves several people speaking different languages presents a particularly delicate situation. The salesperson must be aware that the audience for a particular presentation may include people who will not understand all of the important points as they are being presented. It is critical to allow time for the buyers to digest fully what is being presented to them and to ask all of the questions needed to feel comfortable with what they are being told. The art of this type of presentation is to allow the buyer to ask questions and clarify points without any embarrassment.

Salespeople must be prepared for the sales presentation. This is especially crucial for a presentation made in a country that is foreign to the sales team. Presentations should be made as clearly as possible. The person speaking should be certain to speak clearly and understandably for those who may struggle with the language being used in the meeting. Visual aids should be used to help everyone at the meeting overcome any language difficulties. Illustrations or examples may be helpful, but should be appropriate for the customer and the specific sales situation. Humorous references should probably be avoided since humour does not always translate very well.

Once again, part of the preparation for the presentation should include the study of local customs and cultures. In France, a discussion of pricing or money will make potential buyers uneasy. In Arab countries, financing will be a sensitive subject. In Japan, a sale may be arranged over several meetings with higher level people from each company participating as the meetings progress. A salesperson must expect the developments in each of these areas and prepare for them in advance of the sales meeting.

Having been successful in attracting a customer's interest, the salesperson must be prepared to become a negotiator. The negotiating skills required for further success are very dependent on the specific country or region. It is important for the negotiator to be sensitive to the situation of the buyer. If the buyer is embarrassed or loses face during the negotiation, any potential business may be lost.

The salesperson must be prepared for the negotiation tactics of the buyer and be aware of the rules by which negations are transacted in a particular country. For example, in the Pacific Rim, negotiations may appear to be long and drawn out, but are in fact a reflection of the team concepts prevalent in that region. In Japan, it is considered rude to say 'no', so the customer may give an inexperienced salesperson the impression that there is agreement with a proposal when the opposite is in fact the truth. In Israel, a strong negative reaction may be part of the buyer's negotiating strategy. Chinese buyers will expect significant concessions before a deal is struck. Indonesian negotiators will see concessions made too quickly as a sign of naivety of the salesperson. The negotiation must be amicable, properly paced and planned so that both sides can claim victory. Once more, planning and preparation are the critical elements for success in an international sales endeavour.

What to Expect

To demonstrate some of the concepts that have been discussed throughout this chapter, it is helpful to look at some of the countries that are major contributors to the global economy. The following are examples of what one might expect to discover about a specific foreign marketplace.

The market potential in China for many products is enormous due to the vast population, the growing acceptance of foreign-made products and the steady growth of the Chinese market. The infrastructure of the Chinese market creates a unique challenge to the companies choosing to do business there. China represents not one national market, but several regional markets, each with its own interests. Relationships are important to the Chinese buyer, so quite often American companies will hire local agents who have established ties to buyers in the desired market. It is critical to have direct control of the salespeople representing a company in China, because the relationships being built on your company's behalf are really between the buyer and agent. So if the agent switched allegiance to a competitor, the relationship goes with the agent.

Chinese buyers will appreciate attempts to learn their history and culture, and some preparation on the part of the salesperson will be useful in establishing a relationship. English is the accepted language of international business in China, but knowledge of some dialects of Chinese will be helpful in many situations. Business meetings may begin with some pleasantries, but salespeople must be prepared to get right to business. Quality, in terms of performance of the product and available servicing, is an important aspect of the product itself. One can expect to negotiate on price, and the negotiations can be long and frustrating. The Chinese buyer will push very hard on price, so the seller must know the limits and be prepared to stand firm at those limits.

As in any other country, customers in France are looking for thoroughly knowledgeable salespeople, but treat them differently than buyers in other countries would. Money is a very sensitive subject to the French and, as such, creates difficulties in talking about the pricing for goods and services being sold there. In France, it is expected that salespeople will take the time to get to know the buyer and their situation before a sale can be made. French buyers do not like to be pressured into decisions and may take offence at what they may consider rude behaviour in applying pressure. The esteem in which salespeople are held is fairly low. Many French salespeople are not well educated and sales was not their first career choice. Expect to be kept waiting by French buyers. It is not uncommon to be kept waiting for forty-five minutes or so, and it is not unheard of for a buyer to forget about an appointment with a salesperson altogether.

Unlike France, customers in Germany will keep appointments and not only respect promptness, but demand it. Trust is important to the buyer in Germany. In order to establish that trust, the salesperson must have a thorough knowledge of the product being sold and the points that differentiate the product from its competition. The salesperson must be polite and friendly, but not overly friendly. It is still the business part of the relationship that is important. Entertaining outside of the business meeting is not as common in Germany as in some other countries. In Germany, business etiquette requires that you not use first names when addressing colleagues or associates unless there is a long-standing personal relationship.

The keys for successful selling in Japan are 'listening, observing, patience, and a natural curiosity about the Japanese culture'. This is in contrast to the idea of persuasive argument which is a common sales technique in other parts of the world. Japanese buyers emphasize the quality of the products they buy and the support services that go with them. There is also an expectation of continuing improvement in the quality of products and service if the business relationship is to be ongoing. The salesperson is a part of the product to the Japanese buyer, so it is critical for the salesperson to be completely prepared for Japanese customers from the very first contact. Japanese buyers will respect modesty from the salesperson, but thorough preparation more so. This means not only preparation in terms of product knowledge, but also understanding of the customer's needs before they are stated.

References

Acuff, F. L. (1993) *How to Negotiate Anything With Anyone Anywhere Around the World*. New York: AMACOM.

Anderson, R. E. (1996) Personal selling and sales management in the new millennium. *Journal of Personal Selling and Sales Management*, Fall, 17–32.

Axtell, R. E. (1993) *Do's and Taboos Around the World*. New York: Wiley.

Axtell, R. E. (1995) *Do's and Taboos of Using English Around the World*. New York: Wiley.

Batson, B. (1994) Chinese fortunes. *Sales and Marketing Management*, March, 93–8.

Beeman, F. (1996) Selling around the world. *Selling Power*, November/December, 82–3.

Blackwood, F. (1995) Not-so-foreign concepts. *Selling*, October, 26–8.

Brooksbank, R. (1995) The new model of personal selling: micromarketing. *Journal of Personal Selling and Sales Management*, Spring, 61–6.

Churchill, G. A., Jr, Ford, N. M., Hartley, S. W. and Walker, O. C., Jr (1985) The determinants of salesperson performance: a meta-analysis. *Journal of Marketing Research*, May, 103–18.

Cohen, A. (1996) Small world, big challenge. *Sales and Marketing Management*, June, 69–73.

De Keijzer, A. (1994) China: the sales doors open. *Personal Selling Power*, January/February, 12–22.

Fisher, G. (1980) *International Negotiation: A Cross-cultural Perspective*. Yarmouth, ME: Intercultural Press.

Flynn, B. H. and Murray, K. A. (1993) Your sales force could be your weakness. *Journal of European Business*, November/December, 45–8.

Frank, S. (1992a) Gaining a global outlook. *Sales and Marketing Management*, January, 52–7.

Frank, S. (1992b) Avoiding the pitfalls of business abroad. *Sales and Marketing Management*, March, 48–50.

Frank, S. (1992c) Global negotiating; vive le differences! *Sales and Marketing Management*, May, 64–9.

Gschwandtner, G. (1991a) How to sell in France. *Personal Selling Power*, July/August, 54–60.

Gschwandtner, G. (1991b) How to sell in Germany. *Personal Selling Power*, September, 54–60.

Gschwandtner, G. (1992a) Portrait of a world class sales professional. *Personal Selling Power*, July/August, 54–64.

Gschwandtner, G. (1992b) Selling and marketing in Japan: a blueprint for success in a land full of surprises. *Personal Selling Power*, January/February, 42–52.

Hall, E. T. (1959) *The Silent Language*, Greenwich, CT: Fawcett.

Humphreys, M. A. and Williams, M. R. (1996) Exploring the relative effects of salesperson interpersonal process attributes and technical product attributes on customer satisfaction. *Journal of Personal Selling and Sales Management*, Summer, 47–58.

Johnson, E. M., Kurtz, D. L. and Scheuing, E. E. (1994) *Sales Management: Concepts, Practices, and Cases*, 2nd edn. Singapore: McGraw-Hill.

Klein, J. (1995/1996) Selling to the world: the cultural influence of advertising. *Harvard International Review*, Winter, 62–3.

Kustin, R. A. (1993) A cross-cultural study of a global product in Israel and Australia. *International Marketing Review*, 10(5), 4–13.

Kustin, R. A. (1994) Marketing globalization: a didactic examination for corporate strategy. *International Executive*, January/February, 79–93.

Levitt, T. (1983) The globalization of markets. *Harvard Business Review*, May/June, 92–102.

Marchetti, M. (1997) Selling in China? Go slowly. *Sales and Marketing Management*, January, 35–6.

Maruca, R. F. (1994) The right way to go global: an interview with Whirlpool CEO David Whitwan. *Harvard Business Review*, March/April, 135–45.

O'Brian, J. D. (1991) Focusing on quality in the Pacific Rim. *International Executive*, July/August, 21–4.

Ostro-Landau, N. (1995) Let's grow Europe. *Sales and Marketing Management*, September, 65–8.

Ricks, D. A. (1983) *Big Business Blunders*, Homewood, IL: DowJones–Irwin.

Smith, D. C. and Owens, J. P. (1995) Knowledge of customer's customers as a basis of sales force differentiation. *Journal of Personal Selling and Sales Management*, Summer, 1–16.

Spethmann, B. (1993) Selling the world. *Rotarian*, August, 20–3.

Szymanski, D. M. (1988) Determinants of selling effectiveness: the importance of declarative knowledge to the personal selling concept. *Journal of Marketing*, January, 64–77.

Tse, D. K., Lee, K., Vertinsky, I. and Wehrung, D. A. (1988) Does culture matter? A cross-cultural study of executives' choice, decisiveness, and risk adjustment in international marketing. *Journal of Marketing*, October, 81–95.

Weitz, B., Sujan, H. and Sujan, M. (1986) Knowledge motivation, and adaptive behavior: a framework for improving selling effectiveness. *Journal of Marketing*, October, 174–91.

Wind, Y., Douglas, S. P. and Perlmutter, H. V. (1973) Guidelines for developing international marketing strategies. *Journal of Marketing*, April, 14–23.

10 The Theory and Practice of Sponsorship in International Marketing Communications

NANA OWUSU-FRIMPONG

Introduction

This chapter brings in a separate element of public relations. Sponsorship is a form of promotion, which must be viewed as an opportunity for publicity, as well as a type of sales promotion. Although expenditure on sponsorship has risen sharply over the last decade or so, sponsors are now trying to evaluate the potential benefits of this form of marketing communication.

The essence of marketing and advertising in the area of the mass media is to spend the greatest amount of money where the message reaches the largest number of people. TV was the medium that delivered information and activities of general interest to a large audience. What enhanced the marketing and advertising of TV beyond the large audiences it reached was that the message could be repeated several times. Since viewers had a very limited number of channels to choose from, the 'repetition of the message' was almost unavoidable. The formula was simple: information + TV (large audience + repetition) = recognition and sales. However, the recent emergence of the information highway with several channels, e-mail and other options is quickly removing TV from this equation.

The early criticisms of the advertising value of event sponsorship were no mass audience and no repetition. As the information highway dilutes network TV's ability to provide consistently large audiences on a regular basis, the value of event sponsorship is increasing.

Origins of Sponsorship

The origins of sponsorship lie firmly within the sphere of corporate communication. By associating their organizations or brands with popular events or activities, sponsors sought a spirit of goodwill with the public as a whole or with the employees, clients or suppliers. Sponsorship of sports and the arts has its roots in the ancient practice of patronage – done for both purely altruistic and for more pragmatic image reasons.

There is a growing awareness among companies of the need to communicate or interact in different forms with their many publics, such as consumers, politicians or suppliers, who will impact on the company in a multiplicity of ways. Social, economic and political pressures mean that there are expectations of large multinational companies to be seen to contribute to the fabric of society and, hence, earn or preserve the goodwill of the various elements of the community. Being a good corporate citizen helps to earn the company 'a licence to operate'.

Definition of Sponsorship

The relevance of sponsorship to the community as a whole, has increased interest in finding an up-to-date definition. The Council of Europe, at the Third Conference of the European Members Responsible for Sports, held in Palma, Majorca, in 1981, defined sport sponsorship as follows:

> Any agreement under which one of the parties (the sponsor) supplies materials, financial or other benefits to another (the sponsored) in exchange for its association with a sport or sportsman and in particular permission to use the association with sport or sportsman for advertising, especially, television advertising purposes.

Without rejecting the definition offered by the European ministers, but bearing in mind that this chapter deals with wider aspects than sports sponsorship, the definition which will be used throughout this text is as follows:

> Sponsorship is mutually acceptable commercial relationship between two or more parties in which one party (the sponsor) acting in the course of business, trade, profession or calling, seeks to promote or enhance an image, product or service in association with an individual, event, happening, property or object (called the sponsored).

This definition comprises a number of elements, which when understood, enable the scope of sponsorship law to be understood. These elements are:

- Commercial relationship between two or more parties.
- Sponsor's objective is promotion in the course of business.
- The promotion may be an image, product or service.
- The association may be with an individual, event, happening, property or object.

Sponsorship and Charity

Sponsorship is often confused with charity, but the motives are purely altruistic and it has no returns. Charitable donations are not sponsorship. Companies donate to charity because they are persuaded that they should give back something to the community they serve and, sometimes, this is formalized through membership of organizations, such as in the United Kingdom where a shipping company heavily supported seafaring charities such as 'King George's fund' for sailors and the Royal National Lifeboat Fund.

Promotional Mix

In marketing, promotion has a similar meaning, namely to motivate customers to action. The promotional mix consists of a variety of tools, which are often defined as above the line, below the line and other publicity activities (Wilmshurst, 1993). The above-the-line promotional activities are considered to be all the main advertising media, namely TV, radio, newspapers, magazines, cinema, etc. The below-the-line promotional activities are sales promotion, point of sale, coupons, competitions, trade shows, incentives and 'other publicity activities' which consist of public relations activities involving speeches, events, seminars and sponsorship. The crucial point about using any of the promotional elements described above is to know what messages you wish to send to which audiences. The use of sponsorship provides added opportunities for communication to a very wide range of audiences, but should only be considered on its merits to deal with a particular objective alongside the other media. In order to view sponsorship in this way, it is important to understand its relative performance in particular applications compared to the other three media, as in table 10.1, the range of audiences it can reach and the way it operates to communicate messages.

Table 10.1 Relative use of four media

Audience	Advertising	PR	Sales promotion	Sponsorship
Consumer products	+++	++	+++	++
Company staff	+	+++		++
The sales force	+++	+++	+++	++
Shareholders	++	+++		++
Distributor/retailer	+++	++	+++	++
Suppliers	+	+++		++
Financial institutions	++	++		++
The media	+++	+++		++
Decision makers	++	++		++
Local community	+	+++		++
Pressure groups	+	+++		+

Source: Adapted from Sleight (1984).

Table 10.1 shows the relative uses of four media in reaching a particular audience. The real values will differ depending on the type of company and size, and the type of its particular audiences, but it demonstrates that sponsorship matches public relations in its range of uses. One of the problems of trying to differentiate between the uses of the four techniques is the way they overlap. Sponsorship, for instance, often lives happily under the definition of public relations (defined as a planned effort to establish and maintain mutual understanding between an organization and its public with the main object of acquiring and keeping a good reputation).

Some companies erroneously view the promotional mix as the sole communication link with customers. This view often leads to suboptimization of an organization's total communications effort. Successful marketing requires careful integration of all the promotional and non-promotional elements. Sponsorship offers the potential to support the broader public relations strategy, both directly or indirectly. Directly, it can provide a venue for meeting key customers or suppliers in an informal setting or, more generally, improve awareness and attitudes towards the sponsorship company. Indirectly, it can support employees, government and community relations, emphasizing the sponsor's enlightened sense of social responsibility and good corporate citizenship.

The trend towards integrating marketing communications – the co-ordination of advertising, promotion, publicity, sponsorship, direct marketing and point-of-purchase communication with each other and with other elements of a brand's marketing mix – is one of the most important marketing developments of the 1990s. Sponsorship and advertising should be inseparable friends, not implacable enemies. By using sponsorship with advertising, a company can 'turbo charge' its marketing. Integrated communications yield more effective results. Sponsorship is a deed and advertising tells the public about it. Sales promotion and direct mail are integral too. For example, a Diet Coke campaign used sponsorship of a London marathon as a vehicle for a sport T-shirt offer. Promotional vouchers that were returned had the recipient's name and address filled in. This provided a useful basis for future communication between the company and the consumer.

The Driving Force Behind Sponsorship Growth

While the broadcast and print media put their messages out to the masses, and hope people will find them, people attend and follow events because they have an interest in them. The dramatic growth of commercial sponsorship as a marketing activity is due to the following factors.

1 New opportunities due to increased leisure activity. Increasingly, leisure-conscious societies provide opportunities for sponsorship involvement. This is clear from the wide range of activities currently being pursued in both sports and arts compared with earlier decades.
2 Greater media coverage of sponsorship events. Increasingly, media coverage, particularly on TV, is being directed towards sports and cultural activities, thereby creating opportunities for broadcast sponsorship.

Table 10.2 UK sponsorship market by sector, 1990 and 1994

	1990		1994		
	£m	%	£m	%	% change
Sports	223	79	265	64	+19
Broadcast	7	3	70	17	+900
Arts	35	12	49	12	+40
Others	16	6	31	7	+94
Total	281	100	415	100	+48

Source: Hollis Sponsorship Newsletter, November 1995.

3 Escalating cost of advertising media. Sponsorship provides a cost-effective marketing communication tool compared with traditional advertising.
4 Government policies on tobacco and alcohol. Changing government policies on advertising for alcohol and cigarettes caused manufacturers of such products to seek alternative promotional media. Table 10.2 shows the industry growth of UK sponsorship by market sector.

The above table shows the sponsorship industry's 5 years of fast-track growth. The market for 1995 was worth £439 million, an uplift of over £24 million, representing a 5.8 per cent increase on 1994. The sports market has consolidated its lead position and now takes 64 per cent of total spend, tailed by the fast-growing broadcast sector with 17 per cent.

Product and Service Promotion Through Sponsorship

According to Wilmhurst (1993), almost every type of sporting activity today affords the opportunity for sponsorship of some kind and he believes that '... enterprise, ingenuity and enthusiasm can often make a modest budget go a long way. That marketing companies have achieved remarkable results by shrewed support of a growth sport or growth participants'. Sponsorship allows brands to improve their image with greater impact than some traditional advertising. Traditionally, sponsorship has been an underrated medium compared to its more glamorous cousin, advertising. Times are changing and, increasingly, marketers see this tool as an investment that makes good marketing sense.

According to Sponsorship Research International (SRI) market research company, in 1992, businesses around the world spent £5.9 billion on sponsorship. In the United Kingdom, Allied-Lyons, one of the world's largest drinks companies, boasted £3.3 million sponsorship of the Royal Shakespeare Company. It uses this prestigious alliance to promote its corporate identity and, ultimately, to increase sales of individual brands. Common trends are emerging in almost all European countries. In Germany, however, due to high public subsidy for the arts and punishing levels of taxation, businesses play a lesser role. Those that do participate, however, like Daimler-Benz, BMW and Lufthansa, do seek public recognition and media coverage for their efforts. Sponsorship can be cheaper than advertising. Sunkist's £2 million title sponsorship of a bowls championship generated £7.2 million worth of media impression for the brand in the United States. Smaller sums can also result in spectacular return.

Sponsors of Olympic Games

What exactly does a sponsor get for its money since the Olympics is one of the few sports events that does not allow perimeter board advertising? Sponsorship was practically unknown until the 1976 Olympics nearly bankrupted the city of Montreal. The very low-key nature of the boycotted Moscow Olympics saw sponsorship hardly move, but since then, the International Olympics Committee (IOC) has funded both summer and winter olympics solely by sponsorship and TV rights, with most cities and those bidding for the future assured that any major shortfall they suffer is underwritten.

Even high-selling brands such as Coca-Cola can demonstrably increase sales through well-orchestrated promotions brought to the consumer via media advertising or point-of-sale promotion. A company like IBM will use the event to showcase its latest product and technology, as well as use the hospitality opportunities to strengthen links with clients. Table 10.3 shows the attitude of respondents from three countries towards sponsorship of Olympic Games.

Table 10.3 shows that attitudes towards sponsors of the Olympic Games are extremely positive, with 65 per cent of respondents agreeing that sponsors are leaders in their industries, and more than half of the sample agreeing that they are modern and innovative companies and dedicated to excellence.

Example of cases

In 1992, Visa used its sponsorship of the US Olympic Committee (USOC) to launch a promotion where a percentage of every transaction went to the USOC. Transactions increased by 17 per cent, 14 per cent more than any previous campaign.

In 1992, General Accident (an insurance company) abandoned its expensive golf and turf sponsorship, and refocused on activities that will deliver real gains in image, awareness and customers. As a risk-led business, it identified crime prevention and the Home Office's neighbourhood watch scheme as a more suitable medium and has now committed a £1 million per annum sponsorship until the year 2000. General Accident's support goes towards developing better communications amongst the police, watch coordinators and members through nationwide road shows, conference and improved technology. On the business

Table 10.3 Respondents' attitudes towards Olympic Games sponsorship

	Total agreement with statements about Olympic sponsors (% of respondents)			
	USA	*UK*	*Japan*	*Average*
Without sponsorship Olympics will not be viable	88	80	84	84
Olympic sponsors are leaders in their industries	73	55	67	65
Olympic sponsors are only concerned with profits	55	68	28	50
Olympic sponsors are dedicated to excellence	66	33	66	55
Olympic sponsors deserve my business	56	23	44	41
Only highly reputable companies are allowed to sponsor the games	42	52	45	46
Olympic sponsors are modern and innovative companies	69	53	45	46
Olympic sponsors offer the highest quality products	46	32	36	38
Olympic sponsors care about the community	65	22	47	45
Overall I am in favour of the Olympic games being sponsored	93	80	52	75

Source: Adapted from *Hollis Sponsorship Newsletter*, June 1995.

side, the company offers a specially branded home insurance policy exclusively to neighbourhood watch members. Since becoming available nationally, sales have increased by 40 per cent.

World Cup USA 1994 Sponsorship

International marketers are exploiting sports sponsorship in a big way for both national and international campaigns. Sports like football, tennis and others, as discussed under Olympic Games, have true global appeal. However, achieving international exposure from a single sponsorship is expensive and, with only a few exceptions, this type of sponsorship is limited to the largest companies and requires considerable resources to work effectively. An event like the World Cup offers powerful imagery and awareness to a huge global audience, and provides

Table 10.4 Effect of World Cup sponsor emblem on purchase decision

	Per cent of consumers likely to buy product with logo				
	USA	*Brazil*	*Germany*	*Russia*	*Average*
More likely	50	49	24	32	40
No difference	46	46	68	65	55
Less likely	4	6	9	4	5
Net difference	+46	+43	+15	+28	+35

Source: Mintel (adapted from *Hollis Sponsorship Newsletter*, 1995).

the sponsor with properties that can be further exploited in all communication media. Table 10.4 shows consumers' attitudes towards the 1994 World Cup in the United States. The result shows a favourable attitude in products bearing the World Cup Logo. The emblem provided a vital point of difference in determining a customer's product selection. On the whole, 40 per cent of consumers would be 'somewhat more likely' to select the product bearing the World Cup sponsorship emblem.

One of the problems with most international events is that the sponsor cannot achieve title to the events, but can only take designation within specific categories and has to deal with competition from other sponsors. In addition, there are usually very few opportunities for audience promotions and it is often very difficult to achieve product tie-ins. Several companies often feel harshly treated by the TV stations and the broadcasting restrictions regarding sponsorship. The problem at its most basic is often the gulf between the sponsors wanting value for money and TV companies hiding behind sometimes outdated guidelines and unworkable legislation. There is also the danger of sponsors getting too associated with the sponsored in the eyes of the target market. With issues of, say, the sponsored failing to win or receiving bad publicity, the association can damage the hard-fought image the company was seeking when it took up the sponsorship.

Sports sponsorship can be an important means of entering developing markets where few traditional media are available. In Europe, it is often used selectively to target particular consumer groups or buyers of services. For instance, Alitalia, the Italian airline, sponsors golf tournaments in Italy to reach its upmarket prospects. Similarly, Pepsi Max sponsors extreme sports to reach the young people it portrays in its advertising.

Cause-Related Sponsorship

Sponsorship of good causes may serve various objectives, but it mainly enhances corporate image and brand awareness. It is mostly used locally, but large international companies also use it on a multinational basis. McDonald's sponsors all

kinds of good causes on a local basis, e.g. housing for cancer patients linked to a children's hospital in Amsterdam. British Airways, as a global operator, teamed up with UNICEF, a global charity. A scheme encouraging long-haul passengers to donate unwanted foreign coins raised over £1 million in one year. The airline also donates unfilled seats on flights to UNICEF personnel and allows the charity to use any spare cargo space. J & B Scotch whisky associated itself with raising money to help endangered species, such as the black rhino, by making a donation for each promotional bottle sold. The impact for such activities is greater if there is a clear synergy between the brand and the charity, or at least if the charity has a particular appeal to the same target audience as the brand.

Education

Educational sponsorship is mostly used on a local basis. The objective is mainly enhancement of corporate image and its main user is human resource management. Universities can be sponsored and in some cases change their name. An example is the famous business school at North Western University, in Evanston in the United States, which is now called Kellogg Graduate School of Management.

Broad Corporate Objectives for Sponsorship

It is important that companies must fine-tune their objectives to project a favourable image and survive in a turbulent environment. It is for these reasons that companies engage in sponsorship in fields which sometimes do not bear any relationship with their business. The types of sponsorship objectives formulated by companies include:

- To increase awareness of the company.
- To increase product or brand awareness.
- To alter public perception of the company.
- To counter adverse publicity.
- To build goodwill among opinion formers and decision makers.
- To identify with a particular market segment.
- To be involved in community activities.
- To reassure policy and stockholders.
- To offer opportunities for corporate hospitality so that customers, investors and distributors can be entertained.
- Circumventing advertising regulations for certain products.
- As an aid to staff relations and to assist staff recruitment.

Many sponsorship organizations allow a combination of one or more of the above objectives. In an international aspect, sponsorship affords a good medium for name awareness, especially if the international company uses a global name or trademark in all its operating markets. Sponsorship helps companies respond to changing consumer media habits. The sponsor should look for added value. For example, will a sportsman or famous entertainer be prepared to meet your guests at a social occasion after a game or performance. This adds considerably to the sense of occasion for the guest.

Looking for Sponsorship

Never assume that a sponsor has a bottomless fund of money, or that sponsorship is an act of kindness. It must have a sense of mutual benefit. Sponsorship should not be sought for anything with doubtful legality. One should not hector or criticize organizations for failing to sponsor. Companies exist not to provide sponsorship, but to provide a return for their shareholders who are at the end of the queue for financial return.

The first approach should not be a telephone call, but a letter which states, simply, your organization and its activity, what is being sought in terms of sponsorship, the cost, the audience and the period of sponsorship. There will not be an immediate response other than an acknowledgement, since evaluation of sponsorship can take time. It will be worthwhile asking for a meeting to discuss matters in more detail, especially if there is little opportunity of an early decision in favour of those seeking sponsorship. A would-be sponsor who is interested will need a meeting and visits to the location.

The most common cause of discord between sponsors and those on the receiving end of largesse is failure to produce a comprehensive and mutually acceptable agreement. An agreement must specify the benefits that the sponsor can expect, and the time scale. If extra money is likely to be required during the term of the agreement, review clauses should be inserted. It might also be possible to stipulate that programme and other event advertising is not permitted for the sponsors' competitors.

Commercial Checklist for Sponsors

Sponsors should be certain of their objectives and, as part of this, should have a list of requirements from a sponsorship before agreeing to provide support. Sponsors should look for opportunities which can be maintained for two or more years so that the benefits of being associated with a particular activity are enhanced by repeat exposure, just as advertising often goes unnoticed at first and needs repeat exposure. The secret is not to stick to a sponsorship for so long so that the sponsor's name becomes taken for granted and merges into the background. A good sponsor will always give adequate notice, a year or so, of discontinuing the sponsorship. A commercial checklist for sponsors will have to be undertaken with regard to its viability, goals cost, the product offered and when to pay.

1 *Viability.* What is the target audience of the sport or event? Does this match the company's profile, the product position or the corporate strategy? Will the event or team attract sufficient media exposure to justify the outlay?

2 *Goals.* Is the involvement a whim? If so, write off the investment. What constitutes success? Is the criterion increased product sales, raised profile or revenue?

3 *Cost.* Has the true cost of the sponsorship been considered? Effective sponsorship can cost up to three times the actual up-front outlay. What comparable return could be achieved if the investment could be placed elsewhere? Have the marketing and finance departments agreed the terms of the investment? Has the payment structure been tied to result? In addition to the cost of sponsorship, sufficient funds must be made available to incorporate the sponsorship into advertising, and to produce promotional items and entertainment relevant to the sponsorship.

4 *The product offered.* Can you guarantee that competitors or competitor products will not usurp your company's involvement? Has the event owner ensured that you are offered a first and last option package over other rights (especially TV production)? Have you specified your requirements for name and product displays, and integrated the payment schedule accordingly? Have you ensured that the product will be adequately promoted in all media? Will you be given access to the database of spectators or corporate clients for marketing your product? Can you acquire an option to renew your involvement with the next event and, if so, at what cost?

5 *When do you pay.* Payment must be linked with performance. A careful contract, monitoring the services provided against those required, should be adopted. Have you safeguarded the funds against possible financial difficulties at the event? Payment may be allocated to specific tasks, e.g. drug testing, security, first aid, etc.; by doing so, you can reinforce your investment.

Measuring Sponsorship Effectiveness

The greatest problem with sponsorship is measuring the effect, especially when a large number of different means of communication are involved. As sponsorship is used to achieve basic communication objectives such as awareness and image building, there is a need to evaluate sponsorship results in communications rather than sales terms. The evaluation process is greatly facilitated if measurement is undertaken at several key stages:

1 Measurement is required to determine the company's present position in terms of awareness and image with the target audience.

2 Interim tracking may be necessary if the sponsorship is longer term in order to detect movement on the chosen dimensions of awareness, image and market attitude.

3 Final evaluation must take place when the sponsorship is completed to determine performance levels against the stated objective.

The four methods of measuring sponsorship effectiveness are:

1 Measuring the level of media coverage/exposure.
2 Measuring the communication effectiveness of sponsorship involvement.
3 Measuring the sales effectiveness of sponsorship.
4 Feedback from participating groups.

Measuring the Level of Media Coverage/ Exposure Gained

As stated earlier, in 1992, Visa used the USOC to gain a transaction increase of 17 per cent. In 1994, a staggering total of 188 countries watched the World Cup. The resulting accumulation of viewers from all corners of the globe established an all-time TV audience record of 31.2 billion for the fifty-two matches played. Not only is the World Cup the most viewed competition, but also the most read about. Of the 7000 accredited media that attended the event, almost half represented newspapers and magazines from all over the world. The World Cup means global branding. Perimeter board advertising is a major component of the inter-soccer package. SRI assessed that consumers on average receive up to twelve hours of TV over the course of the competition with the exposure reaching 188 countries throughout the world.

The advertising remains as a component part of the picture, impervious to 'zapping', repeated a thousand times in television highlight programmes and replays – edited into videos and films – revived with each successive World Cup. All this additional exposure is a bonus too great to be measured. Stadium advertising is just one component of the sponsorship programme, but it is perhaps the most important. Sponsor companies know that no other single media purchase can deliver on this scale.

Measuring the Communications Effectiveness of Sponsorship Involvement

As sponsorship is used to achieve basic communication objectives, levels of awareness achieved, attitudes created, perceptions changed or associations suggested are measured against stated objectives. For example, Mastercard's World Cup objectives included increasing awareness within Asia and the Far East. Philips, the electrical giant, wanted to change a negative perception of them no longer being the global brand leader in their class. SRI conducted research on the communication effectiveness of World Cup 1994 which consisted of a comprehensive two-wave adult consumer study in four key countries: the United States, Germany, Brazil and Russia (see table 10.4).

Measuring the Sales Effectiveness of Sponsorship

In commercial sponsorship, as in the case of advertising and marketing commun-ications generally, the matter of keying sales results to given expenditures is highly problematic for a variety of reasons:

1 The simultaneous usage of other marketing inputs.
2 The carry-over effect of previous marketing communication effort.
3 Uncontrollable variables in the business environment, such as competitors' activity or changing economic conditions.

While these factors make this keying of sales results to sponsorship investment somewhat more difficult, many sponsors point to sales results as evidence of sponsorship effects even if conclusive proof of this effect is difficult, although Coca-Cola, the title sponsor of the World Cup festival, had extremely promising results. Consumers responded by drinking 12 per cent more Coca-Cola than they did the summer before. Philips, the electrical giant, trebled its profits during the second quarter of 1994; they attributed much of the growth to increased sales stimulated by the World Cup. The company attributes its 14 per cent increase in turnover largely to soccer-inspired sales.

Feedback from Participating Groups

Measurement by obtaining feedback is perhaps easiest to implement where the sponsorship is targeting a small well-defined audience, e.g. those invited to attend a sponsored concert and its associated hospitality.

Summary

Sponsorship is used by many organizations for enhancing both their image and other marketing communication activities. Sponsorship could be involvement in sports, the arts, broadcast media, charities and other good causes. Sponsorship must be corporate or brand specific and the sponsor's involvement might be plainly obvious or quietly discreet. The sponsor benefits from the public relations spin-off from the activities and public profile of the organization and/or events it supports, while those receiving the sponsorship benefit from cash or benefit in kind.

Sponsorship is not a substitute for advertising. The rich globally recognized companies who sponsor the World Cup and Olympic Games will do so because there is a point where advertising can do no more than sell the product, but sponsorship can continue to maintain goodwill, reputation, understanding of the corporate identity and name familiarity, thus strengthening the advertising that is conducted.

To take advantage of international events, a company should have a logo or brand name that is worth exposing to the global audience. It is not surprising that the most common sponsors in the international arena are companies producing consumer goods with a global appeal, such as soft drinks, consumer electronics, films, tobacco products, alcohol, etc. Through the intensive coverage of sports in the news media all over the world, many companies continue to use sponsorship of sporting events as an important element in their international communications programmes. Successful companies have to track the interest of various countries in the many types of sports, and to exhibit both flexibility and ingenuity in the selection of available events or participants.

REFERENCES

De Mooij, K. and Keegan, W. (1994) *Advertising World Wide: Concepts, Theories and Practice*. Prentice Hall.

FIFA World Cup, USA (1994) *Dossier*. Sweden: ISL Worldwide Marketing.

Fletcher, K. (1990) Role of sponsorship in marketing communications mix. *International Journal of Advertising*, 5(12).

Fletcher, K. (1995) Good causes and effect. *Marketing*, July 20, 31.

Hennessey, D. (1995) *Global Marketing Strategies*. Houghton Mifflin.

Hollis (1995) *Sponsorship and Donations Yearbook*. Sunbury on Thames.

McKeon, M. (1995) Highway swells sponsorship's strength. *Hollis Sponsorship and Donations Yearbook*.

Sleight, S. (1984) *Sponsorship, What it is and How to Use it*. UK: McGraw Hill.

Wilmhurst, J. (1993) *Below the Line Promotion*, 1st edn. Butterworth Heineman.

Wragg, D. (1992) *The Public Relations Handbook*. Blackwell.

Wragg, D. (1994) *The Effective Use of Sponsorship*. Kogan.

11 The Nature, Role and Importance of Publicity in International Marketing Communications

ROSEMARY BURNLEY

Introduction

Increasing internationalization has resulted in firms taking advantage of global opportunities where and when they occur, and reaping the advantages of economies of scale in production and experience and learning curve effects. In the words of Levitt (1983): 'The world is becoming a common market place in which people – no matter where they live – desire the same product and lifestyles.' Behind this trend towards globalization lie the concerns, outlooks and attitudes of increasingly educated, well-informed citizens and customers, influenced by increasingly sophisticated pressure groups and deluged with information by a media whose international scale and speed of coverage is almost breathtaking.

The changing concerns of citizens around the world are the most fundamental changes of all. They are certainly the most crucial for corporate relations. Technology makes things possible but, in open societies, consumers and voters decide how it is used. Even the largest companies compete to understand and respond to consumers' needs and aspirations. This task is even more complex in view of the decline in the power of advertising in terms of influencing consumer purchasing behaviour. The increasing costs of media space and airtime, the increased fragmentation of media audiences, and the intensification of competition for the attention of audiences, have all contributed to an increasing realization that advertising alone can no longer be relied upon to deliver the results that appeared possible during the 1960s and 1970s.

Many firms are now forced to re-examine the basis of many of their marketing strategies and, in particular, their traditional reliance on mass media advertising. This has led to a move towards more narrowly targeted and focused marketing strategies employing other promotional tools like direct marketing, public relations, publicity and sales promotion to a far greater degree than might have been the case in the past. This chapter will focus on one such emerging area of international marketing communications, i.e. international publicity.

Definition and Scope of Publicity

Publicity involves supplying information that is factual, interesting and newsworthy to media such as radio, TV, magazines, newspapers and trade journals, all of which are not controlled by the firm. Publicity is not advertising, since the firm does not pay for time or space. A firm has to earn coverage with interesting, timely material. Publicity is not public relations either. Public relations is a broader task which includes publicity, but involves corporate image advertising, public affairs and opinion making as well.

Most industrial and consumer buyers are somewhat sceptical of advertisements. They know that advertising is an attempt to influence them, and that a great deal of effort goes into making sure the message is 'right'. On the other hand, buyers are more likely to believe publicity because they know it cannot be influenced as directly. This makes positive publicity a valuable asset.

The role of publicity in international marketing, however, can be a complex one since the firm is operating in different environmental conditions with constraints on strategy choices. Hence, the supply of factual, interesting and newsworthy information becomes dependent, to a large extent, on the following factors:

- Cultural differences in various markets.
- Language barriers.
- Different promotion laws.
- Media availability.

These factors present a set of unique problems for international publicity. As noted by Sam Black (1993), 'Even drawing up a simple news release may require a knowledge of local culture, religion and traditional values if it is to ring true and not offend local sensitivities'.

If it is against this background that corporate relations are to be conducted, how can firms respond to it and exercise influence effectively? Fortunately, the basics of corporate communications, public relations and publicity still apply. The task is to apply well-known principles in a new, more complex, environment.

The Nature of Publicity

Publicity is a major tool of 'proactive public relations'. In other words, it is offensively rather than defensively oriented and opportunity seeking rather than problem solving.

Like advertising and personal selling, the fundamental purposes of marketing-oriented publicity are to create brand awareness, enhance attitudes towards a company and its brands, and possibly influence purchase behaviour.

Companies obtain publicity using various forms of news releases, press conferences and other information dissemination. News releases concerning new products, modifications in old products and other newsworthy topics are delivered to editors of newspapers, magazines and other media. Press conferences announce major news events of interest to the public. Photographs, tapes and films are useful for illustrating product improvements, new products and advanced production techniques.

Understandably, all forms of publicity are subject to the control and whims of the media, but by disseminating a large volume of publicity materials and by preparing materials that fit the media's needs, a company increases its chances of obtaining beneficial publicity.

Forms of Publicity

There are three widely used forms of publicity, namely product releases, executive-statement releases and feature articles.

Product releases

Product releases announce new products, provide relevant information about product features and benefits, and tell how additional information can be obtained. A product release is typically aired on TV networks or published in a product section of trade magazines and business publications (such as *Fortune, Business Week, Marketing Weekly, Wall Street Journal,* etc.) or in the business section of consumer magazines such as *Time, News Week, The Economist.*

Audiovisual product releases (called Video News Releases or VNRs) have gained wide usage in recent years. Microsoft received tremendous exposure when it introduced its much-heralded Windows 95 software package in late 1995. It videotaped the launching of the package and distributed tapes to networks all over the world.

Executive-statement releases

Executive-statement releases are news releases quoting chief executives of companies. Unlike a product release, which is restricted to describing a new or modified product, an executive-statement release may address a wide variety of issues relevant to a corporation's publics, such as the following:

- Statements about industry development and trends.
- Views on the economy.
- Comments on research and development or market research findings.

- Announcements of new marketing programmes launched by the company (e.g. Microsoft Chief Executive, Bill Gates, espousing the merits of a new offering from the company).
- Views on foreign competition (e.g. Richard Branson of Virgin Atlantic talking about unfair American competition).
- Comments on environmental issues.

Whereas product releases are typically published in the business or product section of a publication, executive-statement releases are published in the news section. This location carries with it a significant degree of credibility.

Feature articles

Feature articles are detailed descriptions of products or other newsworthy programmes that are written for publication or airing by print or broadcast media. A feature article is usually an exclusive, whereas a news release can be sent to all who may use it. Whilst a news release is factual and free of comment, a feature article is imaginatively written. Feature articles can be written in the following ways:

- They can be written in-house.
- A freelance writer can be commissioned.
- Papers and speeches given by company personalities can be offered as articles.
- A PR/publicity consultancy can be commissioned.
- Facilities can be provided for a staff writer on a journal to visit the organization and write an article.
- They can be produced by EIS International (an international press service which prepares articles for overseas distribution, translating them and distributing them to appropriate editors in the countries chosen by the client).

Although feature articles can be time consuming, they can provide companies with tremendous access to many potential customers.

Constraints on International Publicity

The international publicity programme of a firm is determined by one major constraint, i.e. the international environment. As mentioned earlier, the decision making of the firm is very much dependent on different environmental conditions, such as language and cultural barriers, different government controls and media availability.

Cultural constraints

Knowledge of culture is essential to conducting international publicity. It enables the firm to communicate with its targeted audience through the use of language either commonly known to both parties or leaned. Most importantly, it helps the firm anticipate how consumers in various markets are likely to respond to their actions. According to El Kahal (1994): 'Ignorance of cultural difference is not just unfortunate, it is bad business'. Hence, sensitivity to cultural difference is crucial to successful international publicity.

Ignorance of cultural differences can create problems for a firm. For example, EuroDisney's corporate image suffered initially due to the insensitivity of its executives towards the French people. The Disney personnel were considered to be brash and overbearing. According to Gumbel and Turner (1994), the answer to any doubts or suggestions invariably was: 'Do as we say, because we know best'. For a proud and touchy people such as the French, this attitude by the American company fuelled resentment that led to planning and operational difficulties for the company.

Language barriers

The diversity of languages in world markets is one major constraint facing international publicity. Although some languages are used in more than one country, there are many more languages than countries. There are approximately 3000 different languages and 10 000 different dialects in the world with less than 300 nations (El Kahal, 1994). A firm does not, however, have to know all the languages of all markets, but must ensure that it communicates in these languages. Even in the few cases where the product and its publicity are universal, the language will not be.

A major difficulty often confronting an international firm is the translation of a concept (product, promotional theme) from one language to another, even from one dialect to another. For example, United Airlines, on acquiring Pan Am's Pacific routes in 1985, used the Australian film star Paul Hogan on the cover of its inflight magazine with the caption 'camping it up'. The backdrop was the Australian outback. United was quickly informed by Hogan's lawyers that, in Australia, the caption implied acting in an effeminate fashion. This goes to show that even within major languages like English, the meaning of words and expressions varies from country to country. These differences need to be considered when developing publicity materials and when communications occur between a company and its foreign publics.

Within a country, different classes of people (such as manual workers, white collar workers, managers) use different vocabularies, dialects and accents. These differences also need to be taken into account when developing print and audio promotional messages, especially when these messages are for a particular segment of the market.

When a company enters a foreign market, it can use properly translated product news releases, feature articles and other published information, or it can develop new, market-specific materials. Manufacturers of computers and other high-tech products may find it easier to use materials developed for their domestic markets than would manufacturers of consumer goods. The use of standardized technical language in industry journals means that existing promotional materials for high-tech products are often directly transferable to another market. It is much more difficult to translate the shortened (often slang) expressions used in promoting consumer goods and services.

Media availability

Generally speaking, much of the communication with target audiences is indirect through the media. Almost all newspapers and TV stations are national organizations addressing a national audience. However, an *International Herald Tribune* or a *Financial Times* will have a significant international readership, while broadcasting corporations like CNN and the BBC World Service have an international audience. Currently, dealing with the media internationally is largely a question of dealing with a range of national publications and broadcasting stations in many national markets.

What is even more challenging for the firm is the fact that communications infrastructure varies from one country to another. For example, TV set ownership ranges from one set per two people in countries such as the United States and Japan, to one per twenty in Indonesia, one per fifty in India, one per 330 in Bangladesh and one per 600 in Burma (Terpstra and Sarathy, 1994). Newspaper availability ranges from one daily paper per two people in Japan and one per four people in the United States, to one for every ten to twenty people in Latin America and, in extreme cases, one per 200 people in some African countries.

Managing media relations in a foreign country also requires special skills. The fact that the media has its own agenda and decides what it will print or broadcast, according to its own values, makes it more important than ever to develop a longer term media strategy. An international media strategy will feature a set of consistent messages, directed towards particular channels, underpinned by long-term media relationships, and focused on the international issues which most concern the company.

Government regulations

Local promotion regulations and industry codes directly influence the selection of media and the content of promotional materials. Government restrictions can take many forms. The following are some examples:

1 Some countries have restrictions on the types of products that can be promoted. Tobacco, alcohol and drugs are especially targeted. The promotion of tobacco products like cigarettes is banned in Belgium, Denmark, Finland, France, Germany, Portugal and Switzerland.
2 In some countries, certain media are not available or are very limited. In Austria, the TV cannot be used for the promotion of tobacco. In many African countries, where ownership of a TV set is very limited, promoting a

product solely on TV would not be adequate to reach all the required target market. The firm will need to combine TV promotion with other media such as magazines, radio and newspapers.

3 Some governments are very particular about the language used and the use of comparative promotion. This often necessitates pre-clearance of some promotional materials. South Korea bans plagiarizing of foreign-inspired messages. Many countries regulate the use of words such as gratis, free, low calorie, etc.

Given the above restrictions, it is not surprising that a common target for publicity campaigns consists of government regulatory agencies. This is because, if they have a positive view of the company, it may be easier for the company to conduct business. For instance, Japanese companies like Toyota and Sony have been very concerned that the huge US trade deficit will result in tariffs and other protectionist policies. They have initiated publicity campaigns, including press releases, in order to convince the media, regulators and the public that protectionist policies are not the best solution to the trade deficit.

International publicity is made easier if a firm maintains a good and healthy relationship with its host government. As evidenced by the Japanese companies in the United States, this requires good communications and investment in contacts and relationships.

Some of the ways of forging such good relationships are listed below.

- The government must be made aware of your contribution to output, investment and employment.
- They must be convinced of your standards of behaviour.
- They should find you willing to be helpful, and supportive of the needs of the community.
- They must know that their nationals are well treated and have real prospects of developing themselves.

Planning and Controlling International Publicity

By its nature, publicity entails careful planning, be it at the domestic or international level. A carefully considered plan can benefit a firm in the following ways:

- Reward the firm profitably.
- Put the firm ahead in the competition for space in publications and airtime.
- Help the firm avoid bad publicity later on.

This section will examine some of the key decision areas in international publicity and will attempt to put forward some useful, practical suggestions as to how to design a good publicity plan.

The development and implementation of any publicity plan is dependent on answers to the following questions:

- What are the objectives of the publicity campaign?
- Who are the target audience?
- How should they be motivated?
- How can the audience be reached?
- What procedures should be used for testing and evaluating publicity?

Defining the objectives of the campaign

A company's international, regional and national marketing objectives have a strong and decisive influence on the objectives of a publicity campaign. For example, a company's marketing objectives could be to develop several international brands and to be the dominant competitor in all its markets. On occasion, it may also want to enter a new market or introduce a new or modified product on an international, regional or national basis. Marketing objectives such as these give direction to the company's publicity objectives.

Generally, publicity should help a company accomplish one or more of the following:

- Inform consumers about how to choose, buy and use the product or service.
- Persuade consumers to buy the product or service.
- Counteract misconceptions about the product, service or organization.
- Get information to the public on issues the organization is concerned about.
- Bring consumers to an event or series of events.
- Increase attendance to programmes.
- Recruit highly qualified employees.
- Get people to vote for an issue.
- Attract shareholders to support the company's interests or activities.
- Protect the company from frivolous lawsuits.

The setting of specific objectives helps in deciding which programmes, events and issues get priority. This calls for selectivity on the part of the company, for if the media is deluged with publicity material, the credibility of the company may suffer. In order words, overkill could lead to undercoverage. Not all events call for a full-scale publicity campaign and if a minor event is overemphasized, a company could have difficulty getting coverage for a genuinely newsworthy programme that takes place soon afterward. A good publicist knows the difference between routine announcements and a really interesting product development.

Identifying, analysing and motivating the target audience

Publicity, in a way, involves selling, and like any good salesperson, a firm must identify its target audience. In publicity or public relations, this audience is referred to as 'publics'. Publics are groups of people, internally and externally, with whom an organization communicates (Jefkins, 1992). Publicity is very discriminatory because it is often aimed at carefully selected groups of people, who could be the community, potential and actual employees, investors/share-holders, consumers, opinion leaders, the government and journalists. Each organ-ization has its own special publics with whom it has to communicate internally and externally. External communication necessitates careful selection and under-standing of the publics. It is important to define the publics clearly because it helps the organization to:

- identify all groups of people relative to the publicity programme;
- select media and techniques;
- prepare the message in acceptable and effective forms; and
- establish priorities within the scope of the company's resources.

(Jefkins, 1992)

Identifying an audience is an important part of a publicity plan. The choice of the audience is dependent on the message the company wants to put across. Some of the key decision areas facing a publicity manager are the following:

- Can sales increase more quickly by targeting publicity toward current customers?
- Should the message be aimed at people who never use the company's prod-uct, and provide them with reasons why they should?
- Should the company only target people who agree with the company's stand on certain issues and policies?
- Are there people who are undecided or even segments of the competitors/opposition who might be persuaded to join the company or at least engage in a dialogue? Who are they?

The selection of the target audience requires some knowledge of the audience. A firm needs to be aware of the behavioural and cultural traits of the audience in order to understand and anticipate their reaction. Conducting a survey on the target audience can be useful in ascertaining some possible misconceptions or opinions that the audience has about the organization, product, service or indus-try. Obtaining detailed information on such opinions could indicate precisely what people need to know about the organization.

As a publicist, the firm's task of persuasion in a double one. First, it has to convince journalists to run its material or cover a story. Once that happens, the approach and information must be enticing enough to get the public to act. As mentioned earlier, publicity involves selling. Every time a firm does some publicity, it has to make two sales pitches: one to the journalist and another to the audience.

Audience motivation is an area which many businesses often find difficult. Ironically, the advertising world does an excellent job of motivating and persuad-ing their targeted audience by pointing out product and service benefits. Hence, businesses that are experienced in advertising should find it easier. For those inexperienced ones, the following are some useful tips for audience motivation:

- Be positive, emphasize the facts.
- Avoid reminding people of their fears and dislikes. For example, a publicity piece with so many negative statements like 'children under 12 would not be admitted without an adult, no dogs and push chairs are allowed, and dress must be formal' would only help to make customers anxious or annoyed.
- Promise a benefit, satisfy a need or offer a distinctive service.
- Study some advertisements that are particularly effective. How convincing are these advertisements in terms of putting across the product's benefits? Try to parody the advertisements, substituting your product, service or company's name for the brand in the original and creating parallel product or service benefits to fit your company. This should increase the firm's ability to translate its message into the targeted audience's terms.

Reaching the audience

Once the audience has been chosen, the decision has to be made as to how to reach it. Less experienced firms often use the 'shotgun approach' by sending publicity to every broadcaster and publication in the country. If a firm wants to get teenagers to buy a new line of fashionable clothing, it would be a waste of time directing the material to a radio station with an audience of over-40s. Similarly, a press release about workshops for young graduates in architecture should go to a professional publication and not to a local newspaper whose readership would not necessarily comprise young graduates in architecture.

It is necessary to do some research in order to choose the best media for publicity. Depending on the type of publicity, the choice would be based on answers to the following questions:

- Which radio/TV stations will reach the target audience?
- How much credibility do these media have with their audiences?
- Will the journalists, broadcasters or presenters be interested in the material?
- Will the audience(s) be interested in the publicity material?
- How much lead time is required?

More often, media with large and broad audiences are the most difficult publicity targets. Specialized media seldom get enough material that fits their narrow focuses, so it could be easier to use them. The obvious advantage is that their specialized focus often results in a knowledgeable treatment of the material. So, it is worth searching for the highly specialized newsletters, magazines, trade journals, syndicated columns and even specialized broadcast programmes that reach a specific target audience.

One fundamental problem in dealing with the media is that the firm is not in direct contact with its chosen public; it is dealing with an institution which has, to its own satisfaction, interpreted the public need and interest. Hence, if the firm's publicity material is to reach its target audience, the material must be presented in a way that reflects that medium's interpretation of the audience's interest, otherwise it would be rejected as unsuitable to the medium's editorial policies. There are, therefore, four elements in the situation:

1   The actual need of the audience.
2   The medium's interpretation of the audience's need.
3   The firm's need.
4   The firm's interpretation of the audience's need.

Essentially, effort should be made to align all four, although in reality there are few cases whereby a firm's concept of a public need would correspond to that of the medium.

Pretesting and evaluating publicity

Pretesting publicity material provides vital feedback information which should indicate whether the target audience will receive and understand the message. This is especially necessary in a foreign setting where most publics may not be familiar with the organization, its service, product or cause. A press release that makes perfect sense to the organization, but fails to take into account the behaviour and culture of its chosen public, may result in misperception and hence rejection of the message.

Wherever possible, the group used for pretesting must be selected from the target audience. The size of the group must be large enough to provide more accurate feedback.

Once the publicity material has been used by the media, effort should be made to evaluate its impact, in order to ascertain whether it has been a success, partial success or failure. The importance of evaluating publicity material cannot be overemphasized. Oxley (1989) observes that the consequences of neglecting evaluation will be 'a reduction in the organisation's self-steering capacity – it will have deprived its memory of information needed to guide it into the future'. Evaluation can only be made after all the relevant facts have been gathered and analysed. Evaluation would therefore entail some research – the systematic gathering and analysis of information. Two types of information are especially important: quantitative and qualitative. In publicity, software programs or press clipping services can be used to develop reports that pinpoint the quantity of media exposure, number of mentions of the company's product/service or name, the amount of favourable, unfavourable and mixed coverage, and the number of people the publicity reaches. Some clipping services can even index and store the company's clippings and the publicity materials that generated them on a high-density disk.

Counting clippings is not, however, the only way of measuring success. It is also necessary to measure their impact on the public. Telephone or personal surveys are useful ways of conducting opinion research. Most developed countries have opinion research firms who could provide such information. Information from opinion surveys can help a firm decide whether a publicity campaign has achieved its objectives, whether it was efficiently carried out and whether its overall benefits were worth the campaign's effort.

Summary

Despite the wealth of literature devoted to marketing communications, publicity is one of those elements of the communications mix that has yet to be accorded sufficient recognition in terms of its role and importance. Evidence of this is in the scanty coverage of publicity in most marketing and international marketing textbooks. A comprehensive and consensus definition of publicity has remained elusive.

This chapter has sought to provide a more realistic definition and coverage of publicity by delineating its function within public relations and examining its basic dimensions. It is, however, acknowledged that the tools and processes for a publicity campaign are the same for the domestic and foreign market, although the task of international publicity is more complex given the various constraints posed by different foreign environments. Nonetheless, as with all other communication tools, successful international publicity campaigns are largely dependent on careful planning, taking into consideration the peculiarities of the foreign environments.

REFERENCES

Black, S. (1993) *The Essentials of Public Relations*. London: Kogan Page.

Dunn, W. S. (1976) Effect of national identity on multinational promotional strategy. *Journal of Marketing*, 40(October), 50–7.

El Kahal, S. (1994) *Introduction to International Business*. UK: McGraw-Hill International.

Gregory, A. (1996) *Planning and Managing a Public Relations Campaign*. London: Institute of Public Relations.

Gumbel, P. and Turner, R. (1994) Fans like Euro Disney but its parents goofs weigh the park down. *Wall Street Journal*, March 10.

Hennessey, H. (1992) *Global Marketing Strategies*, 2nd edn. USA: Houghton Mifflin.

Jefkins, F. (1992) *Public Relations*, 4th edn. London: Pitman.

Levitt, T. (1983) Globalization of markets. *Harvard Business Review*, 61(3), 69–81.

Mclver, C. (1964) Formulating media strategy for foreign markets. In S. W. Dunn (ed.), *International Handbook of Advertising*. New York: McGraw-Hill.

Mooiji, M. K. and Keegan, W. J. (1991) The global advertising environment. In *Advertising Worldwide*. New York: Prentice-Hall.

Nally, M. (1991) *International Public Relations in Practice*. London: Kogan Page.

Onkvisit, S. and Shaw, J. J. (1993) *International Marketing: Analysis and Strategy*. New York: Macmillan.

Oxley, H. (1989) *The Principles of Public Relations*. London: Kogan Page.

Phillips, D. (1992) *Evaluating Press Coverage*. London: Kogan & Page.

Prone, T. (1990) *Do Your Own Publicity*. Channel Islands: Guernsey Press.

Terpstra, V. and Sarathy, R. (1994) *International Marketing*, 6th edn. USA: Dryden Press.

Weiner, R. (1982) *Professional's Guide to Publicity*. New York: PR Publishing.

Wragg, D. (1993) *Targeting Media Relations*. London: Kogan Page.

Yale, D. R. (1992) *The Publicity Handbook: How to Maximize Publicity for Products, Services and Organisations*. Chicago, Ill.: NTC Publishing Group.

12 The International Dimension of Direct Marketing as a Communications Tool

Colin Angwin

Introduction

Direct marketing started in the mid-nineteenth century as a means of supplying the needs of homesteaders and others in the American West who were physically distant from retail outlets. From this beginning, it has paid little heed to physical distance or to boundaries. This geographical freedom has obviously been enormously extended by the twentieth-century *globalization* of communications. Globalization has been accompanied by increasing *personalization*. Where once the only way of remote communication between individuals was the mail, in a developed Western society people can be reached directly in their homes from anywhere in the world by a number of channels uniquely addressed to them (mail, telephone, fax, e-mail), each of which can be a carrier for direct marketing.

The objectives of this chapter are to review the basic workings of direct marketing and to show how these well-established processes can be implemented in other countries, whether by taking advantage of national differences or by finding ways of circumventing their effects.

The objectives of this Introduction are to suggest a few principles which will be helpful in approaching foreign markets and to identify the key stages of a direct marketing programme where local variables may cause special difficulties or open up special opportunities.

Direct marketing as a communications tool

The distinguishing characteristic of direct marketing as a communications tool is that it uses marketing and selling methods in combination to build a direct relationship between marketer and customer. This uniquely powerful mechanism can be employed as effectively across boundaries or in several countries as within a single domestic market.

A direct marketing programme may consist of anything from one campaign with a limited objective, such as launching an importer, to a sustained schedule of campaigns and activities intended to generate and maintain a complete new business stream.

The wider context

For many successful companies, direct marketing has been the sole method of building the business. On the other hand, it can also be one amongst an armoury of weapons deployed for the purpose. One reason why specialist agencies have proliferated over the past decade or so is that the need to use direct marketing methods as part of the overall marketing strategy is becoming imperative.

This is in part because of their proven effectiveness, but particularly because their effectiveness is measurable. The desired result of almost any direct marketing campaign can be established as a target number of specific transactions, each with a target value. Whether the campaign has achieved this result, or the amount by which it has exceeded or fallen short of it, can be precisely determined. Following this determination, changes can be made to the programme to improve its effectiveness and its long-term profitability.

For a component of a marketing activity, such measurability is invaluable. It imposes marketing disciplines from which the whole business benefits.

International direct marketing

The phrase 'international direct marketing' is used in this chapter as a generic term for any direct marketing programme which extends beyond the bounds of a single domestic market. Such a programme may involve activity in one or several countries, including or excluding the domestic market, and may consist of programmes carried out within or between countries (e.g. mailings despatched from one country for delivery in another).

Some of the best-known practitioners have built huge worldwide businesses – and worldwide reputations – using only the techniques of direct marketing. Many multinational businesses, not historically users of these techniques on any significant scale, are now moving beyond this and incorporating direct marketing as one element of their global business strategies.

Background to chapter content

This chapter, and indeed the whole book, is in part about moving from the familiar and comfortable domestic market to a challenging alien environment.

		Geographical spread		
		Single foreign market	Several foreign markets	Foreign markets and domestic market
Communications flow				
	Within each country			
	Between countries			

Figure 12.1   Geography and communications.

Inevitably, much of the content is dealing with obstacles in the way of success. The purpose is not to paint a discouraging picture but, on the contrary, to show how, by being aware of potential difficulties in advance and being ready to tackle them with thoughtful attention to detail, the marketer can achieve profitable results and have a lot of fun doing so.

Some points brought up in this chapter echo arguments put forward in other chapters. The intention here is to look at the application of such wider issues in the specific context of direct marketing.

For convenience, and particularly for purposes of illustration, it is assumed throughout this chapter that the present domestic market of most readers is the United Kingdom. However, any particular reader for whom this may not be true should not allow himself to be irritated by the apparent insularity. Which market is actually the 'home' one makes little difference of practice and none of principle.

Some basic principles

Direct marketing, like any form of marketing, depends in part upon getting into the mind of potential customers. Where these are in a foreign country, certain points always need to be borne in mind:

- Basic human motivations do not differ according to race, class or nation.
- However, at a superficial level, there can be significant differences in reactions to verbal and visual stimuli.
- There are substantial practical differences in the ways society and commerce are organized.

In another person's country, you are the foreigner and his or her reactions are the norm. There is no reason why he should adapt to you. You must do the adapting. This is probably the hardest lesson to learn.

Direct marketing has always been an information-based activity. This has been true since long before computers made life simultaneously easier and harder. In seeking foreign information (i.e. information about an unknown marketplace), two questions need to be asked:

- Does the information I want exist?
- If so, does it mean what I think it means?

Making a direct marketing operation work depends upon attention to detail. Getting the detail right may be more difficult in unfamiliar surroundings, but the same logical processes should always be at work. *'Abroad' is not one place.* Two foreign countries are as different from each other as either is from your own home base. All the detailed work must be redone for each new market tackled.

Framework

The remainder of the chapter is constructed as follows.

First, two general sections – *Applications* and *The Transaction Cycle* – on how direct marketing works.

Next, a section setting out the fundamental *language* issues which underpin all international direct marketing.

This is followed by four sections outlining the basic components of any direct marketing activity and showing how each of these – *The Marketing Database, Creativity, Mechanisms* and *Mailing Lists* – has to be modified to allow for the international element.

The chapter concludes with a section on *Putting it Together*.

In each of these *topics*, particular *concerns* which are the consequence of introducing the international element occur and, inevitably, recur from section to section.

Some of these concerns are the following:

- Stage of market development and infrastructure.
- Commercial custom.
- Legal and regulatory environment.
- Language.
- Culture.

The interaction between the section topics and the international concerns (see table 12.1) is really the core of this chapter.

Within Europe, the influence of the European Union is to some extent diminishing certain of these concerns, but this is a slow process and will never be more than partial. While it is undoubtedly true that the four freedoms of movement envisaged by the Single European Act (people, goods, capital and services) have been greatly enhanced and are improving all the time, it is also true that the intrinsic cultural differences between peoples are not diminishing at all. Indeed,

Table 12.1 Topics and concerns

	Market stage	Business customs	Regulation	Language	Culture
Applications					
Transaction cycle					
Language					
Marketing database					
Creativity					
Mechanisms					
Mailng lists					
Putting it together					

in some ways they are becoming more marked. The need for good information as the foundation of direct marketing activity is as great in this continent as in any other.

Applications

Overview

Direct marketing has always proved to be equally effective in selling to consumers and in business to business, and its mechanical and creative flexibility make it equally suitable for any mix of cost and volume. It can encompass mass mailings of millions of pieces and sophisticated, highly targeted programmes using combinations of media to reach minuscule specialist audiences. In either of these cases, or anything in between, the campaign can take place in one country, in a few countries, or in many.

Direct marketing is distinct from the other broad marketing disciplines, such as retail marketing and field sales. It can be, and frequently is, used on its own. However, it can also be utilized in support of these other disciplines, often greatly enhancing their cost effectiveness. Equally, it can serve as an export channel itself or as reinforcement for other export modes.

Specifics

Almost without exception, the principal objective of a direct marketing campaign is to initiate transactions. Amongst the results the marketer may be looking to bring about are:

- A sale, whereby the customer sends in his money, a detailed description of the product or service he wants to buy and a signed order (classic mail order).
- A subscription or club membership, which is an extended form of sale.

- A donation, whereby the customer sends in his money (or a commitment to donate regularly).
- Sign-on to a proxy activity (e.g. to sell from a catalogue).
- A call (physical or telephonic) by a salesman.
- A visit to a retail outlet or to some event.

Any of these types of transaction can be initiated within a local or national marketplace or internationally. Large, successful, international direct marketing operations have been created in, for example, the fields of business publications and luxury goods, and international fund-raising for academic and other institutions with global reputations.

There are also activities specifically related to cross-border trading for which direct marketing has proved very effective and is often the only method used, such as:

- Attracting potential importers/agents.
- Providing importer support (i.e. promoting sales or enquiries).
- Invitations to international conferences, trade fairs, etc.

Sometimes, more than one transaction may be an acceptable result or one kind of transaction may be planned to lead to another. For example, club membership may lead to product sales. In all cases, a by-product is the creation of a list, which can be the source of future activity and should feed into the marketing database.

The promotion may have a more general advertising message not directly geared to transactions, e.g. building brand recognition or reinforcing image. Only very rarely is this the sole or main objective. Usually it is an auxiliary benefit arising out of the primary task, and in the international context it is often at best a marginal consideration.

The promotion may also be a small-scale preliminary exercise designed to test some of the assumptions that are being made. International tests can be a highly cost-effective, controllable contributor to the process of judging whether a market for a new product exists in a particular country.

The Transaction Cycle

Direct marketing is a transaction-based activity (see figure 12.2).

Every business activity is built up of transactions, each one containing the potential for a *new* transaction. A continuing series of repeat transactions between the parties will enhance both the marketer's profitability and the customer's satisfaction.

The marketer's profitability is enhanced because:

- The high costs of obtaining a new customer are progressively amortized.
- Continuity of demand is sustained.
- Early warning can be received of changes needed in the product range.

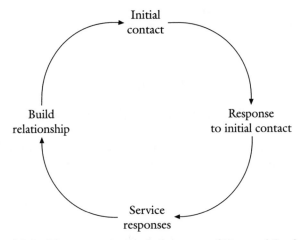

Figure 12.2 The transaction cycle (courtesy of Dun and Bradstreet).

The customer's satisfaction is enhanced because:

- Pricing can become progressively more favourable.
- Continuity of supply and assurance of quality are sustained.
- Influence can be exercised over changes in the product range.

Whether the transaction is a sale or of another kind, it involves the following four basic steps.

1 *Making the initial contact.* This is a communication by one of the parties to the other with a view to initiating a transaction. There may be an existing relationship or the approach may be purely speculative. In direct marketing terms, the initial communication usually consists of an offer and a request for a response, and is sent to a number of recipients.

2 *Response by the other party to the initial contact.* Some of the recipients respond by placing an order or requesting more information. A dialogue has now been established which the initiator can and should extend.

3 *Receiving and servicing the responses.* The initiator must honour any promise made in the opening communication (e.g. to supply the goods ordered) and address any problems or complaints which the responses uncover.

4 *Building the relationship.* The initial expectation having been fulfilled, there is now an opportunity to construct a continuing and mutually rewarding relationship. Repeat and new transactions form an important element of this relationship, and the 'initial contact' is often really a contact renewed following a previous transaction.

The nature of direct marketing is that all the transactions and the entire customer relationship are managed at a distance, using postal and telephone services and other media in various combinations. The fact that the distance may be greater than usual, and may involve crossing national boundaries, does not require any fundamental changes in methodology or approach, although it may well impose major changes of detail.

Language

The importance of language

Marketing hinges upon effective communication. Direct marketing, above all, hinges upon effective direct communication between people. The moment this involves people with different first languages, decisions about choice of language have to be made.

English

'English', it is often stated and sometimes half-believed, 'is the international business language'. This statement is untrue. There is no universal business language, and there is no particular reason why there ever should be one. As a matter of observable fact, even people who are fluent in a foreign language, be it English or another, usually prefer to speak their own when they are at leisure or in the day-to-day run of their lives (which includes when they are being sold to). Anybody who has attended a meeting conducted in a language which some of the participants do not have as their mother tongue will have noticed how every so often, whether to concert an argument, to clarify understanding or even just as an easement of tension, little groups will break back into their own speech.

It *is* true that:

- English is the most widely used second language.
- In some trades/professions, particularly those with a technological/communications orientation, it is the practical working language at a managerial and technical level.
- It is often the official working language of multinationals, including some which are not themselves of Anglo-Saxon provenance. However, even in this case, a visit to a local office of such a company will serve to show the observer that at the practical, day-to-day level, business is carried out from choice in the local language.
- Some countries, for historical, commercial and cultural reasons, have developed a tradition of quasi-bilinguality between their own languages and English. There are, on the other hand, many parts of Africa and the Middle East where the tradition of bilinguality is with French, and in Eastern Europe it is increasingly becoming with German.

Figure 12.3 is a simplistic representation of the likelihood that a given group of people will be sufficiently comfortable with English to be happy to transact business in it.

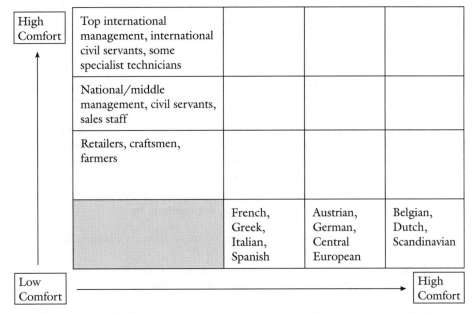

High Comfort	Top international management, international civil servants, some specialist technicians			
	National/middle management, civil servants, sales staff			
	Retailers, craftsmen, farmers			
		French, Greek, Italian, Spanish	Austrian, German, Central European	Belgian, Dutch, Scandinavian

Figure 12.3 Likely comfort levels in English. NB: It seems probable that, if the figure related to comfort in another language, e.g. German, and the British were one of the nationalities on it, they would find themselves displayed towards the left of the table.

Options and considerations

The question the direct marketer has to ask himself is which language or combination of languages will be most cost effective in promoting his product or service internationally. As was hinted earlier, almost all of us, whatever our nationality, react better to being sold to in our own language. This means that the marketer's preference must be to communicate in the customer's language. However, the practical difficulties in satisfying this, particularly if several countries and languages are concerned, are not trivial:

- Translation.
- Cost.
- Availability of lists.
- Identifying preferred language.

There are certainly circumstances in which English is either the best choice or a perfectly acceptable one, including:

- Where the product or service being promoted requires familiarity with English (e.g. some publications, conferences and seminars).

- Where an English-language audience can be readily identified and is large enough to sustain a profitable programme (such as some luxury goods, some fund-raising).
- Some of the 'high comfort' segments in figure 12.3.

Otherwise, everything possible should be done to communicate in the appropriate local languages, bearing in mind that the correct use of styling and honorific can be as important as the language itself.

The European Union has twelve official languages, but getting on for thirty are actually spoken within its boundaries, and of course there are many more within Europe as a whole. On purely cost and practical grounds, a programme covering a sizeable part of the continent may impose the need to limit it to major languages, however defined. This may be unavoidable, but it may in a few instances cause more offence than writing in English, for example by:

- Getting the language wrong (e.g. writing to a Belgian Flemish speaker in French).
- Making insensitive judgements as to what is a major language (including Spanish but omitting Portuguese, including Swedish but omitting Finnish).

Conducting the initial, outgoing communication in the local language implies an ability to handle the responses and all other resultant calls and correspondence in it as well.

Translating

Where the decision is taken to communicate in several languages, the copy will necessarily be written in one of them and translated into the others. This process is a minefield, but there are precautions that can be taken to avoid being blown up.

The original message should be written so as to avoid foreseeable booby-traps:

- Keep it linguistically clear and simple.
- Avoid humour.
- If cultural or topical references are used, make sure they are of universal and not purely local relevance.

Use the right translators (who may not be obtainable from a general-purpose local translation agency). Preferably, they should be:

- Not an expatriate who left home two decades ago, but somebody who still lives in the target country or has kept close and active links with it.
- Somebody who understands the *subject* as well as the *language*. This is particularly important if there is any element of technical or professional jargon. If there is no translator available with the relevant experience, have the translation vetted by a native speaker who does have it.
- Somebody from the right language stream (such as a Québecois rather than a French person if you are promoting into that province).

If you have the right translators, allow them as much freedom as the overall product strategy permits to adapt rather than merely to translate. At this level, you might even indulge in a little levity with a little local colour.

Unless you or your colleagues speak the language well, have the copy translated back into English and review it.

Allow for different language lengths (e.g. German takes on average 30 per cent more space than English to express a given idea). Above all, have the text translated into the longest language in which it will appear before doing designs or layouts.

The Marketing Database

A feature shared by all direct marketing campaigns is that, at some point, a list of names and addresses comes in to play. Commonly, a list is the starting point and is used as a means of contacting prospects. Even where this is not so, the result of the initial contact with prospects, however it was made, is the creation of a list containing details of respondents. The success of individual campaigns depends upon skilful use of prospect lists and skilful handling of respondent lists.

The success of direct marketing as a long-term business builder depends upon managing the lists or parts of them to convert transactions into relationships. This is the principle underlying database marketing, which has become the foundation of most successful direct marketing, domestic and international.

What is a direct marketing database? It is a database of information about:

- Respondents to campaigns.
- Existing customers (including distributors/importers).
- Recent/lapsed customers.
- 'Hot' and other prospects.

As a minimum, it contains name and address information about these. Its value as a marketing tool increases to the extent that it accumulates and processes more profound information. Properly constructed and managed, it is a repository of knowledge about a company's existing and potential markets, and the raw material for plans to develop those markets.

Constructing a good marketing database covering overseas markets as they are opened will provide a secure foundation for building the business in each of these.

What is the database going to be used for?

The underlying purposes of a marketing database are:

- To help the marketer better to understand and service his customers' needs.
- To help him communicate with them more effectively.
- To reduce the cost of identifying and finding new customers.
- To maximize the return on investment in existing customers.

Table 12.2   Probable functions of a direct marketing database

Function	Primary design requirements
Generating mailing/telephone marketing lists and other communications	Efficient search by multiple criteria. Volume production of output
Processing responses (fulfilling orders, passing on leads, etc.)	Quick on-line access to individual customer's case history
Handling enquiries/complaints and other communications from customers	Quick on-line access to customer case history
Customer and market analysis	Efficient search by multiple criteria

Practically, it may be used for several different functions, and some of these may generate conflicting design requirements (see table 12.2). In particular, the need to search the whole database and extract large groups of records according to multiple criteria may be tricky to reconcile economically with the need for on-line access to individual records.

The addition of a multinational dimension may complicate things further because:

- Access to the database may need to accommodate different language needs.
- Different telecommunications regimes in different countries may place obstacles in the way of giving all those who need it access to the database.
- Output capabilities need greater flexibility to cope with national norms and sensibilities.

What information will the database contain?

Depending upon products and markets, the database may contain primarily consumer records, primarily business records, or both. In any case, two broad types of information can be distinguished:

- Demographic.
- Strategic.

These two types exist in all countries, but their availability and structural detail differ considerably.

Demographic information

This is information that is or can be generally known and is not dependent upon any relationship between the customer and marketer. It will include name and address and other geographical reference data, as well as information such as:

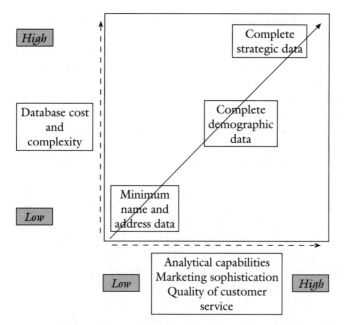

Figure 12.4 The data/function trade-off.

- Details of individuals' qualifications and functions.
- Business activities, size measures and corporate linkages of companies.
- Import/export activity.

Strategic information

This is information about the relationship between customer and marketer. It may include:

- Promotional history.
- Functional relationship (customer/distributor/importer/agent).
- Response and order/sales history.
- Payment history.
- Complaints and other communications.
- Personal contacts.
- Competitive information.

Any marketing database poses a dilemma in that the more information it contains the more useful it is to the marketer, but the more unwieldy it becomes. Function and data may require trade-offs, all the more so where the information originates in more than one country.

Data sources and design implications

Data will be garnered from a variety of sources. Demographic information will be contained on any marketing lists rented or purchased. The extent to which this can be incorporated in another database will depend upon the agreement with the list supplier, and the practice may vary from country to country.

Strategic information and supplementary demographic details can come either from the customers themselves or from in-house sources such as accounts receivable, sales records and distributors/importers.

The variety of possible data sources also carries some other implications.

- Multiple methods of data entry may be required. Some of the data may be delivered on-line or in magnetic formats capable of batch entry. Other items may be supplied in hard copy. Manual entry and visual monitoring of data will require staff with the linguistic skills and geographical understanding to be able to handle foreign names, addresses, titles, etc.
- The risk of duplication of records is constant, particularly where varying character sets and spellings occur. There are no foolproof methods of avoiding this, but it justifies considerable effort to minimize it, because of the high costs it generates, the intense irritation it arouses in customers and the dangerous false conclusions it can lead to. Problems with character sets and variable spellings make multinational duplication even more tricky.
- Reduction of duplication will lead to an increase in inconsistent information about the same records, and rules must be developed for resolving conflicts.

What are its outputs?

The output of the database will consist of:

- Selected records.
- Counts and statistics.

Selected records

The records will be selected for two main purposes.

1 *To facilitate dialogue with an individual customer.* This may be to take an order, to handle a complaint or to answer some query. The person dealing with the case requires to be able to respond in the right language, to find the customer immediately on-line together with the record of his or her most recent dealings, and to update the record with any new transactions.
2 *To communicate with a group of customers.* The communication is most frequently designed to provoke a specific response, such as an order, a donation or an enquiry. Selection of the appropriate categories of customers will be by combinations of criteria, which may be demographic, strategic, or both.

Counts and statistics

The database is a source of detailed knowledge about customers and provides the raw material for analyses of their behaviour and preferences. These require the extraction of statistical data about groups of customers defined by combinations of criteria (demographic, strategic, or both).

How is it going to be managed?

The importance of the direct marketing database to the future of the business is such that it should be given dedicated management. The manager will have to address a number of questions:

- Should the database be developed in-house or externally?
- How does it relate to other systems that may be in use or planned?
- How is it going to be maintained and updated?

Should the database be developed in-house or externally?

There are now several direct marketing database packages available and it may well be more cost efficient to buy one of these rather than to rely on in-house data-processing development resources, since these are often overstretched and focused on other priorities. However, any package being considered must be carefully appraised for its ability to handle multicountry records.

How does the database relate to other systems that may be in use or planned?

To the maximum practical extent, the database should draw upon any existing databases and systems that meet some of the requirements. Similarly, wherever possible, it should take advantage of the capabilities of standard generic software packages, many of which include foreign language options as standard.

How is the database going to be maintained and updated?

Designing a database is one thing. Making it work is quite another, and requires:

- Management commitment.
- Clear rules about how information will be gathered.
- Validation and prioritization procedures.
- Regular and consistent measurement.

Enforcing discipline to ensure that information flows from geographically scattered points of origin to the marketing database is likely to prove quite arduous, the more so because of the need to encompass multiple country requirements.

Handling foreign data

Incorporating records from several countries can have consequences for every aspect of designing and managing the database, some of which have already been touched on. The points that need to be provided for include the following:

Address formats

There is no standardization of address formats within or outside the European Union. Variations include:

- Different postcode structures (alphanumeric variable length in the United Kingdom and a few other countries, numeric fixed length in most countries, but length varying from country to country).
- Different postcode meanings (some countries have more than one postcode for the same address, depending on the use).
- Different postcode positioning (before or after the town or county).
- Different positioning of house numbers (before or after the street name).
- Different positioning of address elements (e.g. town name before or after street name).
- Use of standard abbreviations.

Telephone number formats, including intercity dialling procedures, also vary in length and structure between and within countries.

Character sets

Most Western languages, although they are based on the Roman alphabet, have a few distinctive (accented) characters in addition to the basic twenty-six used in English. The choice must be made between:

1 What is called 'normalizing' (a polite term for anglicizing) these characters by dropping all accents.
2 Constructing the database so as to be able to process them properly.

The former option is easier and cheaper, but it carries significant disadvantages because:

- Incomplete representation of these additional characters may be offensive to recipients of addressed and personalized material.

- Disregarding them may lead to inaccurate sorting of data (e.g. in French, è, é and ê are sorted indifferently together, but in some Scandinavian languages a and å are sorted as distinct letters).
- Mishandling them may lead to incorrect matching and duplication of records.

There is no doubt that, from the point of view of direct marketing effectiveness, taking the time and trouble to handle all characters of the relevant languages is best.

Non-Roman-based languages (Arabic, Farsi, Kanji, Mandarin, etc.) and intermediate scripts (Cyrillic, Greek), which between them are used by the bulk of the world's population and most of its markets, no doubt add a fifth dimension of complexity. Somewhat to his embarrassment, they are entirely beyond the grasp of the author.

Spelling variations

The English spelling of many major town names and countries is different from that in the natural language (e.g. *Firenze* and *Italia* in Italian are represented as *Florence* and *Italy* in English). In some instances, the difference is so great that any affinity between the two variants is scarcely recognizable (*Österreich* for *Austria*) and in rare cases the names are completely different in the two languages (e.g. *Deutschland* for *Germany*).

A further level of complexity is added in countries which are themselves multilingual, such as Belgium and Finland. Switzerland is an extreme example, with three valid spellings in the official national languages (*Suisse, Schweiz, Swizzera*) and the town which Anglo-Saxons know as *Geneva* also having three valid local forms (*Genève, Genf* and *Ginevra*). In fact, of course, the widely recognized English versions are not officially valid in the country itself.

Differences in spellings (as well as those in address formats and character sets) present problems at two stages:

1 *Input.* Data from different sources may carry combinations of spellings and formats, which the computer must recognize for duplication and other purposes.
2 *Output.* Regardless of the original format, output may need to be in one consistent presentation.

Language choice

Another quirk is that there may be a need, legal or cultural, to address an *individual* in a preferred language. For example, Brussels is officially a bilingual city, but any resident (or employee of a business) has the right to insist on receiving official documents in French rather than Flemish, or vice versa, and may well prefer to receive all communications in the chosen tongue. There may, therefore, be a need for the database to contain language codes.

Incidentally, language preference is not exclusively a feature of multilingual environments. In France, for example, it can be illegal, and even if it is not illegal it may cause offence, to send out promotional material in any language other than French.

Titles/qualifications

The English are very sensitive to titles. By contrast, in certain other countries, e.g. the German-speaking region and Southern Europe, much greater weight is given to academic qualifications. These should normally be used in any professional or business communication. The database must be capable of handling these local nuances.

Currencies

At the point of input, information about businesses, and sometimes about individuals, may contain financial detail. This will normally be expressed in the currency of the country where the entity is located, but this is not always so (e.g. foreign banks in the City of London may report their figures in their home currency or in US dollars rather than in sterling). Figures may be in whole numbers or in thousands (or even millions for currencies such as the lira and the yen), with an indicator showing which.

At the point of output, the individual recipient of a mailing may wish to receive any information in a currency with which he or she is familiar.

Data protection

Legislation is more restrictive in some countries than others. In general, regulation is intended to protect individuals. However, it can be interpreted in such a way that some business information (e.g. details of single partnerships in Germany) is protected as if it were personal rather than corporate. It is always worthwhile, before starting to collect information in a country, checking the legality of the process with the regulatory authorities.

A directive is under preparation by the European Commission with the objective of ensuring that similar data protection rules prevail across Europe and thus that information can flow freely between member states. It is likely to be somewhat less liberal than the current UK practice. However, it has not yet been implemented.

Creativity

A direct marketing programme carries a series of messages, each created either to initiate the desired transaction or to move it forward. Some of the issues arising out of the need to *translate*, or preferably *adapt*, the messages from one language into many were discussed in the previous section. The impact can be heightened or at worst nullified by taking cultural idiosyncrasies into account or failing to do so. Good translators will pick up most of these, but the marketer should in any case be alert to the hazards.

Commercial habit

The inhabitants of any country are used to their own way of doing business and regard this as the way any normal person does business (although indeed the practice may vary from the south to the north of a country, let alone between countries). Differences can include:

1 *Shop opening hours.* German rigidity in this field contrasts quite strikingly with the laxity of control in the United Kingdom and perhaps offers interesting mail order possibilities.
2 *Distribution systems.* The well-established wholesaler/retailer pattern which is the conventional channel of retail distribution in the United Kingdom hardly exists in some other countries and is replaced by other methods. Similarly, socially protective legislation in a country such as Italy has resulted in the full-time, salaried salesman virtually ceasing to exist and being replaced by commission agents.
3 *Payment practices.* The methods by which bills are settled, and the speed, can have an impact on cash flow and profitability.
4 *Regulation.* Some countries have strict legislation prohibiting or restricting various forms of promotional offer or limiting the use of 'knocking copy'.

Attitudes and nuances:

1 *Symbolism.* Visual and verbal imagery can have dangerously different significances. For example, the little obelus symbol (†), which in English is commonly used as an alternative to the asterisk to indicate a footnote, denotes death in some Northern European societies.
2 *Formality.* The use of honorifics and qualifications, which is on the whole treated in a rather cavalier fashion by the Anglo-Saxons (apart from a certain British susceptibility to titles of nobility), is an important courtesy in many Continental European societies and perhaps even more so in parts of the rest of the world.
3 *Habit and routine.* Good creative planning will often make it possible to use the same illustrative material in all countries, merely changing the copy. Carelessness in this can have unwanted effects. What is meant to seem a comfortably familiar scene may turn out to look vaguely alien for such simple reasons as the designs of letterboxes and other street furniture.

In one sense, most of these cultural variants are only superficial and have little to do with the real motivations which underlie successful marketing. However, they are unconsciously important and can be sufficient to hamper the relationships that direct marketing is setting out to nurture. Part of the marketer's problem is that it is almost impossible for him to pick up these points without help, because in the nature of things they look fine to him.

Mechanisms

Media options

The strength of direct marketing as a communications tool is that it sets out to build a direct relationship between marketer and customer. It therefore depends upon the availability of media, which permit communication between individuals at known locations (actual or virtual); this availability varies very considerably between countries.

'Direct mail', which *is* the medium most commonly associated with direct marketing, is the use of the postal services to deliver information, advertising or other messages to a group audience. The group may be of any size from very small to huge, and the messages sent to it may be identical or varied to reflect known details about individual recipients. Direct mail is a close-focus medium, in that the marketer exercises control over who receives his message, and it offers many advantages:

- Precision.
- Personalization.
- Elasticity of scale and timing.
- Ease of subdivision into samples.
- Effectiveness at telling a complex story.
- Creative flexibility.
- Two-way operation (equally suitable for outgoing and incoming communications).
- Cost control and measurability of results.

Other close-focus media include telephone, fax, house-to-house distribution, courier services and on-line telecommunications networks such as the Internet. Even telex is still an important mode of communication in some overseas markets. No direct marketing programme can be carried out without the use at some stage of either direct mail or one of these other close-focus media to build the essential personal link between marketer and customer.

However, broad-focus media such as space advertising, TV, radio and billboard advertising frequently make part of a programme. A typical application is as the initial process of soliciting the prospect for the response, which will be nursed by other means into a dialogue.

Thus, while some programmes will be entirely direct mail based, many others will use combinations of mail with or without other close-focus media and broad-focus media.

Choice of media – basic considerations

In a domestic context, where a wide range of efficient media is available, the choice of which or which combination depends upon two different groups of considerations:

* The characteristics of the different media.
* The stage of the programme for which they are being chosen.

The characteristics of the different media available

CLOSE-FOCUS MEDIA.   These will be used for any phase of the campaign which requires communication to go between two identified points. The decision as to which medium is most appropriate will be governed by considerations such as:

* Degree of personalization required.
* Complexity of message.
* Creative demands.
* Timing requirements.
* Test and analytical requirements.
* Cost (total budget and acceptable cost per fulfilled response).

WIDE-FOCUS MEDIA.   Any phase of the programme which can be sustained by a widely disseminated message accessible to anybody who chances or chooses to look at it may be suitable for the wide-focus media. The most obvious and frequent applications are broadcasting the initial request for a response or supporting the close-focus media in this function. Choice of media is governed by:

* Target audience reached by the particular vehicle (a given journal, for example, may reach a mass audience or a tiny one, and the audience may be definable by geographical, class, professional, special interest or other characteristics).
* Complexity of message.
* Creative demands.
* Timing requirements.
* Test and analytical requirements.
* Cost (total budget and acceptable cost per fulfilled response).

The stage of the programme for which the media are being chosen

Every individual direct marketing campaign consists of three stages, corresponding to the first three points on the transaction cycle. The three stages are:

1   Offer stage ('Making the initial contact' in the transaction cycle).
2   Response stage ('Response by the other party to the initial contact').
3   Fulfilment ('Receiving and servicing the responses').

OFFER STAGE.   Delivering to the prospect a message inviting him to take a specified action in response to an offer of some kind.
   Considerations:

*   Ability to match audience to desired profile.
*   Need to modify message to suit individual recipient.
*   Size of audience.
*   Need for test segments.
*   Relative difficulty of explaining the offer.
*   Desired content of message (words, visual material, objects).
*   Type of response desired.
*   Total budget.
*   Cost per fulfilled response.

RESPONSE STAGE.   Giving the recipient of the initial offer a simple means of accepting it.
   Considerations:

*   Nature of product/service to be delivered.
*   Turn-round time required.
*   Need to record and interpret data for development of the transaction into a relationship.
*   Cost.

FULFILMENT STAGE.   Ensuring that what the customer has been promised he receives in a timely, efficient and courteous manner.
   Considerations:

*   Nature of product/service to be delivered.
*   Turn-round time required.
*   Cost.

Choice of media – the international dimension.

Account has to be taken of the foregoing points in all direct marketing planning. Adding an international dimension overlays several other considerations. The assumption cannot be made, in any country, that the media position is identical to that at home. On the contrary, there are always substantial differences that need to be thought through.

Media availability

In the United Kingdom, with a liberal communications regime, we are quite well off for media choice. In other countries, the range may be restricted or the quality of service may not be the same, even in some Western countries. Points that need to be checked include:

- Reliability of postal services.
- Access to mailing lists.
- Reliability of telephone services.

Media structure

There are profound traditional differences in the way media, particularly the wide-focus media, are structured in different countries.

- The relative importance of national and local press (in some countries, a national press scarcely exists).
- The importance of the magazine sector and different methods of distribution (subscription sales versus news-stands).
- The availability of commercial TV and the coverage of terrestrial and satellite channels.

Response services

Most direct marketing campaigns require a reliable response service at some point. Often this is a mail response element free to the respondent (e.g. a business reply card/envelope or a freepost address). It may be a telephone response capability free to the respondent (e.g. an 0800 number) or a premium telephone service for which the correspondent pays according to the time used. Such services may operate differently or may not exist at all in other countries.

At a multicountry level (i.e. where a good mail or telephone response service from a respondent in one country direct to a marketer in another is required), current services are in the main rudimentary.

Support services

A strong infrastructure of support services (print, packaging, lettershop, warehousing) is very helpful in implementing direct marketing campaigns. Such services may exist in only skeletal form.

There are two key issues that underlie not only media choice and planning but all international direct marketing. They are:

- Language and culture.
- Campaign organization.

These are discussed in other sections.

Mailing Lists

The role of mailing lists

Direct mail and direct marketing have never been synonymous, but the former is at the heart of the latter and without the former the latter would not exist.

Direct mail was the first form of direct marketing. There is a complete overlap between their two main functions:

- Their central aim is the creation of a direct relationship between marketer and customer.
- They are transaction based.

In achieving these two functions, both make extensive use of lists.

In fact, direct mail is a form of direct marketing which always begins with a list and which is often the simplest and most effective way of starting a campaign, particularly in a foreign marketplace. The question of selecting and scheduling mailing lists, therefore, assumes considerable importance. It is, in any event, often quite complicated and may be all the more so where several countries are concerned because of the great variations in availability of lists.

List schedules – basic considerations

In a country where the market in lists is well developed, which is true of most although not all of Western Europe, a plethora of lists exists. In putting together a list schedule for any or a number of these countries, several angles have to be considered.

Market segments

The list market is traditionally divided into two segments, consumer and business to business, reflecting a division which is often perceived in direct marketing itself. In practice, the dichotomy is not always so clear-cut. While at one extreme there are lists of businesses and at the other there are lists of individuals at their homes, in between there are many others which may be used equally to sell consumer products/services or those with business applications. Such mixed-function lists include:

- Business managers and executives (who can often be selected from lists of companies).

- Memberships of professional and trade associations.
- Institutional lists.
- People with academic or professional qualifications.
- Lists of politicians and officials (national or local).

Suppliers

The suppliers may be list owners, list brokers or list managers (or sometimes a combination of these).

LIST OWNERS.   For these, the list is often a by-product of another activity and is being made available to generate revenue as a means of offsetting cost. It is sometimes available direct from the owner, sometimes not – if the owner does not wish to be involved in the peripheral activity of promotion and management, a list may not be available directly, but only through brokers or managers.

Contrariwise, some owners will not make their lists available on conventional commercial terms (for rental or for sale), but only in exchange for other lists, which they wish to use in their schedules. These owners must usually be approached directly.

LIST BROKERS.   List brokers make their living by trading in list owner's lists, usually for a commission (which is customarily 20% or thereabouts in the United Kingdom, but may be different elsewhere) on the sale, paid by the list owner. The price is likely to be set by the owner on the advice of the broker and there is probably no price advantage in dealing direct, even if this is possible.

The entry cost to become a list broker is low, with the result that there are many of them and, as in any human activity, the quality varies. A good list broker knows the market or his specialist segment of it inside out and, given a proper brief and an open working relationship, can take from the marketer's shoulders much of the burden of creating the list schedule. This is particularly so for certain international schedules. However, if a schedule is particularly complex, the broker may ask a fee.

LIST MANAGERS.   The section on The Marketing Database will have given the reader an idea of the advantages of managing such a database properly and also of the complexity of doing so. A number of specialist list managers now exist, whose purpose is to maximize the advantages for their clients and minimize the complexity. In most cases, they also handle the sales and marketing of these lists, through list brokers as appropriate.

Types of list

Mailing lists fall into three broad categories, distinguished by how they were created. This may seem a mechanistic approach to classification, but in reality the way a list was put together tells the potential user quite a lot about it.

RESPONSE LISTS. Lists of individuals who have responded to given offers. This may be in either a consumer or a business-to-business context.

Response lists are very popular, particularly with mail order marketers, because:

- In general, people who have responded to an offer have a propensity to respond to other suitable offers, and the more frequently they have responded in the past, the greater the propensity.
- The character of the offers responded to gives an indication of the individual's interests.

On the other hand, these lists are by definition self-selected from a larger universe. They are not comprehensive and may exclude important groups of potential customers. They usually contain only limited supplementary information.

INTEREST LISTS. Lists of individuals or companies with a known interest in a particular subject. Many of these are lists of subscribers to specialist publications or members of associations or clubs.

These lists are also self-selecting and there is no reason to suppose that members have a natural propensity to respond to offers, although well-judged offers relating to strong interests are naturally often effective. They usually contain only limited supplementary information.

COMPILED LISTS. Lists of individuals or businesses put together by collating information from a variety of sources, often including the members themselves. Examples are lists of companies, compiled by specialist business information companies such as Dun & Bradstreet.

These lists often cover most of a given geographic or other universe. They usually contain quite a lot of demographic detail about individuals, but no insights into those individuals' preferences. However, the nature of the list may be that it is constructed of entities, which are commercially important.

There may be overlap between these list types, and indeed database marketing consists in part of profiting from the synergy between them.

Quality of list

Mailing list quality is measured in a number of different ways:

- Does the content of the list correspond to its description?
- Is the information up to date?
- Is the information about each record complete?
- Is the information error free?

The user should realize that mailing list quality is never and cannot ever be 100 per cent, because the universe which a list purports to cover, like anything involving human beings, changes more rapidly than any revision process can keep up with. Levels of quality will be lower in countries where postal and telephone services and direct marketing services generally are less advanced.

List size

The size of a given mailing list is a function of the absolute size of the total universe (i.e. how many people or companies of this type exist in this country) and the proportion of that universe that can be correctly identified, given that the target universe itself is usually a mix of criteria. Different mailing lists may correspond more or less precisely to the criteria mix, so that the largest mailing list is not necessarily the best for a particular programme.

The absolute size of the universe is often very difficult to determine, because of rapid demographic and economic change, and because official statistics tend to be out of date and broad-brush. It is usually sensible to shop around to find the optimum practical list size or list combination, i.e. a combination that gives a worthwhile potential market at an acceptable cost.

Testing subsamples of the lists available is generally recommended, provided that the *sample* is large enough to give a meaningful reading and the *full* list, when rolled out, is large enough to support its share of the whole programme.

Terms

Mailing lists are normally supplied on a rental basis, i.e. the list owner retains his ownership. Rental is usually limited to one-time use only, but it may be for multiple use, which will probably be reflected in the price.

Whether or not the list is rented for one-time use or for multiple use, 'merge/purge' is usually permitted. This is the process of matching against each other lists, which are going to be used in the same mailing, in order to eliminate duplicates. This is very important not only from a cost point of view (postage and print runs, etc.), but also so as to avoid customer annoyance at receiving multiple copies of the same message. No list arrangement should be accepted which does not permit this if there is a likelihood of more than one list being used for the same programme, since duplication is almost certain to occur.

Whether for one-time or many-time use, rented lists cannot normally be legally used to seed marketers' own new databases. Responses to any programme are normally the property of the marketer and, therefore, generally can be so used. Some lists, notably compiled lists, are sold for the purpose of feeding a database; make sure that the contract includes an adequate commitment by the supplier to provide updates.

The effect of technology

Technology, inexorably, changes everything. Obviously, the introduction of computerization, followed by the spread of PCs, made possible huge advances in the management and use of mailing lists and then marketing databases.

Market segments	Consumer	Business-to-business	Mixed-function	
Suppliers	List owners	List brokers	List managers	
Types of list	Response lists	Interest lists	Compiled lists	
Quality of lists	Content	Up-to-date	Complete	Error-free
List sizes	Universe size	Percentage of universe	Optimum size	Sample/roll-out
Terms	One-time rental	Multi-use rental	Merge/purge	Sale with updates
Technology	On-line	CD-ROM		

Figure 12.5   List selection checklist.

On-line and CD-ROM technologies are not only taking this process further (see figure 12.5). They are making it harder for the list supplier to control what is done with the information he purveys, and easier for the user to manage and control his own list applications. The distinction between rental and sale of lists is in practice likely to become increasingly blurred.

The multinational jigsaw

Building a list schedule including several countries is even more like doing a jigsaw puzzle, with several additional possible arrangements.

Local or international

One choice to be made is whether to achieve the desired coverage using 'international' lists, quite a few of which are available from specialist list brokers, or to put together a tailor-made selection from local suppliers.

INTERNATIONAL LISTS.   This is the easy option. Lists will cover whole regions or groups of countries, usually with addresses in a standardized form and with consistent selection capabilities. The lists may be weighted towards English speakers, particularly if they are lists of individuals. Many compiled business lists do not have such a bias.

While the coverage is geographically extensive, it is likely to cover only a small part of the total universe in each country.

The price will probably be consistent across countries.

LOCAL LISTS.   It is much harder work building a portfolio of local lists. Coverage within each country will generally be better than from an international list. However, in some countries, it may be extremely difficult to obtain satisfactory or even any coverage. Mardev, one of the leading international list brokers, has remarked that while there are 10 000 or more lists available in the United States, there are only four in Greece.

There may be large variations in price (lists in Denmark, for instance, typically cost four or five times more than similar lists in Belgium) and there certainly will be linguistic and format variations. One commonplace pitfall is that a list may be supplied in a format suitable for domestic mailing, i.e. without the country name being specified, which makes it unusable for mailing from another country.

It may be difficult to establish consistent selection criteria across different countries. On the other hand, lists may have selection options that are important locally (e.g. language preference in Belgium).

Sources of supply

Where the choice is to go for international lists, the best source will usually be a specialist broker. It may well be worth also considering such specialist help if the decision is taken to build the programme from local supply sources. By no means all countries have well-developed list broking services and, as has been pointed out, there are many details that it is easy to get wrong without a good deal of experience.

Some companies which compile business or specialist lists have local operations in a number of countries and can supply what are effectively composite compilations.

Profiling

The technique of profiling consists essentially of matching a list of customers against a known statistical universe, analysing its demographic structure and selecting other lists, which correspond to that structure. The technique is well developed within the United Kingdom as far as the consumer marketplace is concerned and is becoming so for business to business. It is also possible in several other countries individually and for some areas, such as much of Europe, may also be possible regionally. It is also worth testing whether the demographic structure of the home customer list is an effective starting-point for a new geographical market.

Practical hazards

- Putting together a list portfolio overseas takes *much* longer than doing so domestically, and every extra country extends the time.
- The process is rich with opportunities for linguistic confusion. Local list suppliers may have little English and may be reluctant to acknowledge how slight it is. Try to have everything very simply expressed in writing.

- Some kinds of detailed information that are readily available at home may simply not exist in a market where list sales are underdeveloped.

Putting it Together

The challenge

Putting together any direct marketing programme is challenging because of the diversity of the elements that go to make it up and the need for careful attention to detail. Operating multinationally adds further intensity to the challenge because, to recapitulate points that have already been made:

- The number of marketplaces being addressed is probably larger.
- The variables are certainly increased.
- These additional levels of complexity usually have to be managed by an individual or a team who are unfamiliar with much of the background and who are not fluent in the necessary languages.

Table 12.3, repeated from the beginning of this chapter and completed, illustrates this.

In the final section, we will look at help that is available and lastly review some of the strategies that can be used to cope.

Willing helpers

There are two broad sources of help: professional bodies and service suppliers.

Professional bodies

Within the United Kingdom, the recognized professional association is:

Table 12.3 The actual relationship between topics and concerns

	Market stage	Business customs	Regulation	Language	Culture
Applications		☐			
Transaction cycle					
Language				☐	☐
Marketing database	☐		☐	☐	☐
Creativity		☐	☐	☐	☐
Mechanisms	☐	☐	☐	☐	☐
Mailing lists	☐	☐	☐	☐	☐
Putting it together	☐	☐	☐	☐	☐

The Direct Marketing Association
Haymarket House
1 Oxendon Street
London SW1
Tel: 0171-321 2525

The association will give advice and has a library, and most reputable suppliers of direct marketing services are members.

The other major British professional organization is:

The Institute of Direct Marketing Ltd
1 Park Road
Teddington
Middlesex TW11 0AR
Tel: 0181-977 5705

This body's primary purpose is to provide education and training in all aspects of direct marketing, including international.

Other professional associations, such as the Association of Mail Order Publishers, will also be able to help within their specialist fields.

The principal international organization is:

European Direct Marketing Association
36 rue du Gouvernement Provisoire
B-1000 Brussels
Belgium
Tel: 00-32-2-217 6309

Again, this is a most helpful body and includes many reputable suppliers of services throughout Europe and beyond amongst its members.

Service suppliers

A number of suppliers either specialize in providing international direct marketing services or provide these as an addition to their domestic capabilities.

Royal Mail International has a particular focus on international mailing and delivery. They provide a range of specialist services and also publish an excellent manual: *Marketing Without Frontiers.*

The key areas where it may be worth seeking the services of commercial specialists are:

- List broking and management.
- Creative, copy and design.

- Telephone services.
- Lettershop (the physical side of organizing mailing).

Specialist direct marketing agencies exist which will handle the whole multinational campaign. Many of these are well established with high reputations and great expertise. It is important to check the extent to which claimed international facilities are confirmed by the actual structure and by client references.

Organizational structure

The actual organizational structure adopted will depend in part upon the marketer's existing organization. If this is currently purely United Kingdom based, the options may be more limited in practice than if there is an overseas network which can be called upon.

In any case, there are two main strategies possible, with all sorts of gradations between them: centralization and decentralization.

Centralization

In its pure form, this consists of managing the entire programme from one central location, probably within the United Kingdom. Local services (such as list brokers) may be used, but all decisions – buying, planning, creative and so on – are taken at the centre. Some extremely successful programmes, covering large numbers of countries, are run in this way.

The advantages of centralization include:

- Easier cost control.
- Maintenance of production standards.
- Creative consistency.
- Control of timing.
- Easier collection and management of data.

Some of the disadvantages are:

- Lack of responsiveness to local conditions.
  (a) Difficulty of obtaining local input.
  (b) Possible local resentment.
- Difficulty in establishing acceptable response mechanisms.
- Problems of organization resulting particularly from communications difficulties.

Centralization may be the only practicable way of starting to operate an international direct marketing programme, simply because in the first instance the local infrastructure may not exist. If this is the position, the manager and team must be ready to spend a lot of effort and travel time in coming to grips with the multiplicity of facets which make up local conditions.

Centralization may not always be the most effective approach if the underlying strategic objective is to develop a single business with no local variations across a group of countries or a region.

Decentralization

Decentralization is only possible to a substantial extent where a local infrastructure exists or is created. In its most literal form, it involves delegating planning and implementation of the campaigns to the local management, with the central role being limited to strategic guidance and some coordination.

Its advantages and disadvantages are the mirror image of centralization. In summary, local responsiveness and the suitability of programmes to local needs will be strong, but:

- Costs will be harder to identify and control.
- Information will be fragmented and inaccessible.
- Creative coherence and brand consistency will be lost.

These things may not matter if the primary strategic interest is strong local activity or, indeed, if the nature of the product/service range is such that it differs considerably according to local circumstances.

In between

In practice, many companies operate a hybrid structure, seeking a balance between centralization and decentralization. Properly managed, this can be very effective and can to a considerable extent accentuate the positives and eliminate the negatives of the two extremes.

Making this work requires adherence to three rules of behaviour:

1 Involvement of all the relevant local and central managers from the beginning of the programme and throughout. In this context, 'involvement' means much more than just informing them. It means that the entire group be a party to any decisions taken and, indeed, that the decisions are often initiated locally rather than centrally. This process requires that people who are already overworked must make yet more time available. Consequently,
2 A special effort on communication and motivation, so that all participants can 'see and feel' the results of their working together and the importance of these results.
3 Recognition that there are different levels of resource and expertise in every part of the structure, so that at times some will need more help and support than others will.

. . . and it *is* all worthwhile.

Direct marketing is one of the most rewarding of all business disciplines, because it demands innovation and because it encompasses all modes of thought from the highly conceptual to the most tiresomely pernickety.

International direct marketing is yet more fun. There is an even greater need to be continually learning and what is learnt often adds a spice of the exotic to the potentially mundane. It may seem daunting, but it is an adventure to be accepted with gusto.

13 Advertising Established Brands: An International Dimension

ANDREW EHRENBERG, JOHN SCRIVEN
AND NEIL BARNARD

Introduction

This chapter examines two contrasting theories of how advertising works: the 'strong' and the 'weak'. We favour the latter, based on the evidence of how consumers behave, and what they say about brands.

Most writers on advertising stress that little is known about how it works and that every case is unique. They talk in terms of growth, persuasion and brand building as the aims. The following quote from *The Economist* (June, 1996) is typical: 'Measuring the effectiveness of advertising is much harder than it may seem. To know whether an advertisement is working, you need first to be clear about what it is meant to do. Consumer-goods manufacturers take a simple view: that advertising is about creating and then nurturing brands. If that is what matters, the first thing to look at is sales.'

In the first part of the chapter, we argue that this view of advertising as a strong force – that it is persuasive, aimed at brand building and increased sales – is commonly held but unachievable.

We then present a very contrasting picture of advertising, as mainly for brand maintenance, to defend market share. This sees advertising as a weak force (but effective), reinforcing and at times 'nudging' the number of consumers to whom the brand is salient in the longer term. That is in line with the very extensive evidence on consumers' choice behaviour and attitudes, and with how brands perform, and also with what advertisements themselves are like. This second picture provides a very different basis for planning, evaluating and justifying advertising.

The detailed evidence is set out in the reports from the authors' two-year study on 'Justifying Our Advertising Budgets' (JOAB Reports 1–8) and earlier references given there.

This is a general account of advertising. We conclude with some comments on how this view of advertising impacts on some of the issues raised by others in international advertising practice.

How Advertising is Said to Work

Why spend billions?

Most people agree that a primary job of advertising is to make people aware of the existence of products or brands. (The derivation is from the French *avertir*: to notify.) 'Without advertising, we should not know the range of products available in any field, to buy or not, as we choose' (David Shelley Wright, Advertising).

But is this enough to justify all advertising? What happens when consumers already know about brands and may even have experience of them? Much of the advertising that takes place (well over 50%) is for brands that are already well established (e.g. Coca-Cola, Pepsi, Procter & Gamble and Unilever products, Levis, Ford, Microsoft, etc.).

Taking many advertising people at their word, for the advertising of an established brand to 'work' always means producing something extra: more sales, added values, differentiation, brand building, repositioning, premium pricing and so on. Advertising pre-tests and *post hoc* tracking studies have always to be positive, and sales more profitable than last year. Being accountable would mean adding values and doing better.

This may seem businesslike: how can marketing plans ask for millions and only promise 'no change'? But from our academic vantage point this is sheer make-believe. With established brands in mature markets everyone cannot always win (i.e. sell more). By the self-inflicted goal of 'growth for all', most advertising and also most marketing plans must fail. (It would be like adults eating only in order to grow.) Yet if always chasing the rainbow of extra sales is not on, why do we need advertising and marketing at all?

The answer is, of course, competition. If our competitors market aggressively and we do not, they would slowly gain (other things being equal). Hence, advertising has to be mainly for brand maintenance, an insurance to defend our existing level of sales. Only on occasion will we either gain (as a bonus) or lose (if others gain). How and why this works through reinforcement and nudging, and therefore justifies advertising budgets, is outlined in the second part of this chapter. Here, we first examine the more traditional views, starting with persuasion and going on to differentiation, possible short- and long-term effects, and advertising content.

Persuasion

Most writing on advertising says or implies that advertising works through *persuasion*. Many people (protagonists and critics alike) believe that advertising makes people buy things.

But there is no evidence for that. Few ads directly say or imply 'Buy me'. Consumers show remarkably few signs of being buffeted about in any big way by what the advertising does. A campaign of 30-second commercials is unlikely to persuade people to do something they so far have not wanted or felt able to do, or at least been indifferent to. (Similarly, parents, teachers, the clergy, or any of us often tell other people what to do, but usually they go on as before.)

What is remarkable is that market shares tend to be steady. There is overwhelming evidence in over fifty product categories that consumers' purchase propensities are mostly habitual, steady and predictable, even though individual purchasing records tend to look irregular from week to week (see Appendix). Furthermore, no acceptable rationale or mechanism for such persuasive effects has been given (what would the world look like if most people responded to the last ad seen, say?) This does not mean that advertising does not work, but only that it does not work by persuasion, in the way people think.

The grand-daddy of 'persuasion' models has been AIDA (e.g. see Belch and Belch, 1995), which at first sight may seem to make sense: AIDA says that for each consumer there has first to be *A*wareness, then *I*nterest, then *D*esire, then *A*ction (the purchase). But this 'conversion' view has increasingly been criticized: for instance, no evidence has ever been put forward that potential customers feel strong 'desire' (or 'conviction' even, in some versions of the model) before they first buy the brand (i.e. 'action'). What is more there is nothing in the model – just a blank – *after* that first purchase (no suggestion of post-purchase reinforcement). Yet most advertising for an established brand is seen after it has already been bought at least once. Do we assume that consumers have to be persuaded anew for every purchase, or that they become loyal to this brand until persuaded in a different direction?

Such 'hierarchy-of-effects' persuasion models do not take account of the fact that ads are mostly seen by experienced consumers. AIDA treats each purchase as a sales development exercise of first attracting a cold prospect, then drawing them in, and finally 'closing the sale' (indeed, the model was originally put forward as a sales training model; Strong, 1925). There is no hint in AIDA that some kind of loyalty or relationships might at any stage have developed, whether as a convenient habit/sheer inertia, 'liking after use' or some deeper commitment. Nor does AIDA mention the competition.

Other persuasion views, of course, do very much include competition. A commonly stated advertising goal is to persuade consumers that your brand is best and hence to make them highly *loyal* to it. But the facts show instead that buyers of competitive brands regard them as rather similar and show much the same degree of loyalty (by *any* loyalty measure, as rehearsed in JOAB Reports 1 and 7 and earlier references there). Near-100 per cent-loyal (or 'convinced') customers are rare and equally so for all brands, they are not of special sales importance, are mainly light buyers with few chances of being unfaithful, and occur 'by chance' without any assumption of exclusive commitments (Rosencrantz' run of 'Heads' was *not* due to double-headed pennies).

Differentiation

In a fast-moving world where innovation is perpetually sought, but any product improvement is rapidly copied, advertising is often talked of as the means to achieve the much-desired goal of sustainable competitive advantage through brand differentiation. But is that how it works?

In fact, we constantly read that brands are becoming more and more alike ('mere commodities' even). And advertisers and agencies are often dubbed dull and unimaginative because their advertisements also do not try to say anything different about their offerings.

It is as if product differentiation were very difficult. Yet, in practice, the market supports an enormous variety of functional differences (different flavours; shampoos for dry and oily hair; large and small pack sizes; five-, four-, three- and two-door cars; airbags; business-class travel; variable- and fixed-interest loans; PCs with ever bigger memories; or whatever). But competitive brands are alike in having nearly all of these. Most product differentiation occurs *within* competitive brands (different variants and line extensions), not between them.

There are new-new innovations at times (people-carriers, shampoos for *normal* hair, guaranteed-money-back investments, etc.). But if any of these are sufficiently sales effective, other brands will soon offer them too. Staying competitive means matching your rivals on all the important dimensions. (If not, you have decided to be a niche brand and *small*.) Innovators may gain an early mover advantage and sometimes can hang on to some of that extra market share. But the evidence shows that success here cannot be relied upon.

In some product categories, e.g. cereals, confectionery and holiday destinations, every advertised brand has long been a physically differentiated variety. But even this is eroding (e.g. with Kellogg's Corn Flakes now facing look-alike *private labels* and other me-toos; and with McDonald's, Espresso and pools in every resort). Much advertising is also deliberately focusing more on the umbrella/mega-brands or housenames which comprise highly differentiated items or models (as Kellogg's and Fords do) or even cover different product categories (Sony, Nestlé, Heinz and, more especially, the retail chains, Sears, Wal-Mart, Sainsbury, Marks & Spencer, etc., in general, and their own private label brands in particular; even P&G is now advertising as 'Procter & Gamble' in Japan where it does not have its US-style historical marketing investments of literally billions into individual brands like Tide and Ivory).

Brands always differ in various 'minor' ways, as ingeniously created by the product development people (a nuance of taste, texture or colour in a soup say; the ink flow and the opaque or see-through outers of ball-points; a different bottle top; the car door handles; etc.). When brands are otherwise functionally more or less substitutable, such 'minor' differences may influence brand choice for some consumers (some buy it because of X, some despite X, and some did not notice X at all). They are 'minor' differences because (a) they are overridden by 'major' product differences (such as tomato versus chicken noodle soup, or two-versus four-door cars); (b) they are not slavishly copied by a fearful competition;

(c) they seem to be seldom emphasized or even mentioned in the marketing plan; (d) crucially for us here, most of them never feature either explicitly or implicitly in the advertisements (even in press ads with a lot of small print). In practice, most advertising is created to make the brand name salient, but not the brand's specific attributes, especially not its 'minor' ones.

Given the common lack of overall differentiation between brand A (and its various variants) and brand B (and its similar variants), there is much advertising talk of 'emotional' differentiation and brand positioning. But this does not seem to be at all effective. Consumers' beliefs about established brands and products are notoriously difficult to change (apart from the effects of overall awareness and salience). In practice, the evidence is that consumers' beliefs are *not* a major source of differentiation between similar brands – much the same percentage of users of A say it 'tastes nice', say, as do users of B (see JOAB Reports 1 and 7, and the Appendix). Yet in what many people say about advertising, they still pursue the romantic dream of highly differentiating and 'persuasive' advertising messages, supposedly aimed to give consumers a reason for choosing brand A rather than B.

> Researchers long have observed that attribute-perception shifts are easy to observe while tracking the introduction of a new brand, and devilishly difficult to observe with regard to established brands.
>
> It is ironic to note that repeat exposure to and total recall of such research findings has done little to change researchers' determination to stick with their old perception of the advertising process. (Moran, 1990)

Short and longer term effects

Traditional persuasion-orientated advertising research concentrates on short-term measures: soon-after awareness and recall (of the ad and/or of the brand); persuasion shifts; triggering the next purchase; and weekly or even instant scanner-based purchasing records.

Yet apart from the up-and-down blips of price promotions, the reported short-term sales effects of marketing action are relatively rare and seldom large, and then mostly cases of momentarily refreshed brand awareness. Aggregate sales levels tend to stay remarkably steady.

The short-term sales returns on advertising, as quite widely stated and apparently never questioned, are less than 20 per cent (20 per cent, not *120 per cent*). No one invests $1 million to get back a $200 000 pay-back year after year.

This short-term failure of advertising to shift sales on a large scale can hardly be because consumers are locked into the unique advantages of their brand, since brands tend to be so much alike – 'mere commodities'. Instead, multibrand or split-loyalty repertoires are dominant (as rehearsed in JOAB 1), and for durable goods people have equivalent consideration sets of the brands they *might* buy. Coffee drinkers, say, *could* therefore be readily persuaded by an ad to buy your brand of coffee more and their other repertoire brands less, without their having to drink more coffee. But in practice such 'see ad ∩ buy now' effects hardly ever happen.

There is a good reason. Most individual customers of a brand of frequently bought goods buy that brand very infrequently. (Pareto's old '80:20' rule, reflecting the vast predominance of light or infrequent buyers, has been backed up by all the world's consumer-panel data ever since. And the point that durables are infrequently bought hardly needs making.) Many months or more elapse between most customers' exposure to an ad campaign and their actually buying the brand, usually with intervening purchases of competitive brands, and exposure to *their* advertising and retail displays, etc. Hence, the advertising effects on a brand's actual purchasing have mostly to be long term.

The traditional picture of any direct longer term persuasion effects on sales is, however, bleak. All writers stress that the long term is difficult to measure. In part, this is because of the varying other marketing-mix interventions (such as competitive product improvement, or a new sales director) so that longer term sales movements are not consistently in line with advertising spend. But far more important is that a brand's longer term sales seldom increase anyway: 'Not everyone can always win'.

Nor is there any sort of consensus in the literature on how and why a persuasive longer term sales increase would or should happen, or how this would relate to the *content* of the advertisements (as is discussed much more positively in the second part of this chapter).

> It is difficult to accept a 'time-bomb' effect in which an advertisement now – barely noticed [or] probably forgotten within a very short time – can nevertheless explode 18 months or three years from now so as to induce a sale. (Bloom, 1976)

The discussion so far: what people say and what they do

What people say about advertising mostly seems very logical: the goal is growth. Advertising therefore has to persuade people to buy your brand. It does so by differentiating the brand and bringing out reasons or values for choosing it. This sees advertising as a strong force even in mature markets, with the emphasis on the short term: a differentiating message which leads to persuasion shifts.

In dramatic contrast, there is what actually happens. This is nothing like what is supposed to happen. In mature markets, most advertised brands do not and cannot all grow all the time. In any case, most consumers are already rather experienced with the product (they have used it for years) and a few sales messages cannot 'persuade' them that this brand is now different, or that they should now buy it. In line with that, few ads explicitly seek to persuade by saying 'Buy me now', or strongly imply it. They seldom give any specific or explicit reasons or motivations why one should buy the brand, or why it should afterwards seem like a good thing to have done. Few ads even mention how brand A differs. They rarely seek to communicate attributes or moods, which could not, in principle, also have been adopted by brands B, C or D. The brand has to be distinctive (Pepsi is not Coca-Cola), but not otherwise differ very much, if at all.

In the second part of this chapter, we will now argue that:

- Brands differ greatly in how many people find them salient (and hence in their existing market shares), but *not* in how salient their customers find them.
- Hence the sheer number of consumers to whom brand A is salient is what A's advertising should and usually does aim to reinforce and nudge.
- Despite what people say about advertising, the traditional impactful twopence-coloured publicity which merely says 'I'm a good example of the product category' or 'Here I am' has therefore long been the right thing to do, and still is.

This makes it possible to formulate a positive view of how advertising works which is in line not with what many advertising people say, but with the 'Here I am' advertisements which advertising people do in fact produce.

An Alternative View: Advertising as Weak but Effective

We now put forward an alternative view of how advertising works for established brands. This seems to us coherent, simple and in line with what is known. There are four main aspects: consumers, brands, the ads themselves and the advertising mechanism. In brief:

- *Consumers* are polygamous, with habitual split-loyalty brand repertoires.
- *Brands* differ greatly in their penetrations (or to how many people they are salient), but hardly very much in how their customers see them or in how loyal they are to them.
- Actual *ads* mostly just say 'Here I am' or 'I'm a good example of the product'.
- *The advertising mechanism* is mainly to maintain or occasionally nudge the salience of the brand, by refreshing or adding long-term memory traces and/or associations for the brand.

This calls for a 'weak' view of advertising (which accounts for the fact that there can be so much of it). It differs from the more traditional 'strong' growth/persuasion/differentiation scenario outlined previously. So instead of trying to persuade consumers to do something different and switch to brand A, advertising is expected mostly to reinforce or perhaps nudge their existing propensity to buy brand A, usually when the brand is already part of their existing brand repertoire. Advertisements do not seek to do this by greatly differentiating the brand's image or the like, but simply by influencing the number of people to whom the brand is distinct and salient. It works mainly through linking short-term exposure to the ads to consumers' longer term remembrance of the brand.

Starting with the consumer

The context for advertising is the consumer. The picture is of consumers who generally also buy or use other brands – even for durables, if we take a long enough view. Your customers are mostly other brands' customers who occasionally also buy your brands.

Brand choice is, however, not so much promiscuous as polygamous, with habitual split loyalties to several steady partners. One or two of these will be consumed more often than the others. And occasionally one will try a new brand, or drop an old relationship.

Brand choice from purchase to purchase often appears irregular and may reflect varying marketing inputs and needs of the moment. But all these tend themselves to recur and hence to be more or less regular over time. Consumers are therefore not always re-evaluating their current brand and then switching to another. The overwhelming evidence in more than fifty product categories is of a predominant tendency to restrict oneself to a repertoire of a few habitual brands, presumably because that is convenient yet provides for some variety or choice.

We know of no evidence that there is any deep 'commitment' to such repertoire brands. (A fashionable analogy is to say that brands are *friends*, but *acquaintances* might be better.) Instead, consumers' attitudes just seem to come into line with their buying behaviour ('I use it therefore I like it'; as discussed in JOAB Report 7). The results of attitudinal surveys and tracking studies are largely explained by the fact that consumers are highly experienced. Hence, they know that brands mainly have the attributes of the product category or sub-category, with only occasional divergences (e.g. that it is All Bran which is 'Good for you'), plus minor differences which are however seldom if ever featured in their advertising.

The evidence is that users of brand A generally feel much the same about A as users of brand P say feel about P ('tastes nice', 'good value for money', etc., as summarized in Table 13.2 in the Appendix). Any systematic change in our choice behaviour is likely to be followed by a change in emotional allegiance, rather than preceded by it.

Opportunities and threats

Although consumers generally tend to go on buying much the same brands as before, these brand-choice habits *can* change.

Changing an entrenched habit *radically* is difficult (e.g. taking coffee black rather than with milk, or regularly drinking twice as much as before, or alternatively giving it up altogether). But merely switching from one brand to another is much easier – substituting one habit for a similar habit. Occasionally, adding a further brand Y to one's repertoire need not be a big deal, or substituting Y for X, or buying one of the usual brands a bit less (or more) often. And there are pervasive stimuli to do so – the competitors' remarkable retail availability, plus their in-store displays, advertising, pack designs, (minor) product variations, after-sales service, word of mouth, a neighbour using a different brand and not falling down dead, media mentions, on-pack promotions, price cuts, coupons, price differences more generally, the brands just being 'active', and so on.

Indeed, a degree of consistent erosion of repeat-buying loyalty does occur over time even though consumers generally have steady purchasing propensities (e.g. from one quarter to the next repeat might be the normal predicted 48 per cent, but only 42 per cent or so to a quarter of a year later; see JOAB Report 1). There is, therefore, a *somewhat* leaky bucket, which needs to be topped up even in an otherwise steady market. This occurs across the board – for different product categories, for large and small brands, for heavy and light buyers, etc.

It is also found that individual consumers' *attitudes* are not all very deeply held; for example, on average only some 50 per cent of those giving a positive free-choice response for a brand ('tastes nice' or 'value for money', etc.) say so again about the brand a month or a year later (as in the repeat surveys of the same informants referred to in JOAB Report 7).

All this provides opportunities for your brand to gain share. But it also provides equivalent threats from your competitors, of whom there are more and who in total are bigger. The name of the game has, therefore, to be brand maintenance. Highly active brand support is needed to defend what you have: 'Running hard to stand still'. It is common to talk of 'tired brands', as if it was their fault. But they are probably just undernourished. Any brand that manages to keep its market share steady and still profitable by being active enough is doing very well. Advertising is one tool for doing so.

Some brands are much bigger than others

Competitive brands usually have very different market shares even though the brands are mostly rather similar. This is because they differ greatly in the number of people for whom the brands are salient, rather than in precisely how salient each is to its customers. If 10 million people regard brand A 'well enough' and only 1 million brand B, then about 10 times more people will buy A.

Salience

Marketers are often castigated for not differentiating their brands. Paradoxically, the contrasting view here is that the experienced consumer knows that similar brands are similar (coffee is largely coffee, and brands are brands). Nonetheless, one such brand is salient to *far* more people and sells far more than another (e.g. Maxwell House versus Kenco).

The *salience* of a brand goes beyond any single awareness or recall measure. It is the common factor when all possible brand-performance measures tend to go together, being positive or high for one consumer, but not for another: awareness (by any definition); being or not being in one's consideration set or in one's actual purchasing repertoire (for fast-moving goods); having a significant purchase propensity; *using* the brand; expressing an intention to buy if asked; being willing to pay the price; etc. The brand has to have brand assurance, elicit positive attitudinal beliefs and liking for that consumer, be mentioned more in focus groups, be chosen in 'named' product tests or as the brand I would buy if my usual brand was unavailable, and so on.

'Salience' is the common factor if the different measures tend to correlate, scoring 'yes' for certain consumers and 'no' for the others. (In contrast, Ferrari scores very high on awareness with most people, but *not* on value for money – it is not all-round salient for most.) The numbers to whom a brand is salient would then also tend to correlate with just about everything in the marketing mix that contributes towards purchasing and market share, e.g. the brand's degree of retail distribution, shelf space, being in stock, display, promotions, advertising, media mentions, word of mouth, etc.

To be salient to its customers, the brand has to be distinctive (its name and packaging). But the brand does not have to appear better than all the others (which would be difficult to achieve), let alone 'best'. It only has to be regarded well enough to continue to be in their consideration sets and in effect to continue to be bought by *other* brands' customers (i.e. survival of the fit enough, rather than of the fittest).

This fits in with advertising being for brand maintenance (an insurance or the cost of staying in longer term business). It also fits in with competitive brands striving to be similar through copying success, rather than aiming to be different. The goal is not so much how well your brand is regarded, but how many consumers regard your brand well. The brand is then more likely to be chosen when a relevant product category purchase is to be made, because the number to whom it is salient has been maintained (the brand is still familiar, in one's reper-toire, liked and available, etc.). At times, the advertising and other marketing-mix factors may even work together sufficiently well so that the number of consumers to whom the brand is salient is increased or 'nudged' (a sales bonus).

This is in line with the universal evidence that competitive brands of the same size hardly differ in their major brand performance or loyalty measures, however defined (e.g. how often their customers buy them; how many light or heavier buyers the brands have and how few 100 per cent-loyal buyers; their low shares of category requirements – typically only say three purchases out of ten; or how their customers 'like' them, etc., as illustrated in the Appendix). These loyalty measures are theoretically so predictable that there is nothing much that market-ing or advertising can do to vary them.

This is a dilemma, which many marketing people find difficult to face up to. But all is not lost. Despite these many predictable constraints in the market place on the degree of loyalty a brand has, the sheer numbers to whom the brands are salient and who in fact buy them do differ greatly from brand to brand. By going with the market and aiming to maintain or nudge these numbers, advertising and marketing *can* therefore affect a brand's sales and market share.

Getting started: a trial purchase

As we have just noted, brands differ greatly in how many people buy them, and hence for how many each brand is 'salient'. That is for established brands and experienced consumers. But how did some brands get big? And how do people get to develop their steady habitual purchase propensities in the first place – whether for a new brand, or for one that is new for that consumer?

As discussed in JOAB Report 6, the process can be captured by the box-and-arrow type model A → T → R & N. Here, A (increasing *Awareness*) and then *T* (a possible *T*rial purchase) apply primarily to the previously virtually unknown brand; *R* (*R*einforcement) and *N* (*N*udging) apply to the brand when it is already being used. Each of the four stages of this ATR&N process is potentially affected by advertising (see exhibit 13.1).

EXHIBIT 13.1   A → T → R & N

- *Awareness*: some initial awareness of a new brand X and perhaps some interest.
- *Trial*: a possible and uncertain trial purchase of X ('I might try that', or 'I might try it again').
- *Reinforcement*: use of X and reassurance may lead to a steady propensity to buy it and to liking.
- *Nudging*: existing propensities to buy X may at times be enhanced (or decreased – i.e. *competitors'* nudging).

Consumers usually first come to be *aware* of a new brand (through advertising, other people mentioning or using the brand, sampling, seeing it in a store, etc., and all these things interacting positively).

They may then become interested. But they are already experienced with the category and know that the new brand will be broadly like the brands they already know (unless there are enormous claims that this one is different, and other people are really talking about it).

Even for a rarely bought (but usually fairly frequently used) item such as a pair of pliers, consumers can fairly quickly and adequately make themselves aware of a set of possible brands that are new to them (essentially without much or any media advertising, e.g. from inspection in a store or by asking; or from a 'starred' hotel list for a room in a strange town).

They may then pick a brand as apparently adequate ('That one might do. I think I've actually heard of it. I'll try it.'). The special emphasis in ATR&N is on the first purchase or so of a brand being an uncertain *trial* purchase (being nudged by the brand's retail availability, in-store displays, *advertising*, free sampling, word of mouth, a neighbour using it, media mentions perhaps, etc., and all these things still interacting). This is the situation – the choice usually being narrowed down to some fairly close substitutes and few big decisions still having to be made – where having publicized your brand can do it proud and give some brand assurance ('I think I've heard of that').

If the new purchase seems good enough when it is actually *used*, satisfaction may lead to a further purchase ('Maybe I'll try that again'). And perhaps then to an ongoing tendency to buy it at times – a habit. This would be as an addition to or as a replacement of an existing brand in the repertoire, whether for a somewhat different end use or end user, or just for some variety. Since most brands are fairly similar, one could try, and then adopt, more and more. But in practice, most people slim their choices down to a small repertoire of habitually bought ones, for convenience.

Advertising can refresh consumers' awareness of the brand and keep it salient, and also encourage the retailer, with all the ensuing synergies. This can then reinforce the repeat-buying habit and keep it going. (Even habits decay without encouragement, at least if there are attractive and near identical and available/ publicized alternatives). The same form of advertising can, therefore, sometimes lead some consumers to try a brand when it is new, to reassure and reinforce them afterwards, or perhaps to nudge them to buy a customary brand a bit more often.

For a very infrequently bought product (e.g. a durable), there is of course no short-term repeat buying to develop. But any satisfactory usage experience can still benefit from reassurance through post-purchase advertising ('It's an OK brand to have bought'), since nothing is perfect and there are a lot of good competitors around. And if it's another brand in one's consideration set, it also merits being reinforced or nudged ('Maybe we should have bought *that* one'). The more assured or brand aware the customer remains, the more salient the brand will be next time round, and the better the consumer will be as a word-of-mouth ambassador in the meantime.

What ads say: 'Here I am'

Remarkably, in terms of the customary emphasis on differentiation, the actual advertisements one sees or hears are rarely about differentiation at all. They seldom feature added values or brand images that derive from anything particular to the brand. Despite what is so often said, few ads seek to convey how brand A differs from brand B in any very explicit way.

Instead, most advertisements for established brands aim at attention getting and impactful distinctive ways of saying 'Here I am' (e.g. 'Coke is it') or 'I'm a good/outstanding example of the product' ('Domestos kills all known germs – DEAD'), or the permitted hyperbole 'None better' ('Nothing acts faster than Anadin'). This provides long-term publicity for the brand.

For an advertisement to become potentially effective, it has first of all to be noted ('awareness'). This may initially be just out of the corner of one's eye, and then, or next time perhaps, deliberately looking at it ('What was that ad?'), especially with an ad for a brand or product one is actually using.

Mostly, this is noting with very low involvement. Ads for established brands and for experienced consumers would nearly always need to give very little new information. Consumers expect that since they have seen *lots* of ads before and know what they are like. And they nearly always already know the brand itself, so that there is no call for much information, for heavy persuasion, or for trying to create any new and deep involvement *now*. Hence 'Here I am' reminders can in fact work well by merely reinforcing and perhaps nudging the brand's salience. Few ads in fact say 'Buy me now' (nor even, we think, hint at it, except for reminding the consumer that the brand still exists). This gives great scope for the wide range of effective creative advertising that exists, the objective being to leave a memory trace of the brand, not the advertising *per se*.

How advertising works: the memory mechanism

Since purchases seldom follow shortly after an advertising exposure for the brand – the average interval for those buying a brand of instant coffee, say, is something like 4 months – the crucial advertising effects on behaviour (i.e. on *buying*) have to be in the longer term.

The question, therefore, is whether noting the advertisement at the time will leave an enduring 'trace' of the brand in the mind. This may possibly be a conscious remembrance, or more often just a more or less 'forgotten' memory. But will such memories easily, or ever, be retrieved? (Like recalling someone's name which of course one '*knows*'.) Memories of the brand may then be marginally refreshed or revived by a subsequent ad exposure of the brand (even a 15-second TV flash, or that glimpse in print), or by seeing the name on a can in someone else's trolley, or on a T-shirt, or hearing the name mentioned, or *using* the brand.

Recognizing a well-known slogan can work even better. So can a well-established 'visual' or a jingle, even when only half-seen or heard out of the proverbial corner of one's eye, or just the timbre of the voice-over. It may make the fuller message or treatment 'all come flashing back'.

What is likely to be stimulated in this way is very simply remembrance of the *brand*. The brand name can provide the common link between all the different stimuli (e.g. *using* the brand, glimpsing it in a trolley or on a supermarket shelf, or seeing the ad again). This is not so for remembering the earlier advertisement itself, although ad recall is often what is talked about and measured. There is usually little or no link between an old ad and glimpsing the can in someone's trolley now, especially not if the ad itself failed to make the brand name and/or pack design stick in the first place. The short-term *communication* effectiveness of the advertisement (and measuring it) may therefore be a necessary but not sufficient means to *advertising* effectiveness.

Rehearsal

The literature on 'remembering' is united on *rehearsal* helping to fix an impression (visual, aural, semantic, etc.) in our long-term memory. This can come about in many ways, e.g. through various different kinds of exposure to the brand name (and/or pack design) 'accidentally' becoming linked in our minds.

The *controllable* way is not only through direct repetition of the name in repeat exposures to the identical ad or to different creative executions (e.g. the traditional idea of '4+ exposures'), but also showing the name itself more than once in the given ad, including perhaps hearing it in the voice-over in addition to seeing it. A creative example of rehearsal is the unexpected, if ubiquitous, 'N°5 Chanel' copy. This can slow down the exposure to the name, by making some readers pause fractionally to subvocalize the icon 'It's Chanel Number 5' under their breath. 'Repeating' the name gives a better chance of leaving a memory trace for it.

We stress that memory traces tend to be reinforced, and sometimes even strengthened, by any subsequent exposures to the brand, the brand name, or brand publicity of any kind. Memory even feeds on the sheer act of remembering. This is the opposite to the traditional view that memories of the advertising just fade away and decay unless the ads themselves are explicitly repeated, almost as in rote learning.

Possible memory associations

Once a message or name is in our so-called long-term memory, it seems virtually never to be forgotten (as recognition tests show). But can it be recalled, so that it can reinforce or nudge the brand's salience?

Bringing things out of our memory later is greatly helped by letting *associations* form. These are often highly idiosyncratic for each separate one of us. That is where richly creative advertising should score, and also where that glimpse or tone of voice overheard again can at times make the name come flashing back.

Creative campaigns can provide a wide range of possible subsequent memory associations for the brand. Advertisements quite often incorporate some highly specific property of the brand (or at least a property of the generic product, e.g. that beer can be refreshing) to hang a strong creative treatment on. The purpose is, however, not to publicize that property as such – as a possibly important feature of the brand – but to promote the brand by providing distinctive associations. This is also the role of memorable slogans, jingles or visuals.

For beer, 'refreshing' could be used for *any* brand, although it is typically appropriated by just one or two. But copy ingredients are often successfully used which are strictly irrelevant (like 'natural silk' for a shampoo, or 'flaked crystals' for a *soluble* coffee; see JOAB Report 5). 'Meaningless' but impactful and memorable advertising copy or artwork, which nonetheless provides effective memory associations with the brand, seems to us the essence of creative brand advertising.

The requirement is 'telling a good story well'. This means getting attention, memorability and salience for the brand. But it also implies suitable consistency. Advertising, of course, acts synergistically – it interacts with the rest of the marketing mix and also with consumers' everyday experiences. But that only works when there is sufficient integration for lasting memory links to be formed.

Summary and Discussion

We have argued that what advertisements are like and how they perform differ diametrically from how advertising is mostly talked about (i.e. as always aiming at short-term growth, strong persuasion, differentiating between look-alike brands and directly sustaining premium prices).

In practice, however, most advertisements merely promote their brand as a brand. They mostly show it as a (good) example of the product class or subclass ('None better/cheaper, or great value/new/attractive', or whatever). This is as straightforward publicity for the brand, yet often highly coloured for impact and subtle to help develop memorability. Most advertisements do not carry any special sales promise, or any message that is strictly unique or inherent to just that brand.

Such a sheer 'publicity' view of advertising is consistent with the current emphasis on umbrella branding including house names and private labels, but especially also that a 'brand' traditionally subsumes all its pack size, flavour or model variants. 'Brands' can typically comprise a wide range of differing products under the one name. They usually do so without at all promoting each individual product variant as such.

The aim is, we think, to reinforce or at times nudge the number of people who choose that brand as and when the opportunity arises, or at least *think* of buying it then. That is because a large brand A and a smaller but similar brand B differ greatly in the number of consumers for whom each is salient, rather than in how strongly or differently such consumers think of it. Users of brand A typically like A and users of brand B like B, but there are far more users of the large A.

For most customers, there usually is a long gap (many months) between seeing an ad and buying the brand, even for 'frequently bought' goods. Hence, the main effects of advertising for established brands have to be long term. Good advertising leaves or strengthens a memory trace for the brand in the consumer's mind, so that the brand comes to mind (i.e. is salient) when a purchase is made.

That is quite unlike the short-term up and downs of price promotions. Nor do ads appear to 'persuade' the indifferent or ill-disposed. There is no evidence that advertising makes substitutable brands appear vastly different, or has strong short-term effects to convert the unbeliever. In contrast, competitive brands usually strive to match each other. A brand's goal should not be how well it is regarded by its consumers (which differs little from brand to brand), but how many regard it well.

If competitive brands were heavily advertised and one's own brand were not, the competition would gradually win (other things being equal). One's advertising has, therefore, to be mainly defensive over the longer term. Advertising for established brands need not, and usually does not, pay for itself in the short term, but is an insurance. To keep one's share of the market next week, and even next year, is to us the continually astonishing achievement of successful branding. To sustain this, and to match broadly what the competition are doing, should justify one's marketing budget (with occasional extra sales as a bonus). It also allows one to question or defend one's marketing and advertising costs critically, against realistic goals. Survival may not seem very macho, but it is much better than the alternative.

This makes competitive advertising seem a weak force, acting mainly in the longer term. It does not act as a strong force trying to persuade *now*. Even quite extensive advertising holidays need, therefore, not be a disaster (as long as they are only *holidays*) because the rest of the marketing mix keeps the brand's short- to medium-term momentum going (e.g. the distribution logistics and selling efforts keep the brand widely in supply, and consumers' own ongoing *usage* habits will, for a time at least, sustain demand).

What is special about advertising as a marketing factor is that it is almost uniquely under the advertiser's direct control: how much, when, where and what to say. And while many small brands survive without much or any advertising, in the long run the big brands are the ones that have advertised big and remain salient to more people.

An Application in International Advertising

One of the most frequently discussed issues in advertising brands *internationally* is whether it is better, or even possible, to use a standard approach in all countries (possibly with some local adaptation), or whether it is preferable to develop advertising locally in every case. Many commentators agree that both routes are possible, but argue that the standardized approach can only work in certain circumstances.

Their arguments typically relate to a rather 'strong' persuasive view of advertising. Internationalization or globalization of advertising would, on this view, depend on whether there are major differences between countries in areas such as:

1   *The nature of the products.* What products are available and how has the market developed? Whether the competitive frame is similar in all countries or made up of different brands and product formulations (highly varied competition might suggest a standard approach was inappropriate – but how far does it matter what the competitive advertising actually *says*?). Whether our own brand is the same or is different in some countries, either functionally or in its positioning. What position our brand has in the market, is it big or small (do niche brands need different approaches)? Is the market developing, mature or declining (a standard approach is not appropriate for all circumstances)?
2   *Consumers' needs and usage.* A standardized approach requires consumer expectations of the product category to be similar, particularly the balance between functional and emotional appeal. Also the target group must be uniform.
3   *Culture-based attitudes and emotions.* Needs and usage may be the same, but are there cultural attitudes to products that may influence how they may be portrayed (e.g. is it legal and decent), or advertising styles that cannot transcend boundaries, such as the use of humour, puns, local celebrities?

4 *Is the brand big enough?* A brand needs to have substantial market positions and associated budgets in all markets to warrant standardized advertising (although this seems to run counter to one of the main advantages quoted for standardizing advertising, viz. cost savings).

The arguments for a standardized advertising approach include cost advantages, uniform image, especially where the target audience is travellers, planning and control of objectives, cross-fertilization of good ideas and know-how, and consistent quality standards. Arguments against include heterogeneity of usage and culture, media differences, legal barriers, the nature of the competition, product life cycle, cost of coordination, and perhaps most significantly the 'not invented here' syndrome whereby local management opposes, almost in principle, centrally imposed ideas as undermining their control and authority.

But to us, the arguments can be greatly simplified, knowing that the objective for an established brand's routine on-going advertising is to produce/reinforce its salience. The question of whether a specific advertisement can be used in a specific country then becomes an operational one: can the ad be used (e.g. is it the right medium, legal, etc.) and does it produce the required memory traces of the brand as a good example of the product, which can in principle always be researched. The strategic issue of whether or not to attempt to develop a single ad for use internationally becomes a matter of management philosophy, balancing the drive for synergy with the local tendency to reject things 'not invented here'.

Appendix: The Evidence

Two major strands of evidence underlying the conclusions in this report are that competitive brands differ greatly in how many people buy them (or in any other measure of the numbers of people to whom the brands are 'salient'), but not in how loyal their customers are, or how their customers see them attitudinally. This is discussed in the more detailed JOAB reports (especially JOAB 1 and 7) and the references there.

Table 13.1 illustrates the first point with a classic example for instant coffee from JOAB Report 1. The brand's penetrations vary greatly (four-fold) and predictably so with market shares.

Both the average purchase frequencies (i.e. repeat buying) and how much (or little!) a brand accounts for its customers' product-category requirements in the year, however, vary only a little, and again predictably so just with market share (i.e. as 'double jeopardy', not as idiosyncratic brand-specific values).

Such regular and predictable results are known still to hold twenty-five years later (e.g. Hallberg, 1996; Ehrenberg, 1997; Ehrenberg and Uncles, 1997) and occur across more than fifty packaged grocery products and the like from soap to soup, and also for cars, petrol, retail stores, television viewing, etc.

Table 13.2 for consumer attitudes similarly summarizes how users of different brands see them as similar. Especially after allowing for the small double jeopardy trend with market shares, how many users of one of the biggest brands believe

Table 13.1 Brand loyalty measures: instant coffee

US instant coffee	Annual market share	Penetration (% buying)		Average purchases per buyer		Share of category requirements		Buyers who are 100% loyal	
	(%)	O%	T%	O	T	O%	T%	O%	T%
Maxwell House	19	24	27	3.6	3.1	38	34	20	16
Sanka	15	21	23	3.3	3.0	36	32	20	15
Taster's Choice	14	22	21	2.8	2.9	32	31	24	15
High Point	13	22	20	2.6	2.9	31	31	18	14
All other brands	13	20	21	3.0	2.9	32	31	20	14
Folgers	11	18	17	2.7	2.8	29	29	13	14
Nescafé	8	13	14	2.9	2.7	28	28	15	13
Brim	4	9	7	2.0	2.6	21	26	17	12
Maxim	3	6	6	2.6	2.6	23	26	11	12
Average brand	11	17	17	2.8	2.8	30	30	17	14

O = observed; T = theoretical Dirichlet predictions.

Table 13.2 Users of a brand stating an attribute belief (US products, 30+ brands, 47 attributes, and also in the United Kingdom)

Av. brands[a]	% users	% users stating av. belief	
		Observed	Calibrated for double jeopardy
1st	57	55	50
2nd	50	52	48
3rd	43	50	48
4th	33	42	42
5th	30	47	48
6th	26	44	45
7th	20	41	43
8th	18	48	51
9th	8	43	48
Average	32	47	47

[a] In market share order.

something about it (about 50 per cent) is much the same as how many users of one of the smallest brands believe the same things about that (48 per cent). This is the dominant factor. Subpatterns are noted in JOAB Report 7, but generally there are insufficient idiosyncratic values for specific brands for such attribute beliefs to account for consumers' brand choice generally.

References

Advertising Works. Papers from the IPA Advertising Awards. (Various editors from Simon Broadbent on, and various publishers, in concert with the Institute of Practitioners in Advertising, London.)

Baddeley, A. D. (1974) *The Psychology of Memory.* New York: Basic Books.

Belch, G. E. and Belch M. A. (1995) *Introduction to Advertising and Promotion*, 3rd edn. Chicago: Irwin.

Bloom, D. (1976) Consumer behaviour and the timing of advertising effects. *Admap*, 12(September), 430–8.

Carpenter, G. S., Glazer, R. and Nakamoto, K. (1994) Meaningful brands from meaningless differentiation: the dependence on irrelevant attributes. *Journal of Marketing Research*, 31, 339–50.

de Mooij, M. (1994) *Advertising Worldwide*, 2nd edn. Hemel Hempstead: Prentice Hall.

East, R. (1990; 2nd edn 1997) *Changing Consumer Behaviour.* London: Cassell.

Economist (1996) Which half? June 8, 102–3.

Ehrenberg, A. S. C. (1997) B. E., or not B. E. *Proceedings of the ARF Annual Conference.* New York: Advertising Research Foundation.

Ehrenberg, A. S. C. and Uncles, M. D. (1997) Dirichlet-type markets: A position paper. South Bank University: Working Paper.

Ehrenberg, A. S. C., Goodhardt, G. J. and Barwise, T. P. (1990) Double jeopardy revisited. *Journal of Marketing*, 54, 82–91.

Foxall, G. R. and Goldsmith, R. E. (1994) *Consumer Psychology for Marketing.* London and New York: Routledge.

Franzen, G. (1994) *Advertising Effectiveness.* Henley-on-Thames: NTC Books.

Hallberg, G. (1996) Disaggregating repeat-buying patterns. Presentation: Genootschap voor Reclame, Amsterdam.

Hedges, A. (1974) *Testing to Destruction.* London: Institute of Practitioners in Advertising.

Jones, J. P. (1992) *How Much is Enough?* New York: Lexington Books.

Krugman, H. E. (1965) The impact of television advertising: learning without involvement. *Public Opinion Quarterly*, 29, 350–6.

Maucher, M. (1992) World Economic Forum, Davos.

McDonald, C. (1992) *How Advertising Works.* Henley-on-Thames: NTC Books.

Moran, W. T. (1990) Brand presence and the perceptual frame. *Journal of Advertising Research*, Oct/Nov, 9–16.

Strong, E. K. (1925) *The Psychology of Selling.* New York: McGraw-Hill.

Sutherland, M. (1993) *Advertising and the Mind of the Consumer.* St Leonards, NSW: Allen & Unwin.

van Westendorp, P. (1990) *On the Road to Accountability.* Amsterdam: Genootschap voor Reclame (in Dutch).

Weilbacher, W. M. (1993) *Brand Marketing.* Lincoln, Ill.: NTC Books.

JOAB Reports 1–8 (South Bank University working papers)

1 Ehrenberg, A. S. C. and Scriven, J. A. (1997) Added values or propensities to buy? *Admap*, 376, 36–40 (in press). [Does advertising imbue an otherwise undifferentiated brand with 'added values' as a reason for choosing it? Or do consumers already have habitual propensities to buy certain brands? Cites extensive evidence.]

2 Barnard, N. R. and Ehrenberg, A. S. C. (1997a) Advertising: strongly persuasive or nudging? *Journal of Advertising Research*, 37 (3), 27–35. [Does advertising have to convert 'switchers' into

'loyals'? Or can advertising work by re-inforcing and nudging?]

3 Ehrenberg, A. S. C., Scriven, J. A. and Barnard, N. R. (1997) Advertising and price. *Journal of Advertising Research*, 37 (3) 27–35. [Discusses three pricing issues related to advertising: (a) Price-related promotions appeal only to the brand's existing customers. (b) Consumers generally pay a range of prices for a product. (c) Individual brands have broadly similar price sensitivities.]

4 Ehrenberg, A. S. C. and Barnard, N. R. (1997) Advertising and product demand. *Admap*, 373, 14–18. [Industry seldom invests in generic advertising. Nor does brand advertising affect category demand.]

5 Ehrenberg, A. S. C., Barnard, N. R. and Scriven, J. A. (1997a) Differentiation or salience. *Journal of Advertising Research*, 37 (6) 7–14. [Competitive brands seldom differ substantially. Any differentiation with selling power is usually copied. Yet brands have very different numbers of people to whom each is salient, which can be reinforced and/or nudged by 'Here I am' publicity.]

6 Ehrenberg, A. S. C. (1997) How do consumers come to buy a new brand? (New brands and ATR&N). *Admap*, 371, 20–4. [Consumers have to be aware of a new brand (or a brand new to them). They may then make a trial purchase or two. Both A and T are helped by advertising (usually of a 'Here I am' form). This may subsequently also provide reinforcement and nudging.]

7 Barnard, N. R. and Ehrenberg, A. S. C. (1997b) Attitudes to brands (in preparation). [Consumers' attribute beliefs about a brand mainly reflect its product-category characteristics, except when there is a noticeable physical difference (usually characteristic of a sub-category) and/or advertising replay. Fewer non-users of a brand give a positive belief response about it. Stated attribute beliefs are notably variable over time.]

8 Ehrenberg, A. S. C., Barnard, N. R. and Scriven, J. A. (1997b) Justifying our advertising budgets. *Journal of Marketing* (submitted). [Brings the whole argument together.]

14 Content Analysis of Advertising 1970–1997: A Review and Assessment of Methodologies

GREG HARRIS AND SULEIMAN ATTOUR

Introduction

In recent years, the advertising standardization versus adaptation debate has assumed great importance for both academicians and practitioners of advertising alike. This, in turn, has been reflected in an increasing number of articles reporting cross-cultural/country differences, with reference to the executional elements of advertising.

Content analysis of advertising has gained wide acceptance in both advertising and marketing journals, and has been widely used as a method to detect cross-country/cultural differences.

This chapter is intended as a review of the literature that has employed this method to date. From the results, it appears that, although the recommendations for cross-cultural methodologies have been repeatedly emphasized in previous articles on cross-cultural research, their application in empirical studies has been widely ignored.

In order for future research to make valid contributions to the advertising standardization debate and advance the body of knowledge in international advertising, these methodological issues should be adhered to. This review points out some of the concerns about previous methodologies, and provides recommendations for future research.

> Because of the relative availability of the raw material, many sins have been committed in the name of content analysis. (Berelson, 1954, p. 518)

The present study aims at assessing previous work that has employed the content analysis of advertising. Content analysis is defined as 'a research technique for the objective, systematic, and quantitative description of the manifest content of communication' (Berelson, 1952). The main features that distinguish content analysis from analytical methods are validity, reliability and reproducibility of the results.

The findings of content analysis studies have important implications both for theory and managerial practices. However, the reported results of content analysis studies have so far been inconsistent and often contradictory. For content analysis to be taken more seriously by academicians and practitioners, immediate attention needs to be given to some of the research methodologies.

For generalizable inferences to emerge, the research design should control for alternative explanations of the results. These alternative explanations can be both substantive and methodological (Malhotra et al., 1996). A substantive alternative explanation might be the result of another cultural variable that is not controlled for, while methodological alternative explanations could result from sampling errors, or any other methodological problem.

In this chapter, we aim to draw the attention to these methodological studies, and present some recommendations that will enhance the validity of the findings. The review (covering the period 1970 to 1997) starts with a brief description of the literature followed by a discussion of these criteria:

1   Selection of cultures.
2   Number of cultures studied.
3   Selection of countries.
4   Units of analysis.
5   Number of magazines per study.
6   Selection of publications.
7   Number of product categories.
8   Sampling method.
9   Reliability of the measuring instrument.
10 Methods of analysis.
11 The use of multiple comparisons.

In total, ninety-three articles were found to utilize the content analysis approach. Only three studies (four articles) have investigated the degree of standardization of advertisements that have appeared in different countries.

The majority of the articles (58.07 per cent, $n = 54/93$) make use of content analysis in a single-country setting, while the remaining 41.93 per cent ($n = 39/93$) were studied in cross-cultural or cross-national contexts. Of the cross-cultural/national articles, 56.41 per cent ($n = 22/39$, table 14.1) investigated print advertising, while 35.9 per cent ($n = 14/39$) used TV advertising and 7.69 per cent ($n = 3/39$) multiple media.

The studies under review investigated various elements of the advertisements. Some considered the information content of advertising across countries (e.g. Madden et al., 1986; Noor Al-Deen, 1991; Biswas et al., 1992), sex roles and portrayal of women, visual components of advertising (e.g. Cutler and Javalgi, 1992; Javalgi et al., 1994), etc.

Table 14.1 A breakdown of the media used in content analysis studies

	Multiple media (%)	Print (%)	TV (%)	Billboard (%)	Total (%)
Across cultures	7.69	56.41	35.9		100.00
One country	7.41	72.22	18.52	1.85	100.00
All studies	7.53	65.59	25.81	1.07	100.00

Selection of Cultures

This is one of the most important elements in cross-cultural studies. Adler (1983) noted that for studies to be meaningful, cultures should be selected on a theoretical basis. However, our review indicates that the underlying reasons for the selection of cultures in the majority of the previous studies have not been clear.

Cultural studies have classified and ranked cultures across a number of characteristics. In two-thirds of the studies included in the present review, there is no mention of cultural theory, ranking of cultures, or the way these cultures compare on the aspects under study.

The number of cultures studied is also important. According to Brislin et al. (1973), the number of cultures selected for study should be large enough both to randomize the variance on non-matched cultural variables and eliminate rival hypotheses. For the findings to be generalized, the inclusion of a variety of cultures is needed, as suggested in the literature.

According to Samiee and Jeong (1994): 'Two cultures represent the minimum denominator in a cross cultural sense, not the ideal number'. Studies with two or three cultures should be treated as pilot studies (Sekaran, 1981).

However, most of the studies conducted in the field chose to investigate countries that are of special interest to them. Therefore, the inclusion of more than two cultures in cross-cultural studies has been the exception rather than the rule.

Less than 38.46 per cent ($n = 15/39$) of the cross-cultural studies in the present review have included three cultures or more. Only 10.26 per cent ($n = 4/39$) of these have investigated four or more cultures, while the majority of the cross-cultural studies (61.54 per cent, $n = 24/39$) have used only two cultures (table 14.2).

Table 14.2 Number of cultures examined per study

	Two cultures/study	Three or more cultures/study	Four or more cultures/study
Articles	61.54%	38.46%	10.26%

Countries Studied

The countries studied and the frequency of their inclusion in content analysis research in advertising are shown in table 14.3.

From this table, it appears that most of the previous research focuses on the United States (79.57 per cent, $n = 74/93$). There might be various reasons for this imbalance, but it is clear that most of the research to date is approached from an American point of view, and that researchers might have been using or investigating concepts that are inapplicable to other parts of the world.

The second most researched country is Japan (13.98 per cent, $n = 13/93$). The United Kingdom comes in third place with 8.6 per cent ($n = 8/93$). The inclusion of an English-speaking country was found to be very high, at 86.02 per cent ($n = 80/93$, table 14.4). In addition, the frequency of including a European country was found to be 16.13 per cent ($n = 15/93$), while only 5.38 per cent ($n = 5/93$) of the studies included a developing country, and only one investigated an Arab country.

With the exception of one study (Tse et al., 1989), all the studies that have been conducted so far included one country per culture, and none of these has investigated more than a country per culture.

Table 14.3   List of countries studied

Country	Frequency	Percentage	Country	Frequency	Percentage
USA	74	79.57	New Zealand	2	2.15
Japan	13	13.98	Mexico	2	2.15
UK	8	8.60	Spain	1	1.08
China	6	6.45	India	1	1.08
France	7	7.53	Australia	1	1.08
Hong Kong	4	4.30	Saudi Arabia	1	1.08
Korea	4	4.30	Brazil	1	1.08
Sweden	4	4.30	Indonesia	1	1.08
Taiwan	4	4.30	Hungary	1	1.08
Canada (English)	3	3.23	Dominican Republic	1	1.08
Germany	3	3.23	Italy	1	1.08
Canada (French)	2	2.15			

Table 14.4   Probability of including specific countries

	Frequency	Percentage
Inclusion of an English-speaking country	80	86.02
Inclusion of a European country	15	16.13
Inclusion of a developing country	5	5.38
Inclusion of an Arab country	1	1.08

It appears that the authors have assumed that each culture exists in only one country, and that each country is not only culturally homogeneous, but also represents only one culture. These assumptions might not be justified. It appears that there is certain ambiguity here between the terms nation and culture. Cultural theories indicate that some cultures (e.g. Arabic, Chinese) are manifested in a cluster of countries, and not in one nation.

In order to study Arabic culture, for instance, more than one country has to be investigated for representing this culture. Such a valid representation of cultures, that stems from cultural theory, has been almost absent from the research so far.

Unit of Analysis

This is one of the most important elements of methodology in this area of research, and it is even more crucial for cross-cultural research. The cultural unit of analysis should be clearly defined. When the aim of the research is to investigate cross-cultural differences/similarities, then the unit of analysis should be the culture itself. If a proxy has to be used for culture, then it should be justified in the methodology and accounted for in the results.

Among the cross-cultural studies reviewed, a surprising 81.48 per cent stated that their aim was to conduct cross-cultural research, while in reality, the units of analysis in their studies were countries rather than cultures. In the majority of the studies, there was no clear distinction between cultures and nations. According to Samiee and Jeong (1994), researchers who use countries as proxies for cultures are assuming that each country investigated is dominated by one culture only.

This inaccurate use of the unit of analysis can cause major problems. For instance, using a country as a proxy for culture neglects the existence of within-country differences that can potentially be greater than cross-country differences (Andrews et al., 1991).

Therefore, using a country as a unit of analysis may be appropriate when the country investigated is culturally homogeneous (e.g. Japan), and inappropriate with culturally heterogeneous countries (e.g. India, Malaysia and Belgium). By treating intraculturally heterogeneous countries as proxies to single cultures, it is not always possible to detect real cross-cultural differences (Samiee and Jeong, 1994).

Therefore, when a culture is investigated, a representative sample of the countries where this culture is manifested should be included in the study – unless it is confined to a single country.

Sampling Method

In this type of research, many factors limit the sampling options available to researchers. Among all the studies that employed the content analysis method, only 21 per cent have used a random sample, while the majority chose convenience, judgemental and non-probability samples. For the standardization studies, none of the researchers have used a random sampling method in their study.

This restriction is understandable and even expected in this type of research. Many limitations are faced by the researchers, including the choice and availability of local and foreign publications, the availability of a sufficient number of local and foreign ads, etc.

However, sample equivalence across cultures is required if valid inferences are to emerge. Therefore, research design should control for all the demographic, socio-economic and other salient factors that may influence the results (Malhotra et al., 1996).

Considering that characteristics of the target audience influence the strategic and creative content of advertising, it is relevant factors such as age, gender and socio-economic group that should be equivalent across the cultures under examination.

Academics suggest that 'Any lack of comparability in the samples should be reported as a limitation and incorporated into the interpretations of the data'. It is our belief that the same also applies to cross-cultural advertising research employing content analysis.

The notion of sample equivalence will form the basis for the discussion of the next two elements: the number of magazines and the selection of publications.

Number of Magazines per Study

To achieve sample equivalence across cultures, the advertisements obtained from each magazine category should be compared to those obtained from the equivalent categories from other cultures.

To illustrate this, it would be inappropriate to compare, for instance, an automobile advertisement that appeared in a gay magazine in Australia, showing two male models, with an advertisement of the same brand in a family magazine in the United Kingdom. The resulting differences in the kind of appeals, values and portrayal of people are due to sample inequivalence rather than real country differences.

If the samples are not comparable, i.e. the ads are pooled from more than one magazine category, then the various subsamples (i.e. magazine categories) need to be analysed separately to assess the impact of the differences in terms of the variables examined.

Close examination of the literature shows that 41.86 per cent of the studies have used either two or more magazine categories, and only 16.28 per cent have used one magazine category. Furthermore, in 41.86 per cent of the articles it is not clear how many magazine categories were used (table 14.5).

It is worth mentioning here that the authors should not assume that the readers of the academic journals could recognize the title of every magazine from every country. It would be much clearer if the number and kind of magazine categories selected are pointed out in the methodology.

Table 14.5   Number of magazine categories used per study

	Percentage	Accumulative percentage
NA (not available)	41.86	41.86
Three magazine categories or more	16.28	58.14
Two magazine categories	25.58	83.72
One magazine category	16.28	100

Selection of Publications

As mentioned in the sampling section above, target audience characteristics should be controlled for in order to ensure sample comparability across cultures. Consequently, one would expect that target audience characteristics (also referred to as 'readership profile', 'audience characteristics' and 'target markets') to be a principal criterion for the selection of publications across cultures.

However, our review shows that publications have been selected for examination because of their high circulation in around 71.43 per cent of the studies. In 11.9 per cent of the studies, publications were chosen according to their availability, and only 11.9 per cent have chosen their publications according to the target audience (table 14.6).

Since circulation was the main criterion for choosing publications for the majority of the studies, sample equivalence across the cultures studied cannot be assumed.

The number of magazine issues examined has varied considerably from one study to another. Some authors have been content to use one issue per publication per decade (Belk and Polley, 1985), more than one issue per magazine – whenever possible (Javalgi et al., 1995), one or two issues per magazine (Cutler and Javalgi, 1992), three to four issues per magazine (Neelankavile et al., 1995), four issues per year (Klassen et al., 1993), etc., to the point that some authors have examined all of the twelve monthly issues.

One wonders about the representativeness of the resulting sample of advertisements in cases where less than four issues per year are used, or the extreme case where just one magazine per decade is used.

Table 14.6   Criteria used for the selection of publications

	Percentage	Accumulative percentage
Circulation	71.14	71.14
Availability	11.9	83.33
Target audience	11.9	95.23
Other	4.77	100

Number of Product Categories

It is believed that the product category has an influential effect on the character-istics of advertising across countries. Keown et al. (1989) concluded that there are significant differences between advertisements of durable and non-durable products.

McCarthy and Hattwick (1992) found that the values displayed in advertising are related to the products advertised rather than the cultures studied. Similarly, Samiee and Jeong (1994) suggested that some of the observed differences among countries might be due to uncontrolled variables such as the product category.

The number of product categories used per study also varied from one study to another. Additionally, at least 53.93 per cent of the studies included in this review did not account for the effect of the product categories in their results (table 14.7).

Two other factors further complicate matters. First, 27.59 per cent of the articles did not report the number of product categories used. Second, compari-sons of product differences across studies are further restricted by the various methods of product classification used (i.e. durable/non-durable, high/medium/low involvement, product class and other methods).

Therefore, it can be seen that unless the product category variable is controlled for in the design of the research, observed differences among countries might reflect the differences of these uncontrolled variables, rather than real country differences.

Table 14.7 The number of product categories used per study and whether these were accounted for in the results

	Mean	Range	Not available (%)	Not accounted for in result (%)
All studies	6.68	1–21	27.59	53.93
Across culture studies	6.33	1–16	25.93	62.86

Reliability of the Measuring Instrument

Four aspects of inter-coder reliability will be briefly discussed:

- Measurement method.
- Intra-coder reliability.
- Inclusion of judges from each culture.
- Different reliabilities across countries.

The most common method of measuring reliability is percentage agreement. According to Kassarijian (1977), an inter-coder agreement value equal to or

Table 14.8 Percentage of studies using judges from each culture

	Yes	No	Not available
Judge from each culture	40%	28.57%	31.43%
Different reliabilities across countries	28.57%	–	71.43%

greater than 85 per cent is acceptable in content analysis research. This method, however, has been criticized by many, including Scott (1955), Cohen (1960) and Krippendorff (1980).

By chance alone, agreement increases as the number of categories decreases. Therefore, a higher agreement measure would be expected on a two-category variable than on a nine-category variable. Several methods were suggested to correct for chance agreement, including those by Bennett et al. (1954), Scott (1955) and Perreault and Leigh (1989).

These methods vary along one or more of the following dimensions: (1) sensitivity to systematic coding errors; (2) correction for chance agreements; (3) ability to handle multiple coders; (4) level of measurement represented by the stimuli (Kang et al., 1993).

Of the ninety-three articles examined, only twenty-eight (30.11 per cent) used acceptable, yet not accurate, methods of measuring inter-coder agreement. The majority of the studies (69.89 per cent) have either used percentage agreement (47.31 per cent), a method that has been criticized widely since the 1950s, or have not performed reliability tests at all (22.58 per cent).

To ensure the reliability of the measuring tool over time, an inter-coder test is normally used. However, our review found that less than one third of the researchers have conducted a test–retest as an additional measure of reliability.

Brislin (1980) has suggested that a judge from each culture is required to take part in the analysis, and reach an agreement of more than 85 per cent. The presence of a judge from each culture guards against the possibility of the judges' agreement due to factors specific to their cultural background. In addition, inter-coder agreement involving one culture generally tends to inflate the reliability (Gilly, 1988).

In more than one quarter (28.57 per cent) of the studies reviewed here, the judges did not represent each culture, and in almost one third of the articles it was not possible to assess whether judges from each culture were used (table 14.8).

Many authors have previously warned about the effects of instrument reliability inequivalence across countries (Parameswaran and Yaprak, 1987; Aulakh and Kotabe, 1993). It has been demonstrated that the same scales may have different reliabilities in different cultures (Malhotra et al., 1996). In addition, Davis et al. (1981) showed that two sources of measure unreliability can confound the comparability of cross-cultural findings. Therefore, unequal reliabilities across countries/ cultures/measures should be adjusted for before valid inferences can be drawn (Bollen, 1989).

A considerably large number (28.57 per cent) of the studies included in the present review have reported reliability values that are not equivalent across the countries/measures studied (table 14.8). None of these studies have mentioned this fact as a limitation of their findings, and none of the authors have attempted to adjust for this instrument reliability inequivalence. The vast majority of the studies have not reported the reliability measures per country.

The lack of attention to this crucial issue of cross-cultural methodology is not surprising, considering that only recently have these issues been given attention in domestic research (Malhotra et al., 1996).

Methods of Analysis

A wide range of statistical analysis techniques have been used in the studies reviewed. These techniques are summarized in table 14.9. From this table, it appears that most of the researchers have chosen to use simple and univariate statistical tests. This is rather surprising considering the state-of-the-art statistical methods available, the importance of the findings, and the amount of effort and financial investment in these studies.

Table 14.9   The methods of statistical analysis used in the literature

Method of analysis	Percentage of studies	Accumulative percentage
Frequency tables	19.77	19.77
t-test	8.14	27.91
Chi-square	45.35	73.26
ANOVA	6.96	80.24
Regression	8.14	88.38
Discriminant	2.33	90.71
Factor	1.16	91.87
Correlation	3.49	95.36
Multidimensional scaling	1.16	96.52
Log linear	1.16	97.68
Logit	1.16	98.84
Sign, runs test	1.16	100

The Use of Multiple Comparisons

Multiple comparisons refer to conducting many pairwise tests (e.g. pairwise comparisons for a group of five countries). Statistically, the use of univariate tests can be performed only if a multivariate test indicates that at least one cross-national pair is significantly different (Hummel and Sligo, 1971). Our review has found that the vast majority of studies have not used a multivariate test to justify the use of univariate pairwise comparisons.

Additionally, around 80 per cent of the articles reviewed in the present study have performed multiple comparisons using conventional confidence levels (e.g. 95 per cent). This practice is statistically inappropriate, and does not result in accurate findings, for the reasons explained below.

Three principles should be acknowledged when conducting multiple comparisons:

1   It is appropriate to perform statistical tasts for each pairwise comparison by utilizing conventional levels of significance (e.g. 95 per cent). This is due to the fact that multiple comparisons inflate the overall type-I error rate – the probability of rejecting the null hypothesis when in fact it is true. For independent tests, the overall error is given by:

$$[1 - (1 - a)^n]$$

where $a = 0.5$ for 95 per cent confidence level and n = number of comparisons.

As an example, for every twenty pairwise comparisons each at the 95 per cent confidence level, the overall error rate would be 64.2 per cent. That is a confidence level of 35.8 per cent, which is so low that no findings can be seriously considered at this confidence level.

2   Depending on the nature of the comparisons (i.e. *post hoc* or *a priori*), there are many procedures to control the overall error rate (Klockars and Sax, 1986).

For *a priori* comparisons, a common procedure is to set the confidence level for each pairwise test to:

$$[1 - a/n]$$

where a = the desired overall error rate, and n = the number of multiple comparisons.

As an example, for a confidence level of 95 per cent, $a = 0.05$ and $n = 20$, the twenty pairwise tests should be evaluated at a confidence level of:

$$[1 - 0.5/20]$$

Confidence = 99.75 per cent; error = 0.0025. With such a high confidence level, it would be difficult to reject the null hypothesis if it is not true.

3   An alternative option to adjusting the overall error rate would be to use a method that will perform all the comparisons simultaneously, rather than separately (e.g. SPSS LISREL) (Singh, 1994).

Recommendation for Future Research

1   Cultures (preferably more than two) should be selected on a theoretical basis, and the underlying reasons clearly presented.
2   Units for analysis should be clearly specified (e.g. culture/country, etc.).
3   Samples should be equivalent across cultures.
4   The following should be stated clearly:

(a) method(s) of measurement used for inter/intra-coder tests;
(b) sample size used for reliability tests, time elapsed for test–retest, number and country of origin of the coders;
(c) the country where the research is conducted, number and kind of magazine categories, number of product categories.

References

Adler, N. J. (1983) Cross-national management research: the ostrich and the trend. *Acadamy of Management Review*, 8(April), 226–32.

Andrews, J. C., Lysonski, S. and Duravasula, S. (1991) Understanding cross-cultural student perceptions in advertising in general: implications for advertising educators and practitioners. *Journal of Advertising*, 20(2), 15–28.

Aulakh, P. S. and Kotabe, M. (1993) An assessment of theoretical and methodological development in international marketing: 1980–1990. *Journal of International Marketing*, 1(2), 5–28.

Belk, R. W. and Polley, R. W. (1985) Materialism and status appeals in Japanese and US print advertising. *International Marketing Review*, Winter, 38–47.

Bennett, E. M., Alpet, R. and Goldstein, A. C. (1954) Communications through limited response questioning. *Public Opinion Quarterly*, 18(3), 303–8.

Berelson, B. (1952) *Content Analysis in Communication Research*. New York: The Free Press.

Berelson, B. (1954) Content analysis. In I. G. Lindzey (ed.), *Handbook of Social Psychology: Theory and Method*. Cambridge, Mass.: Addison Wesley, pp. 488–522.

Biswas, A., Olsen, J. E. and Carlet, V. (1992) A comparison of print advertisements from the United States and France. *Journal of Advertising*, 21(December), 73–81.

Bollen, K. A. (1989) *Structural Equations with Latent Variables*. New York: John Wiley.

Brislin, R. W. (1980) Translation and content analysis of oral and written material.

In H. C. Triandis and J. W. Berry (eds), *Handbook of Cross-cultural Psychology*, 2. Boston: Allyn & Bacon, pp. 389–444.

Brislin, R. W., Lonner, W. J. and Thorndike, R. M. (1973) *Cross-cultural Research Methods*. New York: Wiley.

Cohen, J. (1960) A coefficient of agreement for nominal scales. *Educational and Psychological Measurement*, 20(1), 37–46.

Cutler, B. D. and Javalgi, R. G. (1992) A cross-cultural analysis of the visual components of print advertising: The United States and the European Community. *Journal of Advertising Research*, January/February, 71–80.

Davis, H. L., Douglas, S. P. and Silk, A. J. (1981) Measure unreliability: a hidden threat to cross-national marketing research. *Journal of Marketing*, 45(2), 98–109.

Gilly, M. (1988) Sex roles in advertising: A comparison of television advertisements in Australia, Mexico, and the United States. *Journal of Marketing*, 52(April), 75–85.

Hummel, T. J. and Sligo, J. (1971) Empirical comparison of univariate and multivariate analysis of variance procedure. *Psychological Bulletin*, 76, 49–57.

Javalgi, R., Cutler, D. and White, D. (1994) Print advertising in the Pacific Basin. *International Marketing Review*, 11(6), 48–64.

Javalgi, R. G., Cutler, D. and Malhotra, K. (1995) Print advertising at the component level: a cross-cultural comparison of the United States and Japan. *Journal of Business Research*, 34, 117–24.

Kang, N., Kara, A., Laskey, A. H. and Seaton, F. B. (1993) A SAS MACRO for calculating intercoder agreement in content analysis. *Journal of Advertising*, XXII(2), 17–28.

Kassarijian, H. H. (1977) Comment analysis of consumer research. *Journal of Consumer Research*, 4(June), 8–18.

Keown, C. F., Synodinos, N. E. and Jacobs, L. W. (1989) Advertising practices in Northern Europe. *European Journal of Marketing*, 23(3), 17–28.

Klassen, M. L., Jasper, C. R. and Schwartz, A. M. (1993) Men and women: images of their relationships in magazine advertisements. *Journal of Advertising Research*, March/April, 30–9.

Klockars, A. and Sax, G. (1986) *Multiple Comparisons*. Beverley Hills, Ca.: Sage.

Krippendorff, K. (1980) *Content Analysis: An Introduction to its Methodology*. Beverley Hills, Ca.: Sage.

Madden, C. S., Marjorie, J. C. and Shinya, M. (1986) Analysis of information content in the US and Japanese magazine advertising. *Journal of Advertising*, 15(3), 38–45.

Malhotra, N. K., Agarwal, J. and Peterson, M. (1996) Methodological issues in cross-cultural marketing research. A state of the art review. *International Marketing Review*, 13(5), 7–43.

McCarthy, J. A. and Hattwick, P. M. (1992) Cultural value orientations: a comparison of magazine advertisements from the US and Mexico. In J. F. Berry and B. Sternal (eds), *Advances of Consumer Research*, 19. Association for Consumer Research, pp. 34–8.

Neelankavile, J., Mummalaneni, P. and Sessions, D. (1995) Use of foreign language and models in print advertisements in East Asian countries: A logit modeling approach. *European Journal of Marketing*, 29(4), 24–38.

Noor Al-Deen, H. (1991) Literacy and information content of magazine advertising: USA versus Saudi Arabia. *International Journal of Advertising*, 10, 251–7.

Parameswaran, R. and Yaprak, A. C. (1987) A cross-national comparison of consumer research measures. *Journal of International Business Studies*, 8(1), 35–49.

Perreault, W. D., Jr and Leigh, L. E. (1989) Reliability of nominal data based on qualitative judgements. *Journal of Marketing Research*, 26(2), 125–48.

Samiee, S. and Jeong, I. (1994) Cross-national research in advertising: an assessment of methodologies. *Journal of the Acadamy of Marketing Science*, 22(3), 205–17.

Scott, W. A. (1955) Reliability of content analysis: the case of nominal scale coding. *Public Opinion Quarterly*, 19(3), 321–5.

Sekaran (1981) Methodological and theoretical advancements in cross-cultural research. In S. Samiee and I. Jeong (1994) Cross-national research in advertising: an assessment of methodologies. *Journal of the Acadamy of Marketing Science*, 22(3), 205–17.

Singh, J. (1994) Measurement issues in cross-national research. *Journal of International Business Studies*, 3rd Quarter, 597–619.

Tse, Belk and Zhou (1989) Becoming a consumer society: a longitudinal and cross-cultural content analysis of print ads from Hong Kong, The People's Republic of China, and Taiwan. *Journal of Consumer Research*, 15(March), 457–72.

Wiles, C. R., Wiles, J. A. and Tjernlund, A. (1996) The ideology of advertising: the United States and Sweden. *Journal of Advertising Research*, May/June, 57–66.

15 The Internet and Marketing Communications in the Twenty-first Century

SYLVESTER O. MONYE AND PETRA MAYER

Introduction

The Internet represents the most exciting, yet challenging, medium of marketing communication in history. It offers unique features, which include individuality and interactivity – dialogue, reaction and a self-selecting audience. It currently stands as the fastest growing medium ever with the potential to threaten the very existence of some of the well-established marketing media. Advertising on the Internet only started in 1994 when the first commercially available web browser, Netscape Navigator 1.0, was realized, and has generated the most phenomenal interest among marketers. In 1996, the Internet generated US$3.5 billion of revenue by providing services to about 22 million users worldwide. All indicators suggest that its growth over the next five years will be exponential, and advertising on the Internet is expected to take up a large chunk of marketing budgets.

Industry experts argue that the Internet alone has the potential to deliver what the notion of electronic commerce had always implied. It extends beyond the transaction itself to everything that comes before and after, from marketing and product display to order tracking and sometimes even delivery. It is, therefore, not surprising that the Internet has experienced an exponential growth around the world over the last two years, with an increasing number of private and commercial users.

Web sites are becoming a basic business requirement for companies. It is estimated that, by the end of 1996, 80 per cent of America's Fortune 500 firms had a website, compared with only 34 per cent a year earlier. The primary reason given by these companies for the acquisition of websites is to market their products and services, and help their customers, saving them money in the process. If this trend continues, and it is expected to, it will certainly influence people's lives and work, as well as the way companies do business and deliver services. The purpose of this chapter is to assess the role and impact of the Internet on marketing communications in the twenty-first century. It examines the key issues and forces likely to influence future developments in this important field.

The World Wide Web

The growth and commercialization of the Internet would not have been possible without the creation of the world wide web, which was developed at CERN, the European Council for Nuclear Research near Geneva, in 1990. The world wide web, 'the web' or WWW for short, is an interactive, common front-end interface which organizes text and accommodates graphics and multimedia information such as full colour images, sound and even full motion video (Manchester, 1996, pp. 7, 28). Another important innovation of the web is the concept of 'hypertext mark-up language' (HTML) which allows cross-reference of contents of different documents. Therefore, hypertext makes it possible to move through different sources of information irrespective of computer and operating system. The user is able to move from one source of information to another by simply clicking on a hypertext link, which is usually blue and underlined. This mouse click will then move him or her to the desired source without knowing and typing the exact computer address or other information.

To be able to use the web, a user needs to install navigation software, called a web browser. Netscape Navigator is by far the most popular and most widely used browser, and dominates the web browser market worldwide. According to Durlacher Multimedia, Netscape has more than 80 per cent market share in Europe (Durlacher Multimedia, 1996, p. 19), despite the existence of approximately twenty web browsers in the market. However, in future, it is expected that the web browser function will be incorporated into operating systems such as MS Windows.

The web has clearly fuelled the growth of the Internet and is itself the fastest growing area of the Internet. The growth of the Internet is illustrated by the number of hosts worldwide. In 1995, there were 9.5 million hosts supporting 33 million users. Available evidence suggests that the number of hosts increased dramatically with the arrival of the WWW. The web is currently doubling in size every 3 months, measured by the number of websites, with the vast majority of these sites (approximately two-thirds) located in the United States.

The Nature of the Internet

The Internet is a collection of LANs (local area networks), WANs (wide area networks) and stand-alone computers around the world. By using a set of protocols, the Internet protocol (IP), the transmission control protocol (TCP) and the file transmission protocol (FTP), different machines and networks can communicate with each other, irrespective of their operating system (DOS, Windows, MacOS or Unix).

The Internet is not a single network and it is not operated by a single vendor. The networks connected via the IP/FTP are operated independently and there is no single organization that owns the Internet. The Internet may be likened, in a way, to the telephone and TV broadcasting with public and private infrastructures, a growing subscriber or user base, certain types of access devices and various services.

The Internet is a hybrid medium, both in terms of data types transmitted as well as its status as an individual or mass-communications medium. Given its attributes, the Internet may be described as a composite of other networks such as broadcast and telephony.

Despite the commonly held belief of a 'free' Internet, this is not the case, because both the users and vendors pay service providers and network operators for access, communications and storage. This means that the Internet is also unique in terms of revenue generation, since both users and vendors make payments for services provided.

In contrast, voice telephony derives its revenues primarily from subscriber charges – for access and usage – and TV broadcasting charges its subscribers a flat annual rate and generates its revenues primarily from companies advertising in the medium. Exhibit 15.1 summarizes the hybrid attributes of the Internet.

EXHIBIT 15.1   THE INTERNET – A HYBRID MEDIUM
(Scales, 1996)

- Multiple networks
- Communications
  - One-to-One
  - One-to-Many
  - Many-to-One
  - Many-to-Many

- User *and* vendor payments
- Multimedia/bandwidth variable
  - Data
  - Voice
  - Image
  - Video

As at January 1996, the total number of Internet host computers worldwide was about 9.5 million, with the vast majority (more than 60 per cent) located in the United States. Slightly more than 2 million hosts were in Western Europe,[1] making it the second largest Internet market behind the United States. Although Europe lags behind the United States, the question is to what extent. Some industry commentators argue that the time lag is between eighteen and twenty-four months, others claim it is even between three and five years. On average, the delay is believed to be about three years.

Uncertainty also surrounds the number of users per host. However, anyone will agree that there is at least one user per host. Most surveys or estimates assume that there are three to five users per host, others suggest a figure of seven to eight users per host. It seems reasonable to assume that there are several users per host, since many of the hosts connected to the Internet are provided by commercial, governmental, educational or private organizations with several people

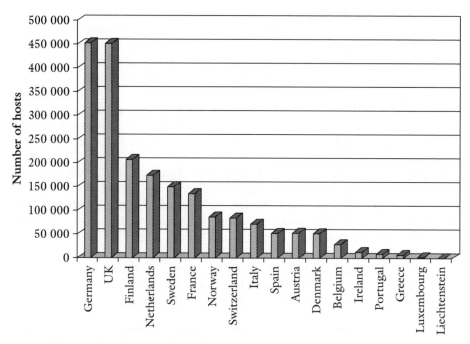

Figure 15.1   Breakdown by country of European hosts in January 1996
(cf. Network Wizards: http://www.nw.com/).

accessing the Internet via that host. This would suggest that Europe's 2 million hosts as of January 1996 could have provided between 6 and 16 million individuals access to the Internet in Europe.

Despite the lack of definitive statistics, it is clear that the Internet has experienced exponential growth across Europe over the last 18–24 months with Germany and the United Kingdom with the highest number of hosts, followed by Finland, The Netherlands and Sweden (cf. http://www.nw.com/). A breakdown of the European hosts is given in figure 15.1.

As at January 1996, 44 per cent of all Western European hosts were located in Germany and the United Kingdom. Another 32 per cent of hosts were located in Finland, The Netherlands, Sweden and France. Italy and Spain accounted for only 7 per cent of the Western European hosts, less than Norway and Switzerland. At the slower end of the market are Austria, Denmark, Belgium and the rest of the Western European countries, with each recording less than 1 per cent. Although the Internet is expected to grow across Western Europe, Germany and the United Kingdom will remain the biggest Western European markets and will also account for approximately 45 per cent of the Western European Internet hosts in the future.

Although Finland, The Netherlands, Sweden and France accounted for 32 per cent of the Western European Internet hosts in January 1996, it is expected that France will become more prominent in the long run, simply because of its size.

This depends on whether and to what extent Minitel, the widely used national electronic information system, can fight off its glamorous rival, the Internet. France Telecom's response has been to launch new Minitel terminals with a colour screen, a higher kbps rate and a secure credit card reader. Italy and Spain, the two remaining countries out of the European 'big five', will need a major boost to progress faster to the more advanced countries. In Italy, this boost might come from the planned investment of roughly $6 billion in fibreoptic networks by the government. Whether this will go ahead remains to be seen. In Spain, there is not even such a boost in sight and it seems as if the liberalization of the Spanish telecommunications sector will be one of the slowest in Europe. Moreover, Spain and Italy's telecommunications tariffs are among the highest in Europe (Capel, 1995).

Most of the other countries, however, are probably too small to increase their shares and are therefore not expected to exceed 5 per cent of the European Internet market. This means that Germany, the United Kingdom, Finland, The Netherlands, Sweden and France, accounting for more than 75 per cent of European Internet hosts, are anticipated to lead Europe into the information age.

The Uptake of the Internet Varies

The uptake and penetration of the Internet varies greatly across Europe with an adoption pattern similar to that of mobile phones and PCs. For instance, mobile phones have a penetration of approximately 40 per cent in Finland, Denmark and Sweden, whereas in Germany the figure is around the 10 per cent level (Wheatley, 1996). If host counts are done on a per-capita basis, the Scandinavian countries, The Netherlands and Switzerland would be among the early adopters of the Internet in Europe, with Finland having a clear lead and countries like the United Kingdom and Germany further down the line.

There seems to be a clear north–south divide in Western Europe. It is particularly noticeable that all the Latin-speaking and Mediterranean countries are at the far end. This picture is also reflected in the level of awareness of the Internet and actual access to it. According to surveys, awareness of the Internet in Europe is highest in Sweden with 91 per cent, and lowest in Spain and Cyprus with 44 and 39 per cent, respectively. These differences are also reflected in the percentage of the adult population with access to the Internet. There are certainly linguistic and cultural reasons for this pattern, since the Internet is clearly dominated by the English language and US-specific content. So non-English-speaking nations are lagging behind. France has been particularly slow in uptake of the Internet, which may be due to the linguistic factor already mentioned, but also due to the widespread use of the Minitel system, the national on-line teletext service network. However, it is not only linguistic reasons that are responsible for this north–south divide. PC penetration and information technology expenditure per capita, which is generally lower in the Mediterranean countries than in the Northern European countries, are also problematic. It needs to be recognized that information technology expenditure is certainly linked to national income levels.

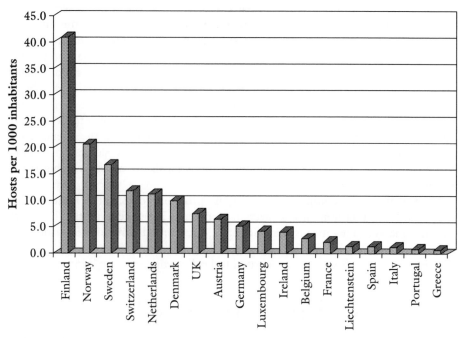

Figure 15.2 Hosts per 1000 inhabitants (calculated on the basis of host count done by Network Wizards and population figures).

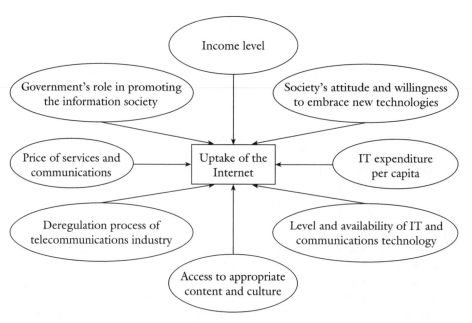

Figure 15.3 Factors influencing the degree of Internet uptake across Europe.

Moreover, the capacity and number of telephone and data lines in place across Europe vary greatly, as do prices of communications and Internet services. This also plays an important role for the varying degree of Internet penetration across Europe (European Information Technology Observatory, 1995). Another reason for the north–south divide is the diverging attitude towards information technology and the digital revolution among governments. The Swedish government, for instance, has a clear goal of promoting the information society in Sweden and is providing substantial resources to put Sweden into a leading position for the information age.

Internet and Marketing Communications

The erosion of the network TV audience during the 1980s and 1990s has changed media plans for ever. In a wide-ranging study of advertising on the Internet, Forrester Research Inc. (1997) observed that television's recent history has demonstrated that media budgets, ultimately, are pragmatic. As audience migrates, media plans follow, acknowledging that the ultimate goal of any brand is to reach its target audience effectively and efficiently. Not surprisingly, media planners are adapting their plans to account for the ever-growing numbers of people spending increasing amounts of time on-line at the expense of other media. Top websites have TV-sized audiences of millions of viewers per day. For example, America On-line, the US Internet service provider, is reported to have more than 8 million subscribers – which is more than any cable TV network or newspaper can boast of.

Types of Marketing Communication on the Internet

The Internet has been used extensively for various forms of marketing communications in its relatively short history. It presents new challenges to the marketer as it is difficult at this point to gauge the extent to which the various forms of marketing communications have been successful or satisfactory. The key objective for each technique, however, is to attract and maintain customer attention and interest by creating excitement and value. As marketing communications on the Internet begin to take up a respectable portion of marketing budgets, attention is now being focused on the nature and effectiveness of the variety of techniques being used for the communication of marketing campaigns on the Internet. In the following sections, we examine the various approaches to marketing on the Internet.

Infomercial

This is a high-involvement approach to marketing communications which is best suited to the discerning customers who are willing to spend a considerable amount of time to research and retrieve information on products and services in which they are interested. Infomercials have proved extremely attractive in the marketing of products for which customers require a lot of information to support their decision-making process. They are particularly useful where product information is highly perishable as details provided through this medium can be updated regularly. It is also possible to have direct contact/communication with the company's employees. Unlike the unidirectional communications of traditional mass media, the Internet is based on a two-way communications flow, which gives a more active role to the user. Increasingly, companies are being attracted to infomercials because of the possibilities of reaching a global audience and the relatively low costs of setting up and maintaining a website. Despite these obvious benefits associated with infomercials, available research evidence suggest that companies are still struggling to make the most of them.

Sponsorship

Sponsorship is a fast-growing technique in corporate communications on the Internet. A well-known brand can sustain its visibility through website sponsorship instead of constructing a big and expensive website. This is particularly effective because logos and positioning lines are sufficient to create the required impact. Various types of sponsorship are now available and include the sponsorship on-line schedules of league matches, sport results information services, news and current affairs. In the United Kingdom, for example, Carling Lager sponsors Carling Net football. Usually, sites with a high number of visitors generate the greatest interest in prospective sponsors. One of the advantages of sponsorship is that users who would not actively seek the advertiser's website are 'ambushed' through the sponsorship of a popular website such as the BBC On-line, CNN and ESPN SportsZone.

Display advertising and advertainment

Advertainment offers companies the opportunity to maintain a corporate site. Experts suggest that companies need a 'face to the public' that catches search engine queries and serves investor relations and recruiting groups. Advertainment offers the opportunity for advertisers to achieve this objective. It is suitable for products of low involvement and low information intensity. The content of these advertisements is often designed in such a way that it enhances brand equity. It is particularly appropriate for lifestyle products such as Levis, Rolex, Coca-Cola and feminine hygiene products. Often, competitions and games feature in advertainment to create a sense of entertainment and involvement.

Electronic mail

One of the most exciting developments in the use of the Internet as a marketing communications medium is the use of electronic mail (e-mail). E-mail exhibits attributes similar to those used in printed mail shots. It is an effective direct and personal form of advertisement because of its power to induce attention from recipients. It employs the same principles as direct mail. By using e-mail databases, advertisers try to develop and sustain a personal relationship with their target audience through a process of ongoing communication. Users receive regularly updated product information and it fosters a sense of importance in them.

Banner advertisements

This is the most widely used form of marketing communication on the Internet. Banner advertising is described as a rectangular clickable graphic, which enables users to search through a company's web pages. Jupiter Communications reports that advertising banners comprise 80 per cent of all on-line placement and ad spend. The impact of banner advertisement extends beyond the search process. Banners can create an instant and effective impression on surfers without a 'click-through'. Further, consumers have no problem with claims made on banner advertising. It is as credible as the traditional media. Banner advertising exhibits the same characteristics as printed poster advertisement, but with the additional benefit of interactivity. It is, therefore, not surprising that the benefits it offers include significant brand communications prowess, which can lead to the formulation of a positive attitude towards a brand by consumers – with the potential to increase sales.

Studies on the effectiveness of banner advertisement suggest that it is more likely to be noticed than TV advertisement. Although TV advertising may be more intrusive because of the combined effect of sight, sound and motion, it is still a passive medium because there is no element of audience involvement in the process. Banner advertisements have the benefit of user involvement as they create a sense of adventure and help the inquisitive surfer.

On-line Publications

On-line publication is increasingly becoming a popular vehicle for advertisement on the Internet. It has characteristics similar to the traditional print media, but with a further dimension of interactivity. The attractiveness of this medium stems from the fact that advertisers have a guaranteed number of visitors to a particular website such as the *Financial Times On-line* which is attracting an audience from 180 countries worldwide. Other attractive on-line publications for advertisers include the *Wall Street Journal*, *Time Magazine*, *New York Times* and the *Economist*.

On-line Sales

This form of marketing communication combines both the advertising and sales roles. On-line sales enable a company's products to be sold on-line. It follows the same principles as home shopping, popularized by the American TV shopping network QVC (Quality, Value and Convenience). The volume and value of sales generated by companies through on-line sales are increasing phenomenally. Its growth is only restricted by the fear induced by on-line crimes such as the misuse of credit card information. It is believed that when it becomes safer to conduct on-line transactions, on-line sale will really take off in a big way.

It is now clear that the Internet will have a profound effect on international marketing communications over the next twenty to thirty years. Although it is not expected to replace the traditional advertising media such as TV and print and outdoor facilities, the Internet will support and strengthen the industry. It will make it not just possible, but easier, to reach and communicate with potentially interested audiences. By using keywords, it is quite easy for customers to access websites with specific products for which they have a specific interest. By using the keywords 'search for airline tickets', for example, a list of travel agents, prices and destinations is generated, making it possible for a potential traveller to communicate with travel service providers. Thus, the Internet combines the advertising and direct marketing functions simultaneously.

Perhaps one of the most important aspects of advertising on the Internet is its capacity to provide immediate and accurate measurement of its effectiveness. Bill Wanamaker, an American marketing executive, once remarked that 'Half of advertising expenditure is wasted, but the difficulty is knowing which half'. On the Internet, it is very easy to know which half because each 'click-through' is recorded. It makes it possible to evaluate the effectiveness of each advertising campaign.

Revenues from advertising on the Internet have been very slow in coming. Against the trend of growing popularity of the Internet, advertisers have been too cautious in making substantial budgetary allocation to it because of the uncertainties surrounding this new and exciting medium in terms of value for money. It is too new a medium for advertisers to be sure they will get their money's worth. Indeed, the total global Internet advertising revenue for 1996 was just $267 million compared with $33 billion spent on TV advertising in the United States alone (*The Economist*, May 10, 1997). However, analysts remain optimistic that as the popularity of the medium continues to grow, so will the confidence of advertisers.

Despite the impressive statistics on the development and growth of the Internet, it is highly unlikely that, in the short to medium term, it will replace other marketing communications media. The technical capability required to make widespread use of the Internet possible may not be available for some time to come.

Political and Legal Framework

As the Internet grows into a unique communications medium, which transcends national borders, the question of regulation will continue to arise, with opinions both pro and con. It is worth pointing out that, throughout history, new communication technologies have always been met with fears and concerns regarding the powerful influence they exert on audiences.

The problems of pornography, libel, copyright, trademark, racist propaganda, just to name but a few Internet-related legal issues, have received extensive media coverage. It seems that due to the greater anonymity of the Internet, people are much more daring in what they write and do over a computer network than they are in real life.

This has brought about a heated debate as to who – service providers and/or computer owners – is to be held responsible for cases of libel, pornography or infringements on copyright. Some service providers interviewed, however, regarded the legal issues surrounding the Internet as being exaggerated in the press and receiving a lot of media hype.

The problem of law enforcement

One of the biggest problems of Internet regulation is the issue of law enforcement. Owing to the global and decentralized nature of the Internet, regulation and censorship attempts are extremely difficult to police. Furthermore, what is legal in one country, may be illegal in another. So, posting neo-Nazi material on the Internet is anti-constitutional in Germany, but falls mainly under the freedom of speech act in the United States.

Moreover, the Internet community tends to interpret 'censorship as damage, and routes around it' as happened with the well-known case of CompuServe in Germany. German prosecutors pushed CompuServe to block pornographic photo and chat groups with the effect that almost instantaneously some resourceful users publicized tips on how to get around that ban on the Internet as well as in Internet-specific magazines.

These legal issues have continually raised the question of regulation, which now seems more and more inevitable. Yet there may be two options, state regulation versus self-regulation, with the Internet community favouring self-regulation and many governments being inclined towards state regulation.

Self-regulation through technology and rating

In order to block sites unsuitable for children or other vulnerable groups, several methods have been available so far. Unsuitable sites can either be blocked by Internet access providers, as happened in the case of CompuServe in Germany, or by software.

The software either screens sites for suspicious words and then blocks sites containing these words, or the user can set his or her own criteria according to which the software blocks access to a list of known sites.

However, these approaches all centre around list making, which in the face of the rapidly growing number of Internet hosts becomes an impossible task. In addition, these methods have other drawbacks.

Word-screening software, for instance, blocks off sites irrespective of the meaning and context that the word appears in. This lack of semantic and contextual sensitivity caused America On-line to 'accidentally shut down a forum for discussing breast cancer, because it mentioned breasts'.

PICS – a proposal for self-regulation

Since all these methods have proved inadequate, a self-rating scheme called 'Platform for Internet Content Selection' (PICS) was proposed in May 1998 by a group of Internet and software companies, scientists from the Massachusetts Institute of Technology and the WWW Consortium. However, some say that its origins lie in the American Communications Decency Act, and that this Act threatens to impose strict standards on electronic information.

PICS is a new system for grading websites, similar to the film industry's movie rating. It consists of four rating categories – sex, violence, language and nudity – and each category is rated on a scale from zero to four. A site is rated either by its author or by the publishing service provider by answering a detailed questionnaire about the site's content. How effective this self-rating is remains to be seen.

Having received its four grades, the site is then electronically marked as PICS tested. This means that Internet navigation software itself can recognize whether a PICS-tested site is within the decency or tolerance level pre-programmed by a parent, a teacher or a government. If it is not, the browser will automatically deny access.

The rating list is held at another Internet address with the browser software pointing to this address and being set to accept the ratings given by the list. This means that this rating list can be provided by an organization or a single person, who can update and change the list according to requirements. Parents or teachers trusting a certain rating service will accept their advice for suitable websites.

The only web browser so far available that can use the PICS system is the new beta version of Microsoft's Explorer. Nevertheless, it is predicted that 'By the end of this year, PICS will probably have become a standard across millions of sites and tens of millions of browsers'.

By and large, the proposed self-regulation scheme may well work out for content rating, but whether the above optimism can be shared remains to be seen. PICS certainly does not solve all the other legal problems surrounding the Internet and even PICS itself may be viewed as a pre-emptive action of self-regulation in the face of the new legal situation in the United States.

State regulation

Despite the proposed self-regulatory scheme, governments across the world are gearing up to regulate the Internet. The United States is ahead of Europe in imposing laws and regulations, but many expect Europe to catch up soon.

GLOSSARY

ADSL	asymmetric digital subscriber line	LINX	London Internet Exchange
ATM	asynchronous transfer mode	M-bone	multicast/multimedia backbone
BBS	bulletin board service (full on-line service with packaged content)	Minitel	widely used electronic information system in France
DAB	digital audio broadcasting	OEM	original equipment manufacturer
e-mail	electronic mail	PICS	platform for Internet content selection
e-zine	electronic magazine		
FCC	Federal Communications Commission (USA)	PoP	point of presence
		PSTNet	public switched telephone network
FTP	file transfer protocol	PTO	public telecommunications operator
GSG	Government Systems Group (Motorola)	SDH	synchronous digital hierarchy
HTML	hypertext mark-up language	SPS	Semiconductor Products Sector (Motorola)
HTTP	hypertext transfer protocol		
IP	Internet protocol	TCP	transmission control protocol
ISDN	integrated services digital network	WAN	wide area network
LAN	local area network	WWW	world wide web

NOTE

1 Western Europe includes the following countries: Austria, Belgium, Denmark, Finland, France, Germany, Greece, Ireland, Italy, Liechtenstein, Luxembourg, The Netherlands, Norway, Portugal, Spain, Sweden, Switzerland, the United Kingdom.

REFERENCES

Capel, J. (1995) *Telecoms in Europe*, December, no. 3.

Manchester, P. (1996) Cern. In *FT Surveys: A–Z of the Internet*.

Scales, I. (1996) Surely some mistake? *Communications International*, February, p. 44.

Wheatley, J. (1996) Telecoms consortia on hold for Brazilian bidding. In *Financial Times*, 28 June 1996, 32.

16 The Practices of Multinational Corporations and Advertising Standardization

GREG HARRIS AND SULEIMAN ATTOUR

Background

The issue of international advertising standardization versus adaptation has been a focus of discussion for over three decades. A review of the literature dealing with advertising standardization reveals the following points:

- Limited available empirical data regarding the practices of multinational companies.
- Questions about the operationalization of standardization – various definitions were used.
- Polarization of the issue.
- Confusion between companies' policies and practices.

There are, therefore, indications that there is a need to measure empirically the extent of advertising standardization practised by multinational corporations (MNCs), in order to find out how three decades of debates about advertising standardization are reflected in their practices.

In the past, one of two methods was normally used to measure the extent of standardization. The first method was achieved by questionnaires sent to executives of MNCs, asking them to describe, or rather estimate, the extent of standardization practised by their companies. The second method was content analysis of advertising. In this chapter, we analyse both methods and illustrate why we find the second method to be more appropriate. In addition, by reviewing the literature, we examine the methodologies that have been employed, and illustrate the need for major modification of these methods.

The countries investigated in this study include France, the United Kingdom, Germany, Spain, Italy, Greece, Saudi Arabia, United Arab Emirates (Dubai), Kuwait and Lebanon. The European segment of the sample covers almost 80 per cent of the population of the European Union. The Arab segment of the sample represents a major consumer market that has been neglected in the literature.

Introduction

The issue of international advertising standardization versus adaptation has been a focus for discussion for over three decades. Almost one-third of the international advertising literature deals with the specific issue of advertising standardization. The importance of the issue is illustrated by the large amount of money spent on advertising.

From figure 16.1, we can see that the total worldwide advertising expenditure in 1993 was $312 billion, and that the pattern of advertising expenditure continues to increase substantially over time. The MNCs' share of this expenditure is considerable. For example, one company, Procter & Gamble, have spent almost $4.3 billion on international advertising in 1993 alone. Examples of the expenditure of other MNCs is also shown in table 16.1.

Given this high level of expenditure, it is crucial for MNCs to ensure that their budgets are deployed in the most effective manner. International advertising standardization is one policy option that is considered by many as a solution to the problems raised by international coordination.

One of the critical issues facing MNCs is the extent to which they should attempt to influence/control the advertising policies and campaigns of the various advertising subsidiaries. This issue is important given the expenditure involved. Over the years, three schools of thought have emerged. The first is that advertising standardization is the optimal policy (Elinder, 1965; Flatt, 1967; Levitt,

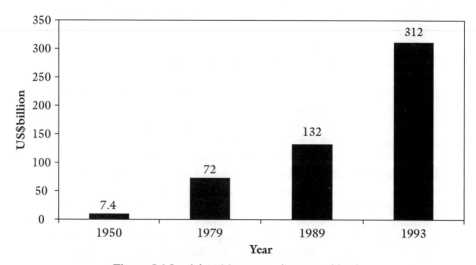

Figure 16.1 Advertising expenditure worldwide.

Table 16.1 Advertising expenditure by selected multinational companies

Multinational company	1993 ($ million)
Procter & Gamble	4298.5
Unilever	2626.2
Nestle	1916.4
Philip Morris	2557.5
General Motors	2139.8
Ford Motor	1492.5
Toyota Motor	1112.6
Pepsi Co.	1383.7
McDonald's	1034.6

1983; Kirpalani et al., 1988), the second was that some form of advertising adaptation or localization is optimal (Buzzell, 1968; Ricks et al., 1974; Reichel, 1989), and the third school argued in favour of the contingency approach, and contended that the efficacy of standardization depends on various factors, such as the specific markets and products involved (Miracle, 1968; Kotler, 1986; Porter, 1986; Sheth, 1986).

The aim of this research is to find out how three decades of debate about advertising standardization are reflected in the practices of MNCs, i.e. which school of thought is supported by the practices of MNCs. In other words, do MNCs standardize or adapt their advertising for the same brands across the countries studied?

A review of the literature dealing with advertising standardization reveals the following points:

1 Only limited available empirical data regarding the practices of MNCs have been presented.
2 Questions about the operationalization of standardization, since various definitions of standardization were used.
3 Polarization of the issue – in most instances, the focus has been on either complete standardization or complete adaptation.
4 Confusion between companies' policies and practices.

The majority of the researchers who wanted to examine the practices of MNCs, with reference to whether and how they standardize or adapt their international advertisements, have chosen to ask the executives about the policies and practices of their companies (questionnaire surveys). The opinions of these executives were then used as a proxy to their actual behaviour. A second approach was content analysis of advertising. The articles for both methods are shown in table 16.2.

We analysed both methods and found that the content analysis approach measures *actual* practices of MNCs, while the questionnaire survey method falls short

Table 16.2 Previous articles (surveys)

Authors	Journals
Ryans et al. (1969, 1970, 1977)	*Journal of Marketing*
Ward (1973)	*Journal of International Business Studies*
Weichmann and Sorenson (1975)	*Harvard Business Review*
Dunn (1976)	*Journal of Marketing*
Killough (1978)	*Harvard Business Review*
Boddewyn et al. (1986)	*Business Horizons*
Kirpalani et al. (1988)	*International Journal of Advertising*
Riesenbek and Freeling (1991)	*The McKinsey Quarterly*
Hill and James (1991)	*International Marketing Review*
Sandler and Shani (1992)	*International Marketing Review*
Harris (1994)	*Journal of International Marketing*

on this criterion. The problem with the questionnaire method is the difficulty the respondents face in describing or summarizing their company's policies and practices. For example, in many instances, executives are asked to generalize about their company's practices across all their brands and in all their markets. Responses to such questions represent at best generalizations. Alternatively, if the respondents are asked simply to describe their company's policies/practices for one brand, while the responses may have more descriptive validity, how representative will they be of the company's policies? Therefore, it was decided to employ the content analysis of advertising for the purposes of this study.

Studies that Investigated the Similarity/Difference of Advertisements Across Countries

Only three studies used an approach different to survey to investigate the degree of standardization versus adaptation of international advertising: Mueller (1989), Whitelock and Chung (1989) and Seitz and Johar (1993).

Mueller (1989)

In Mueller's study, the author '. . . compared pairs of advertisements to determine the degree of similarity between foreign messages and US baseline advertisements. The instrument designed to investigate the degree of standardisation of print advertisements focused on the advertising theme, slogan, headlines, subheads, body copy, models and spokespersons, visual/background scenes, product attributes, product packaging, product name, product(s) portrayed.'

The articles did not specify what aspects of these elements were evaluated. For instance, it is not clear whether the researcher was measuring the presence/absence of a slogan in the advertisement, or whether the slogan in one ad is the exact translation of its baseline advertisement. The same ambiguity applies to the headline, subheads and body copy.

As for the measurement scales used, the author noted that 'Polar opposite terms anchored the five-point scales without spelling out the meaning of the intermediate scale points. Pairs of advertisements were presented to coders in random order. Once each element rated, the advertising pair received a mean rating reflecting the degree of similarity between the messages. The closer the mean rating to "1", the greater the similarity (standardisation) between the two advertisements. The closer the mean rating to "5", the greater the difference (or specialisation) between the two messages.' According to Mueller (1989): 'This classification scheme represents an innovation in the ability to analyse the level of similarity between advertisements'.

As for the sampling strategy, samples of advertisements were requested from American advertising agencies in the United States, Germany and Japan, as well as from major US advisers. Because of this strategy, the sample used was vulnerable to bias for many reasons. To give examples, the samples of advertisements obtained might not have been representative of all advertisements in the relevant markets, or the advertisers who responded to the request for advertisements probably share some characteristics that are related to the elements being investigated, and therefore affect the results. To quote Mueller: 'The letter specified an interest in obtaining pairs of television and magazine advertisements reflective of campaigns in which the foreign message was *identical* to the US advertisement (other than translation), campaigns in which the foreign advertisement was *modified* in part, and campaigns in which the foreign advertisement was *entirely different* from the US advertisements'.

This means of soliciting advertisements with specific characteristics introduces an additional kind of bias and limits the value of the findings. Mueller acknowledges the inadequacy of such a sampling strategy by stating that: 'This sampling strategy is purposive . . . Subsequent research will emphasise external validity using sample strategies that ensure representativeness of the advertisements selected in the nations studied.'

The results of this study showed that standardized messages were more transferred among Western markets than between Western and Eastern markets.

Product type was found to be more influential on the use of standardized messages than market distance. Another finding was that, regardless of the country, message standardization was more common for TV advertising than for print advertising.

At the end of the study, the author highlighted the importance of conducting a similar experiment in some developing nations by noting that: 'The factors highlighted in this analysis require further explication and exploration. For example, it would be of value to investigate the degree of standardisation versus specialisation of commercial messages transferred to developing countries versus those transferred to other industrial nations.'

Whitelock and Chung (1989)

The purpose of this study was to compare advertisements in the same medium for the same brands in two culturally diverse European countries: France and the United Kingdom. These two countries were chosen because they are considered to be economically similar and culturally different. However, the choice of countries was not based on the available cultural theory, but mainly on convenience.

Advertisements for the same brands were obtained from one magazine category (women) in both countries. The magazines were *Marie-Claire* (France) and *Woman's Journal* (United Kingdom). The study was conducted between July 1985 and June 1986. These specific magazines were chosen according to the following criteria: availability of back issues and readership profile. The researchers initially intended to use the following seven categories for their experiment:

- Beauty and toiletries.
- Fashion.
- Food and drink.
- Household requisites.
- Miscellaneous.
- Shopping gallery.
- Travel.

However, there was not a single common advertisement for six out of the seven categories. Advertisements for the same brands in both countries were found only in the beauty and toiletries category, forty-three brands in total.

A model was developed by the researchers to evaluate the degree of standardization of advertisements across the two countries, where the following points were taken into consideration: picture size, colour, general layout, caption, explanatory text. A score was given for each difference, while a difference in the picture (of the advertisement) was given the full ten points and considered as total adaptation. For the remaining elements of the ad, a total of nine points is divided as follows: one point for size difference; one point for colour difference; one point for general layout difference; three points for caption differences (one point increment); three points for explanatory text (one point increment).

To measure the degree of standardization, the total score is subtracted from a total of ten (standardization = 10 – total score). Therefore, an ad that is awarded ten points will receive a 10 – 10 = 0 points on standardization (i.e. total adaptation).

The results of Whitelock and Chung's study have shown that 16.3 per cent of the ads have difference in their general layout. It was also found that 11.6 per cent of the ads (all fragrance ads) did not have a caption. Of the remaining ads, 14 per cent had identical captions. The majority of the advertisements (60.8 per cent) had a caption written in the language appropriate to the country. Only seven advertisements (13.5 per cent), all for perfumes, were found to be exactly the same in both magazines, while nine advertisements (17.3 per cent) were

considered to be cases of total adaptation. The results of Whitelock and Chung's study have demonstrated two points. The first is that advertising standardization should be viewed on a continuum, as was previously suggested by many authors. The second point is that total standardization is the exception rather than the rule.

Seitz and Johar (1993)

In this article, the same model as Whitelock and Chung (1989) was used, and no methodological changes to it were introduced. Only four months (Nov. 1991–Feb. 1992) of women's monthly publications were used, employing just nine products (three for perfume, three for apparel and three for cosmetics). It was suggested in the results that perfume, cosmetics and apparel products exhibit high standardization, moderate standardization and high localization, respectively.

Proposed Content Analysis Model

Our proposed model is based on the one developed by Whitelock and Chung (1989). We have introduced significant modifications to the elements analysed, and also added additional ones. A major development on their model is the meaning and measurement of 'differences'. In this case, elements were judged to be either similar or different from the baseline advertisement. However, this is not always the case. Very often, when the need arises to adapt an element to local specifications, a local replacement (i.e. a local version) of that element is normally used. A local replacement of an element indicates an adaptation to the advertising *execution*, while replacement of an element with a completely different one could also result from an adaptation to the advertising *strategy*. These are crucial differences that should be accounted for in the model.

In the Whitelock and Chung (1989) model (exhibit 16.1), the picture of the advertisement was treated as one [undividable] element. However, it is often the case that specific parts of the picture, e.g. model(s), visual background, etc., are modified, and not the picture as a whole. Therefore, in order to sensitize our model to these fine differences, it was decided to break down the element 'picture' into its more basic components, namely visual background, model(s)/spokesperson, and an additional factor to allow for minor or major modifications to the picture.

Whitelock and Chung's model did not examine the portrayal of product and packaging. These elements are very important. When an MNC is introducing an established product into a new market, even if the original advertisement does not portray the product or packaging, it is customary to show the product and/or packaging in their advertisements, in order for the prospects to be able to recognize the product. Therefore, in our proposed model, we will examine the portrayal of product and packaging with reference to whether these are present or absent, and whether there is a difference in the size or number (i.e. the number of times the product is shown).

Exhibit 16.1 Modifications to the 'Whitelock and Chung' model

1 Definition of differences
   - Similar
   - Different: replaced by local
   - Completely different
2 The elements
   (i) Picture
      - Visual background
      - Model(s)/spokesperson(s)
      - Modifications:
        – Minor
        – Major
   (ii) Product portrayal:
      - Absent/present
      - Difference in size
      - Difference in number
      - Replaced by local
      - Other differences
   (iii) Product packaging:
      - Absent/present
      - Difference in size
      - Difference in number
      - Replaced by local
      - Other differences
   (iv) Text:
      (a) Headline:
         - Same/translated/different
         - Present/absent
      (b) Subhead:
         - Same/translated/different
         - Present/absent
      (c) Body text (copy):
         - Same/translated/different
         - Present/absent
      (d) Slogan:
         - Same/translated/different
         - Present/absent

A preliminary analysis of a number of international advertising campaigns showed that some components of the verbal content of an advertisement may vary, e.g. body text, while others do not, e.g. slogan. This is similar to one of Harris's (1994) findings. Therefore, it was decided to break down the verbal contents of an advertisement into its basic components, namely headline, subhead, body text and slogan. These will be evaluated with reference to whether the components are present/absent, translated into a different language but keeping same meaning, or completely different in meaning.

A first round of modifications are introduced to enhance the sensitivity and objectivity of the model, which is later tested on various international advertising campaigns. A second round of modifications resulted in a universal model capable of detecting the slightest advertising differences in an objective manner. The initial version of our model is presented in exhibit 16.2. This model will be used for the pilot study to test its suitability as a method of analysis.

Exhibit 16.2 The model

1 Picture (40 points):
- (a) Visual background (20 points):
  - Local (10 points)
  - Different (20 points)
- (b) Model(s)/spokesperson (10 points):
  - Local (5 points)
  - Different (10 points)
- (c) Modifications (10 points)
  - Minor (5 points)
  - Major (10 points)
2 Text (32 points):
- (a) Headline (10 points):
  - Same language/different meaning (3 points)
  - Translated/same meaning (6 points)
  - Completely different (10 points)
- (b) Subhead (6 points):
  - Same language/different meaning (2 points)
  - Translated/same meaning (3 points)
  - Completely different (6 points)
- (c) Body text (copy) (10 points):
  - Same language/different meaning (3 points)
  - Translated/same meaning (6 points)
  - Completely different (10 points)
- (d) Slogan (6 points):
  - Same language/different meaning (2 points)
  - Translated/same meaning (3 points)
  - Completely different (6 points)

---

3 General layout (10 points):
   - Minor differences (5 points)
   - Major differences (5 points)
4 Product portrayal (6 points):
   - Difference in size (1 point)
   - Difference in number (2 points)
   - Replaced by local (2 points)
   - Other differences (2 points)
5 Product packaging (6 points):
   - Difference in size (1 point)
   - Difference in number (1 point)
   - Replaced by local (2 points)
   - Other differences (2 points)
6 Colour(s) of the advertisements (3 points):
   - Colour versus black and white (1 point)
   - Different colour (3 points)
7 Size of the advertisement (3 points):
   - As original + extra section (1 point)
   - Different size (3 points)

Total score = sum of points from all the elements
Degree of standardization = 100 − total Score

From the pilot stage, we found that some MNCs employ the same advertising layout for a number of brands. For example, Nivea Visage uses the same layout with the logo centred in the middle of the page, dividing it into two halves – the top half contains a photograph of the model and the lower half contains a photograph of the product. Therefore, an advertisement for a different Nivea Visage brand would contain a different photograph of the product to portray the new brand, but not necessarily a different photograph of the model, depending on the age group of the target prospects.

To complicate matters further, some advertisers often use the same visual of the product, for the same brand in the same country, but a different visual of the model. This practice is sometimes adopted by advertisers in order to avoid boredom in the target prospects that may result from multiple exposures to the same advertisement. Similarly, when the advertising strategy calls for multiple exposures to the same advertising message, advertisers often create different versions of advertising copy, using the same advertising claims, but presented differently.

These and other tactics of creating variations around a theme are sometimes used to counteract the potential boredom that might result from multiple exposures to the same message. Therefore, there is a chance to develop the model further and render it more sensitive to these fine differences. For the visual part, various modifications are introduced to increase the sensitivity of the model in a quantitative way, without compromising its objectivity. The analysis of the visual background will be carried out for the product and the model separately. Further modifications to the element 'model' include breaking it down into the following four subelements at two points each:

1   *Pose of the model:* advertisers employ different poses of the model to convey different meanings, e.g. relaxing, attentive, etc. Since these different poses convey different meanings, they should be accounted for in the model.
2   *Photographic distance:* this element is also used to create different effects. For instance, a close-up is more personal, while a long shot not showing the face conveys mysticism.
3   *Relation of the model to the product:* whether the model is looking at the product, using it, holding it, etc.
4   *Relation of the model to the reader/viewer:* whether the model is looking towards the viewer, or away to the side of the page, etc.

These tactics convey different meanings to the reader and therefore should be accounted for in the model. While any such scaling is to some extent subjective, our model serves the primary purpose of highlighting differences in a more replicable and verifiable manner than prior research.

The research sample

The following ten countries are proposed for this research: the United Kingdom, France, Germany, Spain, Italy, Greece, the United Arab Emirates (Dubai), Saudi Arabia, Kuwait and Lebanon. The European segment of the sample covers almost 80 per cent of the population of the European Union, while the Arab segment of the sample represents a major consumer market that has been neglected in the literature.

In 1990, these Arab markets accounted for 26 per cent of all European exports, 22 per cent of all Japanese exports, 27 per cent of the exports of all South-East Asian countries and 14 per cent of all American exports. Furthermore, these countries accounted for 50 per cent of world sales of luxury watches, and are considered to be major markets for luxury products (Baker and Abou-Ismail, 1993).

The selection of the European countries was based on the following criteria:

* Together they constitute 80 per cent of the EC population.
* They share similar media characteristics and availability.
* They are at a similar economic developmental stage.
* They have similar political systems.
* They exhibit similar consumer behaviour patterns.

The Arab countries chosen have many elements in common, including:

- Similar media characteristics and availability.
- Similar economic developmental stage.
- Similar political systems.
- Similar social and cultural characteristics.
- Same religion.
- Geographical proximity.
- Membership in the same community (except Lebanon).
- Same language.
- Major consumer markets for image and luxury products.

To control for the effect of the publication category, only women's publications (monthly/weekly) are used. The criteria for selection and publications are readership profile and high circulation.

The period of the study covers twelve months (Jan. 1996–Dec. 1996) and all twelve issues are used. All advertisements of all sizes, colour and black/white are selected, with the exception of classified advertisements. To control for the effects of the product categories, the results are presented for each product class separately. This sampling category is designed to lead to the selection of advertisements for companies:

- That are large MNCs.
- Where international sales are important (at least 20 per cent).
- Where sales performance is influenced by advertising.

The magazine *Vogue*, which was also used by Seitz and Johar (1993), is considered the most appropriate magazine for this research, as it enjoys similar readership profiles across Europe. In addition, women's apparel, perfumes and cosmetics are the most advertised products in this publication. Therefore, in order for our study to result in findings that are comparable to those reached by other authors, it was decided to use publication titles comparable to those used in previous research. For Greece and the Arab world, since *Vogue* magazine is not available, women's magazines with matching readership profiles were chosen.

Research question

Given the existing country/cultural differences among the markets studied (as shown below), we anticipate that MNCs will practise substantial adaptation to their advertising across markets. Some of the differences include:

- Different languages.
- High/low context cultures.
- Hard sell/soft sell.
- Different brand positioning.
- Different marketing environments.
- Difference in socio-economic stratification.

- Different advertising regulations.
- Difference in advertising expenditure.
- Differences in the portrayal of elderly/youth/children.

This research aims to find out:

1 Whether the key executional elements were standardized, to what extent and in how many markets.
2 Whether advertising standardization is standardization of advertising related to other factors, e.g. product.
3 The trend over time.

Initial results and discussion

In order to avoid the problems associated with the use of different versions of the same advertisement as discussed above, the results of this study will be presented in a matrix format, where each country's advertising will be compared to all other countries, including the country under investigation itself (table 16.3). This method will enable us to measure the within-country variation, including the variation resulting from the use of multiple versions of the same advertisement. Therefore, in order for the advertisements of any two countries to be considered different, the between-country differences should exceed the within-country differences.

To illustrate, from table 16.3 we can see that the standardization measure between Lebanon and Italy is very low at 3 per cent. However, we cannot conclude that the advertisements for brand (1) between the two countries are different simply because the within-country advertising standardization (for brand 1) in Lebanon is also very low at 3 per cent. As indicated above, to consider two countries different, the between-countries differences should exceed the within-countries differences. This sensitive measure of between-countries differences is considered an innovation, since none of the previous methods that were used to measure country differences accounted for the within-country differences.

An advertising standardization index (SI) will be calculated as the average standardization score of all brands across all countries for a specific year. This SI will, in the future, be calculated for different years on a regular basis, in order to show the trends in advertising standardization, and to indicate whether the trend is towards more standardization or the opposite.

A subindex will be calculated for each product class to investigate whether consumers' needs and values for specific product classes, as perceived by the advertisers, are in fact converging/or diverging over time, and whether these product classes are in fact moving from their local or regional boundaries, to attain a more global status. The results obtained will be discussed in detail once all brands have been analysed. The final analysis will include factor analysis, cluster analysis and multidimensional scaling.

An initial look at the results in table 16.4 reveals that one brand (6.6 per cent) was found to be a case of total standardization. Seven other brands (46.67 per

Table 16.3 Similarity matrix for brand (1)

	UK (%)	France (%)	Germany (%)	Spain (%)	Italy (%)	Greece (%)	Saudi Arabia (%)	Lebanon (%)	UAE (%)
UK	100	94	96	94	94	92	97	97	97
France	100	100	100	97	100	91	3	3	3
Germany	96	100	100	97	100	91	3	3	3
Spain	94	97	97	100	97	91	3	3	3
Italy	92	100	100	97	100	91	3	3	3
Greece	97	91	91	91	91	0	92	92	92
Saudi Arabia	97	3	3	3	3	94	100	100	100
Lebanon	97	3	3	3	3	100	100	100	100
UAE	97	3	3	3	3	100	100	100	100
Total	92.5	61.37	61.62	60.62	61.37	93.75	50.12	38	50.12

UAE = United Arab Emirates.

Table 16.4 Summary of advertising standardization score for different brands

	UK (%)	France (%)	Germany (%)	Spain (%)	Italy (%)	Greece (%)	Saudi Arabia (%)	Lebanon (%)	UAE (%)	Total (%)
Brand 1	92.5	61.37	61.62	60.62	61.37	93.75	50.12	38	50.12	63.27
Brand 2	93.9	93.9	93.9	93.9	93.9	93.9	90	90	90	92.6
Brand 3	90	90	90	90	90	90	80	80	80	86.87
Brand 4	94.7	94.7	94.7	94.7	94.7	94.7	96	96	96	95.13
Brand 5	94.44	91.11	91.11	91.11	91.11	91.11	94.44	94.44	94.44	92.59
Brand 6	96.7	96.7	96.7	96.7	96.7	96.7	93.33	93.33	93.33	95.58
Brand 7	100	100	100	100	100	100	100	100	100	100
Brand 8	55	–	47	–	56	83	85	85	85	70.86
Brand 9	87	–	87	87	84	84	–	–	–	85.8
Brand 10	89	89	89	89	–	–	100	100	100	93.71

Table 16.4 (cont'd)

	UK (%)	France (%)	Germany (%)	Spain (%)	Italy (%)	Greece (%)	Saudi Arabia (%)	Lebanon (%)	UAE (%)	Total (%)
Brand 11	93	97	95	–	–	97	–	–	–	95.5
Brand 12	91	91	91	91	91	91	93.25	93.25	93.25	91.75
Brand 13	88	88	88	88	88	88	91	91	91	89
Brand 14	74	81	75	72	65	–	–	–	–	73.4
Brand 15	39	39	39	39	39	39	33	33	33	37
All fragrances	94.61	89.68	89.72	89.58	89.68	94.31	86.27	84.54	86.27	89.41
All watches	90.25	91.25	90.75	89.33	89.5	92	94.75	94.75	94.75	91.93
All cosmetics	71	–	67	87	70	83.5	85	85	85	79.19
All apparel	56.5	60	57	55.5	52	39	33	33	33	46.56
All brands	85.22	85.6	82.6	84.08	80.83	87.86	82.85	82.84	83.85	83.85

UAE = United Arab Emirates.

cent) obtain a score higher than 90 per cent, indicating a very high level of advertising standardization.

Furthermore, from the results shown in table 16.4, we can see that a pattern is starting to emerge. The advertisements for watch and fragrance product classes obtained very high standardization scores at 91.93 per cent and 89.41 per cent, respectively, indicating very high levels of advertising standardization. This indicates that either these product classes are universal, and not vulnerable to cultural and country differences, or that MNCs are inclined to standardize their advertising for these products, regardless of the efficacy of international advertising standardization.

Advertisements for cosmetics products obtained an average standardization score of 79.19 per cent, indicating medium levels of adaptation. This result suggests that cosmetic products are, in a relative sense, more affected by cultural/country differences that require a medium level of advertising adaptation than watches and fragrance product classes. This is probably due to the fact that people from Southern and Eastern countries have, on average, a darker skin colour and complexion that calls for different cosmetic products and colours.

The advertisements for apparel brands obtained the lowest standardization score of 46.56 per cent, indicating relatively high levels of advertising adaptation. This result confirms the belief that apparel and fashion products are culture bound, hence requiring higher levels of advertising adaptation, as suggested in the literature (Seitz and Johar, 1993).

The initial advertising standardization index (SI) for the sample examined was found to be 83.85 per cent, indicating a generally high level of advertising standardization. The reason behind this high standardization, which runs against expectations, is that the brands investigated so far are the most standardized brands in all of the markets investigated. Once the remaining brands are fully analysed, a lower level of advertising standardization is expected to emerge.

REFERENCES

Baker, M. J. and Abou-Ismail, F. (1993) Organisational buying behavior in the Gulf. *International Marketing Review*, 10(6), 42–60.

Buzzell, R. D. (1968) Can you standardize multinational marketing? *Harvard Business Review*, September/October, 103–13.

Elinder, E. (1965) How international can European advertising be? *Journal of Marketing*, 29 April, 7–11.

Flatt, A. C. (1967) The danger of local international advertising. *Journal of Marketing*, January, 60–2.

Harris, G. (1994) International advertising standardisation: what do the multinationals actually standardise? *Journal of Marketing International*, 2(4), 13–30.

Kirpalani, V. H., Laroche, M. and Darmon, Y. R. (1988) The role of headquarters control by multinationals in international advertising decisions. *International Journal of Advertising*, 7, 323–33.

Kotler, P. (1986) Global standardisation – courting danger. *Journal of Consumer Marketing*, 3(2), 13–5.

Levitt, T. (1983) The globalisation of markets. *Harvard Business Review*, May/June, 92–102.

Miracle, G. (1968) International advertising – principles and strategies. *MSU Business Topics*, Autumn, 29–36.

Mueller, B. (1989) Multinational advertising: factors influencing the standardised vs. specialised approach. *International Marketing Review*, 8(1), 7–18.

Porter, M. E. (1986) The strategic role of international marketing. *Journal of Consumer Marketing*, 3(Spring), 17–21.

Reichel, J. (1989) How can marketing be successfully standardised for the European market? *European Journal of Marketing*, 7, 60–7.

Ricks, D. A., Arpen, J. S. and Fu, Y. M. (1974) Pitfalls in advertising overseas. *Journal of Advertising Research*, December, 47–51.

Seitz, V. A. and Johar, J. S. (1993) Advertising practices for self-image projective products for the new Europe: a print advertising content analysis. *Journal of Consumer Marketing*, 10(4), 15–26.

Sheth, J. (1986) Global markets or global competition. *Journal of Consumer Marketing*, 3(Spring), 9–11.

Whitelock, L. and Chung, L. (1989) Cross cultural advertising: an empirical study. *International Journal of Advertising*, 8, 291–310.

Index

Page numbers in *italics* refer to exhibits, figures and tables.